f2-

Understanding Computers

Understanding Computers

Richard Stevens

The
Leisure
Circle

For S.E.S.

Oxford University Press, Walton Street, Oxford OX2 6DP

Oxford New York Toronto
Delhi Bombay Calcutta Madras Karachi
Kuala Lumpur Singapore Hong Kong Tokyo
Nairobi Dar es Salaam Cape Town
Melbourne Auckland
and associated companies in
Beirut Berlin Ibadan Nicosia

Oxford is a trade mark of Oxford University Press

© *Richard Stevens 1986*

This edition specially produced for
The Leisure Circle Limited
by Oxford University Press

Printed in Great Britain

Contents

Acknowledgements

Many people have helped by reading the manuscript at various stages. In particular, I would like to thank Len Adams, Colin Carmichael, Clive Cookson, Simon Dismore, David Dodwell, Robert Edwards, Ian Graham, Meg and Robin Greenwood, Steve Lewis, Eduardo Olier, Henri Roussel, Ronald Stevens, Susan Stevens, and Julian Ullmann, who have read the manuscript from beginning to end and suggested many improvements. Microtechnology companies, particularly Bell Laboratories, Intel, and IBM, have been very helpful and have contributed photographs and background information. I owe a particular debt of gratitude to Angus Phillips of OUP, who has put an enormous amount of constructive effort into the book.

Introduction

A fundamental change in human affairs is under way, as important as the Industrial Revolution or the invention of the Gutenberg press. The technical nature of microelectronics clouded this from general view until the late 1970s, but as it pervades almost every aspect of our society, the importance of the microelectronics revolution is becoming apparent to everyone.

The power of a computer can now be brought to bear on a problem at a negligible cost, providing us with an extension of our intellectual, rather than physical, capabilities. The cost of computers has fallen by a factor of a million in thirty years, changing them from an esoteric luxury into a disposable item. As a result, for almost every industry, profession, and product, microelectronics is now the dominant force for change. Most of us are wisely suspicious of change, but we are being forced into it, for if we do not adopt the new technology with enthusiasm, others will. Companies who treat microelectronics as a passing phase are destined for economic oblivion.

Microelectronics has three main areas of application. The first is conventional electronics equipment such as video recorders, radio, and television. The second is the computer industry itself, now a business with a turnover of more than £60bn. a year. The third, and key, area is products and services that require intelligence of any sort, including those in the first two areas. Any product with controls such as levers, latches, switches, or motors must inevitably change over to microelectronics technology. Within a few years, complex mechanical machines will be historical curiosities, to be admired in museums.

Microtechnology should be regarded as an enabling technology, in the sense that it enables improvements to be made to most of the products that underpin the whole of our industry. It gives an edge to other products, for example by controlling aircraft flaps to make a plane more fuel-efficient, or improving the performance of a camera, typewriter, copying machine, or car engine. The processing power that a large-scale computer had in 1960 is now available from a far smaller machine, which can control a soft drinks machine, a dishwasher, a cash register or cardiac arrest equipment in a hospital. Electronic mail will displace many postal services, since it is ludicrous to cut down trees and make paper in order to send messages from one end of the country to the other when these can be sent along a wire. Many more examples of the introduction of microtechnology into established products can be given, but it is already clear that few products will be exempt: the cheapest microelectronics product I have seen is a £1 greetings card that plays an electronic tune.

A two-edged sword

The new technology can enrich our lives, ridding us of boring tasks and the drudgery of repetitive work, but it is a two-edged sword. The same circuits can monitor a child's incubator and guide a missile. Overall the world will benefit economically from the technology, but wealth will undoubtedly become even more concentrated in the advanced countries. In particular, economies of the Third World are under severe threat from microelectronics, because the technology is dominated by the USA, a few countries in the Far East, and Western Europe. The industries that underdeveloped countries have struggled to create are about to be devalued by robotics, mass production, and information technology.

The introduction of microelectronics is destroying many traditional industries. Mechanical watches and calculators are well-documented examples of products whose industries have been made obsolete by microelectronics. Robotics and automated machinery are starting to reduce labour requirements in modern factories—a process that will accelerate as new products are designed to be manufactured by robots. In the UK, tens of thousands of jobs have been lost through the introduction of the self-service petrol-pump, a relatively trivial piece of electronics. In future, the arrival of intelligent computer systems will put professionals out of work, in the same way as labourers were previously affected by machinery. Some programs can already diagnose ailments as well as the best doctors. The original victims were individual and mute, but how will those concerned react when microtechnology affects professions such as accountancy and medicine?

The most severe future changes could well come in office work, where techniques for easily storing large amounts of information and for the electronic transmission of mail will improve productivity, but also reduce employment. In advanced countries 50 per cent of the work-force is organizing and manipulating information in one form or another. Hence intelligent, computer-based equipment for manipulating, storing, and transmitting information—**information technology**—will improve efficiency but destroy jobs. The conventional printing and paper industries will be pushed aside by electronic competitors in the time taken to invest in the new technology. Economic forces are driving these changes—just as they spread printing technology within China, and then across to Europe.

But microelectronics will also start new industries. It is already the driving force behind a range of equipment as diverse as the digital audio disc, electronic car ignition, music synthesizers, and video games. One new industry is the manufacture and application of personal computers themselves, which has developed into a major business in only a few years. Within three years of its introduction, the IBM personal computer was selling at a rate of 200,000 per month—a single home computer producing a business turnover as large as that of the UK car industry.

Technologies allied to microelectronics will also have important economic effects—for example, digital optical disc drives will store information at a cost one hundred times cheaper than paper.

Microelectronics is causing large-scale economic restructuring, and times of change present new opportunities for individuals, firms, and nations. For example, an expanding industry is providing electronic **data bases**. Customers who need to carry out a survey of scientific research, search for a magazine, or find the manufacturer of a specific product, can access all the information they require over a telephone line. The data base comes with a set of programs to help track down the wanted information. Shrewd companies are buying up these data bases, while the more traditional suppliers of such information sit back and do nothing.

The soft machine

If there is a single reason for the impact of microelectronics, it is the general nature of the computer. We are used to machines that perform only a single function, such as drills, lathes, bicycles, and typewriters. The function of a computer is determined by its controlling **program**, and the machine itself is important only as a vehicle to enable the program, or **software**, to run. Each time a computer is supplied with a new program, it becomes a different machine, without any change in its physical form. The same computer can be programmed to perform arithmetical operations, synthesize speech, act as an electronic drawing-board, run video games, or operate as a word processor. Because programs are so powerful, their use can simplify the mechanical design of machines. A modern electronic typewriter has far fewer moving parts because the old latches, levers, and cogs have been replaced by a much simpler machine controlled by a complicated program. Despite the mechanical simplicity, the new machine is able to do more than the old. The complexity is encapsulated in the program, which is easy to mass-produce and test; mechanical complexity has been exchanged for program complexity.

We hear anguished cries that the computer is invading everywhere. This pervasiveness of computers derives from the fact that the same machine can have many different applications—only the controlling programs need to be changed. An author buys a machine on which to write a novel, an accountant one to help prepare accounts, a draughtsman one to help produce drawings. Each purchases the same computer, which, in seconds, is transformed by a program into the tool required.

It is a very costly process to design a computer. However, the fact that a single type of machine can tackle an unlimited range of problems means that computers can be mass manufactured, and thus their development cost spread over thousands of sales.

Computer systems are mimics, with the facility to simulate any aspect of life for which the rules can be provided. Each program creates a model world inside the computer, which may be as simple as a video game or the operation of a lathe, or as complex as an analysis of natural languages or a simulation of a nuclear war. But computers are not just restricted to such internal simulation: the machine can control external equipment; it can reach out and affect the world. The robot arm reaches out and moves the chess piece, under the control of the same micro that worked out the best move.

Computers should never be thought of as simply glorified 'number-crunchers', solely for arithmetic—this is an illusion created by the early use of computers for scientific calculation. Computers manipulate a wide range of information represented in symbolic form. The data being processed can be as diverse as details of patients' illnesses, words in a dictionary, or a colour range for paints.

The growth of microelectronics

To most people, the emergence of microelectronics is seen to be a sudden technological breakthrough, but it actually results from a continuous research effort extending back to the 1920s. Since the 1950s this research has reduced the cost of a large computer system by about 25 per cent each year. Originally computers were economically sensible only for a limited range of tasks, such as working out repetitive calculations for army weaponry or nautical tables. But continual improvements in their design and a steady drop in their price has allowed them to develop from devices undertaking a few specialist tasks into a powerful and general-purpose technology. When microtechnology was a small industry, the 25 per cent annual increase in performance was not particularly important, but it has enormous effects now that the industry is worth a hundred billion dollars annually. The technological progress has generally been evolutionary, extending well-known techniques; it is the cumulative results of this steady evolution that are revolutionary.

The most significant, and perhaps most disturbing, aspect of the microelectronics industry is that it is still far from reaching its full potential, and hence the main impact of the technology has yet to be felt. The rate of technological change is so rapid that every piece of electronic equipment currently in production is obsolete. At least ten more years of development can be found in the laboratory, and even the effects of today's technology have not yet worked their way through to the market-place. If microelectronics technology developed no further, there would still be many years of implementation, delayed by a shortage of skilled people. On the basis of past trends, the next decade will see prices fall to one-twentieth of their present level, and computer processors should become several hundred times faster.

The integrated circuit

'Wherein all components of the electronic circuit are completely integrated into the body of the material.' Jack S. Kilby, Patent Application for the Integrated Circuit, 1959

The key to the steady development of microelectronics has been the relentless improvement of **integrated circuits**, or 'microchips'. A complete electronic circuit can be built on to a small square of silicon. Each individual circuit is only one of many **chips** being simultaneously formed on a thin disc of silicon (a **wafer**). All component parts of a circuit can be made by a sequence of chemical processes on the wafer surface, involving etching with acids, adding impurities, and evaporating aluminium. In particular, millions of small electronic switches—**transistors**—can be made on a wafer.

Each chip, which is about the size of a child's finger-nail and may form a complete electronic circuit, could be a radio, a computer, or a telephone. Chips are continually becoming smaller, faster, cheaper, more reliable, and more powerful. A single integrated circuit replaces many older chips, as well as circuit boards, plugs, and sockets. Reliability goes up and the consumption of electricity goes down. The initial investment needed to design and perfect such a chip is very large, but the circuits can be replicated at negligible cost. Wafer processing is a highly complex, but well-understood, technology, the cost of which stays the same, regardless of the complexity of the chips being made.

In 1964 Gordon Moore, now president of the American company Intel, pointed out that the number of transistors that could be made in a single integrated circuit had doubled every year since the first chip had been produced

Moore's Law

In 1964, Gordon Moore, now the president of Intel Corporation, pointed out that the number of transistors that could be made on a silicon chip had doubled every year since the integrated circuit had been invented five years before. His 'law' stayed approximately true until the early 1980s, which meant that by 1970 a single chip held about 1,000 transistors, and by 1980 approximately 1,000,000.

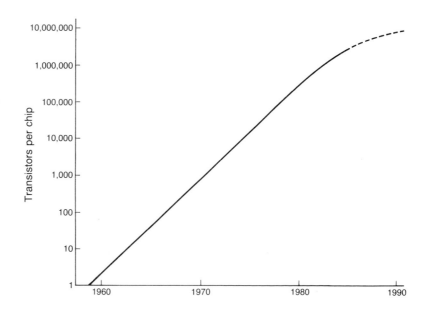

in 1959. At the time this was not a very spectacular claim, for the number had risen from 1 to about 30 in five years. But 'Moore's Law' is still approximately true, and so integrated circuits with more than one million transistors can now be built. Few people within the industry doubt that individual chips with tens of millions of transistors will soon be made.

The validity of Moore's Law has meant that the number of transistors possible on a single chip increases by a factor of a thousand every ten years, and by a million every twenty years. The circuit itself becomes smaller, and more can be produced on one silicon wafer. Clearly there must be a physical limit to this shrinkage, and the mid-1980s may see Moore's Law failing as the curve levels out. In the unlikely event of Moore's Law still holding by the year 2000, there would then be as many transistors on a single integrated circuit as there are neurons in the human brain (about 100,000,000,000).

Microprocessor = computer + integrated circuit

As the number of transistors on a single chip grew, the threshold of complexity was crossed at which a small computer could be made. Only a few thousand transistors, correctly connected, are needed to make a useful computer. By the early 1970s, microelectronics technology had advanced sufficiently for that many transistors to be formed on a single chip, and the whole of the processing section of a small computer could be fabricated on a single piece of silicon— the **microprocessor** (often shortened to 'micro'). Instead of being built for a specific task, the function of this electronic circuit could be changed by altering the computer program controlling the microprocessor. The more transistors that could be built on to the silicon chip, the more powerful the microprocessor would be.

Even the early, primitive microprocessors were comparable in power to the first of the modern computers, the 100-foot-long ENIAC, built in 1945. Today this processing power costs pennies instead of millions of pounds. Since 1971, the single-chip microprocessor has become increasingly powerful, first to match the power of small computers (minicomputers) and then that of more powerful (mainframe) machines. As a result, whole computer systems are rapidly disappearing into a single silicon chip. In retrospect, the simple application of Moore's Law should have enabled us to predict and prepare for the arrival of the microprocessor, but the event still seems to have come as a surprise even to those involved in the computer industry.

The microtechnology industry

The rapid development of microelectronics can be analysed, and to some extent understood, by examining the history of other industrial advances. An article by Robert Noyce in the September 1977 *Scientific American* showed that as industries mature, the cost of their products steadily falls in real terms. For every tenfold increase in the total number of units that have been produced, the cost per unit product falls by approximately 30 per cent. Thus the thousandth steam-engine will have cost 70 per cent of the hundredth, or half the cost of the tenth. This rule seems to apply to a large range of industries.

The unit product of the microelectronics industry is the transistor, and the cost of transistors has indeed followed the trend pointed out by Noyce. What is unique about the development of microelectronics is the speed with which vast numbers of such transistors have been produced. The industry had already produced fifty million million transistors by the end of the quarter century after the invention of the integrated circuit in 1958. The production rate doubles every fifteen months or so, and the decline in price of a transistor, from £20 each to a penny for 100, has consequently been concentrated into only a few years; and the saturation point is still not within sight.

How the cost of a product declines with mass production

When a product is mass-produced, its cost in real terms falls steadily. Every time the total number of units that have been produced increases by a factor of ten, the cost declines by approximately 30 per cent. This cost reduction is caused by improved manufacturing experience and increased competition as the market expands. The prices of electronics products seem to conform fairly well to this 'experience curve', which has been found empirically to apply to a whole range of products. The unusual aspect of the microtechnology revolution is the rapidity with which the industry has produced vast numbers of the unit product—the transistor.

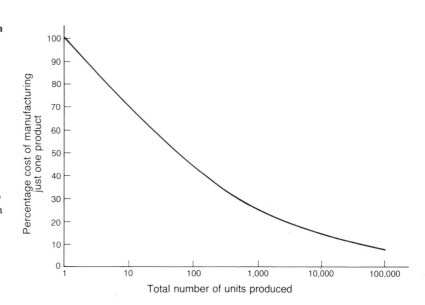

The price of a given electronic circuit decreases each year by about a quarter. After ten years, a chip might cost ten times less than its introductory price, but sometimes the price decline is even more precipitous. Simple microprocessors (computers on a chip) cost £200 in the early 1970s, but within five years cost only 50p each. With each fall in cost, the computer has become economically viable for more and more applications. The industry has improved performance, increased production, and cut costs faster than any other industry in history. The costs of a computer system of a given power have decreased by a factor of ten every six to seven years, and faster than this in some specialized areas. After three to seven years, maintaining an old computer system becomes more expensive than buying a better replacement.

Economic effects of microtechnology

The rapid and remorseless decrease in the price of electronics has important economic consequences which forbid delay in the introduction of new technology. A firm, or a nation, with a one-year advantage in microtechnology has a 25 per cent price advantage over rivals. This enables a rival to be undercut while it remains in profit. Hence there is positive feedback tending to maintain any technological gap. Without large-scale, and initially uneconomic, investment this gap can never be bridged. For this reason, governments in many countries that do not normally intervene in industry are, by a variety of means, subsidizing their indigenous microelectronics firms. Microtechnology is the ideal industry for nations which have seen the problems of heavy industry—there are many advantages in making high-value products primarily based on human, rather than natural, resources.

In traditional industries, productivity savings through innovation are much lower, and are usually in the range of 2–4 per cent per year. Consequently, the natural diffusion of knowledge leads to evolutionary developments becoming generally known before any significant price gap opens. Any price advantage caused by research is not normally critical, and indeed may be nullified by problems caused if products are prematurely introduced. In microelectronics technology, however, because of the 25 per cent price advantage per year, the early introduction of microelectronics equipment is merely risky. For a manufacturer introducing a completely new product, one of the major problems is educating the customer. When both the microprocessor and the personal computer were introduced, the first question asked of the manufacturers was 'What can I do with it?'

If a country delays introducing this new technology in order to allow its obsolescent industries a breathing-space, the effect is to undermine its own ability to produce and export new technology, permanently consigning itself to importing foreign equipment.

Employment in traditional industries will continue to decline, especially clerical employment, since productivity in repetitive office work can be most easily enhanced by introducing new equipment. The loss of these jobs is inevitable, and the choice we have to make is whether they are lost to equipment produced at home or abroad. Some of this employment can be replaced by work produced by the new technologies. The manufacture of integrated circuits in itself does not require much labour, but feeder industries are formed which create large numbers of jobs. Computer repair and maintenance, the development of software, the supply of discs, computer magazines, and even the production of boxes for computer equipment all need a range of labour skills. The wiring of our homes for services such as electronic mail will involve major investment in the last decade of this century. Robot factories will require a mass of supporting industries outside the factory. As these subindustries flourish, they evolve into an infrastructure that makes future microtechnology expansion easier. The long-term employment effects of microelectronics are unknown, but some studies have doubted that the changes in employment will be as rapid as was first thought. The combination of international competition and an apparently insatiable human demand for material goods means that predictions of much lower working hours (for those still in work) are unlikely to come true.

For the individual firm producing microelectronics equipment, being a short distance ahead of rivals is critically important. The most profitable phase in the life of an electronic product occurs before the maximum sales are reached. The first manufacturer of a popular microelectronics product can charge high prices and enjoy large profits, but only until rivals appear. Thereafter a steep price decline follows, and cut-throat competition drives most of the manufacturers from the business. There is thus an enormous economic incentive for the leading firm to ramp up production quickly, while profit per unit sale is high. Firms that enter at a late stage in the product cycle are in a hopeless position, entering a declining, low-profit market. The firm with the technological lead in microtechnology will almost always succeed, because of its lower manufacturing costs and better product. Microelectronics is market driven, but by tomorrow's products rather than today's. Success in microelectronics involves predicting tomorrow's market-place—any company that merely responds to today's market-place will inevitably produce obsolete equipment and fail;

The profits cycle of an electronics product

Over the past thirty years, the microelectronics industry has experienced unbridled competition. Microtechnology has never been stable enough for companies to form comfortable pricing agreements between themselves. When a new product is developed, the first firm in production has a high profit for each sale, and therefore tries to increase production as rapidly as possible. Often teething troubles delay mass production. If a market proves lucrative, then other companies soon move in, the production problems are solved, and prices tumble due to the over-capacity. The unit profit declines rapidly, and so the profit rate for the product reaches a peak before the maximum sales are reached. Any firm entering late in the cycle will make little profit; and for some products, such as video games, the cycle may be complete in a year. Meanwhile, the leading firm is announcing a more advanced product . . .

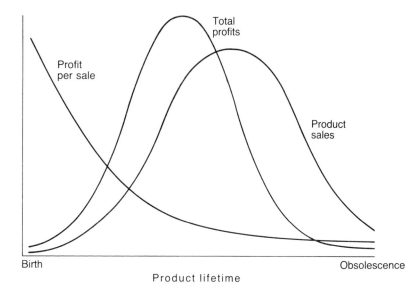

Total profits

Profit per sale

Product sales

Birth

Obsolescence

Product lifetime

Introduction

companies seeking finance for products with a proven history of success are necessarily committing themselves to failure. Because the USA has traditionally held a two-year technological lead over European companies, it has reaped the benefits from this profit cycle.

Dividing the growing market for microelectronics

As the overall supply of microelectronics products increases, the European share is being steadily eroded by the USA and Japan. The total value of the basic components consumed by the microelectronics industry worldwide is shown for 1978, 1983, and 1988 (estimate). The pie charts illustrate how European production of microtechnology is a dwindling proportion of the total.

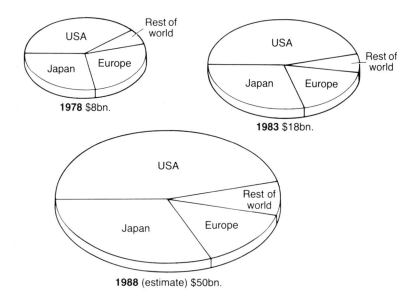

1978 $8bn.

1983 $18bn.

1988 (estimate) $50bn.

The calculator is a prime example of such product evolution within the microelectronics industry. Hewlett-Packard had a virtual monopoly when it introduced its calculator in 1971—and the price was £180. Within eighteen months, the market saw a price-cutting struggle resulting in many company bankruptcies. Hewlett-Packard continue to make profits, but does this by producing a range of up-market calculators with which other firms do not compete, rather than operating in the mass-production market. When calculator technology stabilized in the late 1970s, the mass market in calculators had fallen to Japanese manufacturers, who had the lowest production costs.

Cultural colonialism

Powerful machines cannot help but contain the cultural values of the societies that produce them. America has been dominant in the field of microtechnology, especially for the first ten years of the microprocessor. Europe has now slipped to third position, behind Japan. The rest of the world is scarcely involved, except as cheap labour during the manufacturing process, and as customers for electronic 'goodies'. Individual countries have a stark choice. Embracing the new technology cuts total employment in old industries; however, failure to modernize will have the same effect in the long term, but with no prospect of jobs being generated in, and by, the new technology.

Microprocessors are imposing scientific culture on the population of the USA, Japan, and Western Europe, even invading professions such as law and medicine. A decade ago could we have dreamt that ten million personal computers would be sold in one year? The culture of First World science is being imposed on the rest of the globe, just as the American entertainment industry has weakened local cultures. The present power of microelectronics has led to cultural colonialism. For example, programmers must learn English-based computer languages. In technical areas, the American spelling of words (program, analog) has ousted the traditional English spelling. The French faced an essentially Gallic crisis in 1981 when their new identity cards could not be printed with accents (naturally they were scrapped). The Americans use imperial units of measurement, and so the pins of integrated circuits are spaced one-tenth of an inch apart. Engineers from Vladivostok to Buenos Aires have had to learn a new measurement system, one that even the UK, where it originated, had abandoned. After several decades of sharing the technology, America has now realized its economic and military power, and imposed restrictions on the export of computers, chips, and software.

Infrastructure

Although the microelectronics industry is largely controlled by American and Japanese companies, microelectronics and computer manufacture is a world-wide industry. Electronic components are small and light, and hence easily transported. Chips may be made in California, assembled in the Philippines, tested in Europe, and sold in Japan—the choice of factory site is simply a matter of economic arithmetic. A colossal infrastructure of equipment, experience, investment, and education is necessary for technological independence, and only the USA, Japan, and perhaps Western Europe are large enough to sustain the necessary network.

Any attempt outside these leading nations to go it alone is futile, as can be seen by failures in computer manufacturing in Russia and India. These countries have attempted to replicate obsolete Western technology, and stifle imports of up-to-date components. The results have been more catastrophic than they yet realize—they have fallen further and further behind in the technology, despite both countries having a tradition of programming excellence. It is better to import such components, than to put the whole of your industry at a disadvantage. Microtechnology is not an end in itself, but a tool for all other industries, as necessary a part of the industrial infrastructure as a reliable electricity supply. The smuggling of high-technology chips to such countries may well weaken local research efforts. Think of the effect on the morale of Russian scientists struggling to build microprocessors, when the latest smuggled American technology arrives—and imagine the servicing problems with the equipment that is made from the smuggled components.

Russia has put considerable effort into microelectronics, and closed the design gap, but it is still two to five years behind the West. As usual, the Soviet failure lies in poor mass-manufacturing techniques, and the lack of true customers—the dominant consumer is the military, which absorbs the production of the few chips that are made. Monolithic bureaucracies are necessarily conservative, and they can scarcely be expected to welcome the widespread availability of microtechnology. In the West, the demand for advanced technology has been generated by individual customers, who can see the possible economic benefits.

A capitalist industry

The present power of the microelectronics industry can be seen as a monument to capitalist competition, and the success of the USA reflects the power of competition in that country. Since the mid-1950s, developments have come from commercial companies, rather than from universities or government laboratories. The industry provides high profits for the firms with the most advanced products, and little reward to the also-rans. The customer chooses chips almost purely on the basis of technical performance, and comparison is relatively easy—if your chip is 25 per cent slower than its rivals, or more expensive for the same performance, you will sell no chips at all.

Entrepreneurs have been quick to see the profits available to manufacturers of advanced products, and risk capital has been freely available to the best engineers. Time and time again, small firms have been founded by individuals who left bigger, slower-moving companies to build advanced chips. Indeed the first microprocessor was built after Dr Robert Noyce and his colleagues left Fairchild to form Intel in 1969. It is not unusual for new firms to reach a turnover of $100m. in two to three years. The fastest to reach that figure is Compaq, a firm making small computers compatible with IBM equipment; its turnover was $110m. in its first year.

The industry exhibits the virtues of capitalism, but also the faults. All the early, uneconomic, development work had to be funded by governments, because it was too long-term for individual companies. The results of research are hoarded by each company, and not dispersed for the benefit of all. The development of necessary standards for hardware and software is grossly underfunded, because universal standards would require co-operation between firms. For example, there are dozens of different, incompatible, standards for organizing information on a single size of computer disc. Vital goals, such as to develop and standardize computer languages, or devise methods for linking computers, are underfunded because they yield no short-term profit for individual companies. This lack of resources for communal objectives actually holds up progress in the industry, to the detriment of all. Standards are presently only generated by enthusiasts devoting scarce time to committees—sometimes this works, sometimes not.

The enabling technology

The applications of microcomputer equipment are now primarily limited by our imagination in programming. With more and more powerful computers becoming available, the limitations imposed by the machine itself are falling away, leaving a new challenge to create programs that exploit the technology's full potential.

Microtechnology will intrude whenever we need to store, process, or communicate information. Technologies such as paper, oil paint, film, and television all provided new and exciting opportunities when they were introduced. The challenge now is to exploit the opportunities offered by computers. From their early years we teach children to read and write, principally in order that they should comprehend and shape the world they live in. With the onset of the microtechnology revolution, a knowledge of computers is similarly important. All of us should take the trouble to explore the fascinating world of this new tool.

One Basics of the Computer

A computer differs from all other machines in its generality. It is capable of attacking any problem, provided that the rules for solving the problem are clearly specified. The computer is much more than a calculator—it can process in symbolic form an enormous variety of information. Until the advent of computers, the notion of such general-purpose equipment was alien, because machines were designed and built for a single task. A few basic ideas that lead to this flexibility are now discussed. These will all be covered later in more detail.

Hardware

The **central processing unit (CPU)** is the core of the computer, the part that manipulates information. The individual operations of the CPU mimic simple arithmetical and logical operations. Computers tackle problems by finding and following sequences of **instructions** or **operations** that are stored in their own **memory**. If we change the instructions, we can make the machine perform another task. The CPU selects each operation in turn, performs it on some information, and then moves on to the next one. Computers are called serial machines because of this method of processing single instructions one after another. Before and after it is processed, the information is stored in the computer memory, intermingled with the processing instructions.

A single computer instruction is not very powerful; it might add two small numbers together, compare two numbers to see which is the larger, or move the answer to a calculation from one part of the computer to another. Many thousands of instructions may be necessary to perform even a trivial task. Processed results can be displayed on a screen or **output** to a printer, and the user can also **input** information to control the computer. The CPU, memory, and the input/output sections are the three basic elements that constitute the **hardware**, or physical components of the computer.

The computers discussed in this book are **binary** machines, in which the individual elements that make up the computer can, like a switch, be either on or off. Simple arithmetical or logical operations are replicated perfectly by these binary switches, or **bits** (binary digits). All information stored in the computer is represented as binary numbers, stored by a series of these bits. We can view the processing of instructions either as an electrical operation or, with equal validity, as a mimicry of a logical operation. A key to the power of the computer is that the bits can satisfactorily represent an enormous range of information from the real world—such as text, numbers, addresses, pictures, lists of industrial parts, or even the complete specification of a product, such as a car or an aeroplane. Of course, in order to be operated on, the information represented has to be converted into the binary code of computers.

The computer performs an operation on several bits of data at the same time. The number of bits operated on is called the **data width** of the machine, and modern computers usually have data widths of 8, 16, 32, or 64 bits. It is convenient to take 8 bits as a basic unit because they can hold one letter, or two numbers (between 0 and 9); a group of 8 bits is called a **byte**.

Switches—the building blocks of computers

The first computing machines used electrical **relays** as their binary switches. Relays are electromechanical devices—they have mechanical parts which can be moved by electricity. In one position (on) the relay conducts electricity, while in the other (off) it does not. An electrical doorbell is an example of a relay; by pressing the switch we cause a small current to flow, and this in turn makes the hammer of the bell operate. Computers were next built from valves, which are an electronic type of switch, once familiar because radios and televisions were made from them. Each valve was 2 to 3 inches long, and usually 3/4 inch in diameter. To make a working computer, a few thousand switches are needed; it is the pattern of electrical connections between the switches that determines which computer operations are performed. Early computers, constructed from large numbers of relays or valves, were necessarily large, expensive, and unreliable.

The **transistor** is an electronic switch built from a **semiconducting** material, such as silicon. Semiconductors are a class of materials whose electrical properties can be tailored to produce switches. Transistors were invented in 1947, since when they have steadily become smaller and faster. A modern computer, which uses transistors for its switches, can perform exactly the same functions as a valve machine, but is smaller, more reliable, operates faster, and is cheaper to make. In the late 1950s, techniques were invented which allowed a complete electronic circuit (the **integrated circuit**) to be built on to a small **chip** of silicon, perhaps $\frac{1}{4}$ inch square. Integrated circuits developed rapidly, and by 1971, the **microprocessor** had been invented—those few thousand switches necessary to build a complete computer were made on a single chip the size of a finger-nail. Within five years, small computer systems made with microprocessors were inexpensive enough to be sold for individual use—the **personal computer** had arrived. By 1985, a powerful microprocessor containing nearly one million transistors could be made on a single chip.

The **memory** of a computer is organized into a long line of individual cells, each holding the same amount of information (normally between 1 and 8 bytes). The computer can directly examine or alter one of these cells in about one-millionth of a second. This type of memory is built from integrated circuits, each of which can store hundreds of thousands of bits. However, this **primary memory** is too expensive for storing large amounts of information, and so computers also use slower **secondary memory**, storing information in the surface layer of magnetic **discs**. Data is copied from the discs into the memory chips when it is needed.

Software

Software is the generic name for the various types of programs that control the function of the computer. Much computer terminology is poor or outdated, but 'software' is an excellent descriptor. Software is easily moulded, and it also shapes the actions of computer hardware.

A **program** is a sequence of instructions that specifies a task for a computer. One program might cause a computer to play a video game; another could make it transfer information over a telephone line or store data in an electronic filing system. Each machine instruction occupies one, or perhaps a few, cells of the computer memory. Each complete program forms a file on a computer disc, which can be copied into the semiconductor memory in seconds when it is needed. The combination of hardware and software makes up the complete **computer system**.

The programs that control computers are long and difficult to understand, and a machine must follow thousands of detailed machine instructions in order to perform a simple task. Therefore, so that programs are more comprehensible, they are written in **programming languages**, instead of in the form of a list of instructions that the machine could directly perform. A programming language contains a variety of functions that can be combined to specify a task, and can also be easily comprehended by a human user. Although it is really only a rigorous specification of what we want the computer to do, the text written in the programming language is also called a program. The computer cannot understand the language of such a program; it has first to be translated into the machine instructions. Fortunately, the translation task is straightforward— and it is performed by the computer itself, using a program called an **interpreter** or **compiler**. This takes the program written in the programming language, and turns it into a sequence of instructions that will fit in the computer's memory.

If a **high-level language** is used to write a program, a programmer is able to express problems in clear terms, remote from the simple operations of the computer. Examples of such languages include Pascal, Prolog, FORTRAN, and BASIC. Conversely a **low-level language** corresponds more closely to the instructions that the computer actually follows to perform a program.

A substantial part of computer software helps programmers to create, improve, and run other programs. These are usually called **systems programs** to distinguish them from **applications programs**, which are the programs that the computer follows in order to perform directly useful tasks. A particularly

16

Transforming a task into a computer program

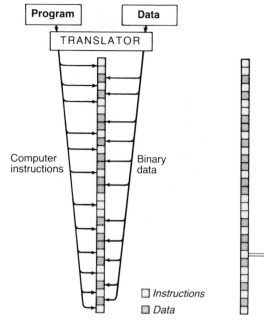

Task

A task is to be performed,
and a computer needs to be
programmed to perform it.
The task requires the
manipulation of information;
for example, adding up a
series of bills.

Program in
high-level
language

Data

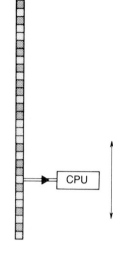

Computer
instructions

Binary
data

Program   Data

TRANSLATOR

☐ *Instructions*
▦ *Data*

CPU

The task is specified by a
program in a high-level
language, and the data to be
operated on is identified.

The memory of the computer
is a line of cells, each of
which can contain the same
amount of information, for
example eight bits (a byte).

The program in a high-level
language is translated into a
stream of binary instructions
that the particular computer
can perform; the data is also
translated into binary form.
The instructions are then
dovetailed into the memory
with the data; the
positioning is organized so
that the data is in the right
place for the instruction that
will process it.

The central processing unit
(CPU) of the computer takes
a copy of each instruction
from the memory in turn,
and performs it on the
relevant data, also copied
from the memory. An
instruction can not only
cause the CPU to operate on
data, but also make it go to
other instructions in the
memory, or write new data
into the memory. The **program
counter** register enables the
CPU to distinguish
between instructions
and data in the memory.

important systems program is the **operating system**, which exercises detailed
control over the computer hardware and its interaction with the user. The
range of applications programs for the computer is effectively limitless, since
the computer's power can be applied to almost any problem or situation.

Thus three major elements are brought together in a computer: serial control, information processing, and programmability. Together these create a
new class of machine, predominantly shaped by an easily varied specification—
the high-level language program. Computer hardware is only important as a
vehicle for running software; it may affect the time a computer takes to run a
program, but not the result of the processing. For many problems, the power
of computer mimicry is now primarily determined by our ability to symbolize
the problems in programs, rather than by the physical form of the computer.

Two The History of the Computer

The computer was not created in a single step, but was the result of a slow development process taking hundreds of years. Human imagination very often takes only small evolutionary steps, and the notion of a general-purpose machine that could perform an unlimited range of tasks was not one that came in a blinding flash. The technical expertise to build computers existed many years before they actually came into being. However, the overall idea of the computer could only be understood after its separate elements had been developed. Two important steps were the development of simple machines for calculation and for industrial control.

Calculators

The first mechanical calculator was built in Germany between 1620 and 1623, by Wilhelm Schickard, Professor of Mathematics at Tübingen University. Schickard was inspired by the astronomer Johann Kepler to build a machine in order to reduce the effort involved in astronomical calculations. This machine could add, subtract, and multiply two numbers using a system of rods and gears. Later in the seventeenth century, Blaise Pascal built an automatic adding machine to assist his father in preparing taxation accounts, and Gottfried Leibniz developed a sensible mechanical scheme to perform multiplication.

Wilhelm Schickard's calculating machine

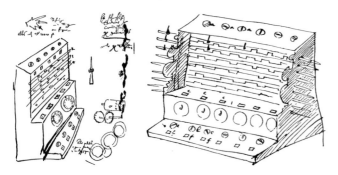

Two drawings by Wilhelm Schickard give an outline of the numerical calculating machine he built between 1620 and 1623 (when it was unfortunately destroyed in a fire). Schickard designed the machine to automate astronomical calculations.

A reconstruction of Schickard's machine.

Numbers were represented in these calculators by the position of gearwheels. Two numbers were added by meshing two gears, and turning them together. The answer was displayed on the gears when they stopped rotating. Such machines were the precursors of computers—any computer can be turned into a calculator by making it work on a fixed set of programs. Until the advent of accurate machine tools in the late nineteenth century, they remained expensive, hand-built curiosities, because of manufacturing difficulties.

Program-controlled operation

The concept that the actions of a large machine could be organized by a small, separate control was understood as early as AD 100. Hero of Alexandria describes a variety of machines existing at that time, including a mechanical toy that shot arrows at a hissing metal snake. Such a machine must have needed a mechanical control of its various actions. This knowledge of sequence (or 'program') control was acquired, or relearnt, by Muslim scientists, and transmitted to Europe by the fourteenth century. Here it was first applied to clock-making, and enabled cathedral clocks to strike the hours and vary the tunes they played.

Clock-making was the harbinger of the Industrial Revolution, being in advance of other medieval engineering by many hundreds of years. It remained a craft skill for many centuries, only becoming a mass-production industry in the nineteenth century. In the eighteenth century such skills were applied to the making of exotic, lifelike automata. Brilliant engineers, such as Vaucanson and the Jaquet-Droz family, made small humanoid dolls that could play flutes or keyboards, or write messages and draw pictures, pausing occasionally to dip a pen into a pot of ink.

Industrially, program control was first introduced into weaving, and the earliest-known machine is from Bohemia, built by Broesel in 1740, but probably invented sixty years earlier. Small wooden bars stuck on a closed loop of linen controlled a loom; as the loop rotated, the bars struck a control that altered the weaving pattern. The best-known machines of this type, using a more sophisticated loom control, were invented by the Frenchman Joseph-Marie Jacquard in 1805. In Jacquard equipment, a sequence of punched cards controlled the threads of the weaving machine, producing complex patterns in the cloth. If a different set of cards was substituted, then the program of the machine, and hence the weaving pattern, was altered. This was a psychological as well as a technical advance, because the two functions of machine action and control were for the first time clearly delineated. The sequence control mechanism of the Jaquet-Droz dolls was an extension of the internal machinery, but Jacquard's looms were controlled by holes in a piece of card, clearly different in character to the mechanical parts of the loom.

It was a very lengthy process to produce the cards for each weaving pattern—the program for a portrait of Jacquard's own face needed 25,000 cards.

The Jaquet-Droz dolls

This little eighteenth-century doll can write any sequence of forty letters under the control of a set of pegs in a plate in his back. He dips his pen into the ink, and follows the writing with his eyes. His wrist is controlled in three axes rather than being restricted to a flat plane, to give more subtlety to the writing. Hence he is a program-controlled robot, although the programming involved is difficult and slow. Only recently have industrial robotic arms been able to match this performance. On the first Sunday of every month, he is one of several automatons that come to life at the Neuchâtel Museum in Switzerland.

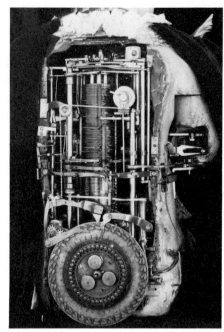

Control mechanism for the writer

Soyez les bienvenus a neuchatel.

Welcome to Neuchâtel—a sample of recent writing

Much of it was repetitive and predictable, and therefore ideal for a computer. Today the computer does in fact assist in the preparation of the program that will later control it. The computer translates each program from a language intelligible to a programmer into its own, more detailed, machine language.

Charles Babbage

We may consider computing history to start with Charles Babbage, the English scientist who developed many of the ideas behind the modern computer between 1820 and 1870. Babbage combined the two operations of sequence control and automatic calculation, using punched cards to represent both the numbers to be processed and the type of calculation to be performed on the numbers. The same machine was designed to produce tide-tables for the British Admiralty, life expectation statistics, or astronomical data, and then print out the results. Simply by changing its stack of punched cards, Babbage's machine could work on a completely different formula. In post-revolutionary France, Baron de Prony had already shown that many mathematical calculations could be reduced to a few repetitive steps of addition and subtraction—the 'method of differences'. De Prony had employed seventy people, double-checking one another, to produce mathematical tables, and Babbage realized that such an approach could be adopted by a machine. He rapidly built a demonstration 'Difference Engine' to show the feasibility of his idea—the only machine of his that ever worked. He knew that program control would give far more flexibility to his machine, and so next designed a more general-purpose machine, the 'Analytical Engine', designed to have 50,000 moving parts.

Babbage's Analytical Engine

The remnants of Babbage's Analytical Engine are on display in the Science Museum in London. About 50,000 moving parts were required, and prospects of a working machine were finally destroyed by a row between Babbage and his engineer in 1833. Babbage had already constructed a working Difference Engine; less flexible than the Analytical Engine, but much easier to make.

How a Difference Engine works

Many complicated tables of numbers can be produced by simple sequences of additions and subtractions, because adjacent numbers in the tables have simple **differences** between them. As an example, look at the series 1, 4, 9, 16, 25 ... formed by squaring 1, 2, 3, 4, 5 ... The differences between the squares are 3, 5, 7, 9, 11, ... moving steadily up by two each time. Since we know the first number (1) and the first difference (3) in the series of squares, we can calculate subsequent values with pairs of additions—without any multiplications.

Two Swedes, George Scheutz and his son Edvard, read about Babbage's work in 1834, and over the next three years built a working version of the Difference Engine (below). By 1843 the machine was able to print the results of calculations. In the 1850s, such a machine was used in the Dudley Observatory in Albany, New York State, and by the British government.

We start by adding the first number to the first difference, to obtain 4—the second value of the series of squares. The second addition is to add 2 to the first difference, and make the difference ready for the next step—increasing it to 5. We now have 4 and 5 as our new number and difference respectively; when they are added, we obtain 9, the third value in the series of squares.

The process can be continued: for $9 + 7 = 16$, $16 + 9 = 25$, etc. Thus the squaring of numbers has been reduced to the addition of pairs of numbers by the **method of differences**. Both the Babbage and Scheutz Difference Engines worked on this principle. Extensions of the same technique allowed more complicated formulae to be processed. Other calculations, such as for the range of guns, were converted into a series of squares, cubes, etc. which the Difference Engines could then process.

Babbage's Analytical Engine had mechanical gears, which were to perform the calculations, and was designed to be driven by a steam-engine or a falling weight. Unfortunately, his somewhat impractical nature and the limitations of early nineteenth-century engineering prevented Babbage from completing the equipment. Finance was initially provided by the British government, but in 1833 this was withdrawn. The rest of Babbage's life was spent in developing computing theory and in further vain attempts to build a working model of the Analytical Engine. Augusta Ada, Lady Lovelace (1815–51), Lord Byron's daughter, acquired a thorough grasp of the Engine, became the world's first programmer, and prepared complex mathematical programs. Because the Engine never functioned, these programs were destined not to be tested. Her name, however, lives on in the programming language Ada, adopted as the standard language for the 1990s by the US Department of Defense, the world's largest software 'consumer'.

Many of the features of today's microprocessors can be seen in mechanical form in Babbage's unfinished Analytical Engine. For example, Babbage was forced to split the design of his computing machine into the 'store' and the 'mill', the former storing the information and the latter altering it. This pair correspond directly to the **memory** and **central processing unit** of a computer. Temporary storage of the results midway through a calculation was possible, pre-dating the internal **registers** of the computer. The Engine was also designed to check intermediate results during the process of a calculation, and change the direction of a calculation depending on the value found—a computer follows similar **conditional branching** instructions. If it had been finished, Babbage's machine would have been the first computer.

George Boole

In the mid-nineteenth century, a self-taught Lincolnshire schoolmaster, George Boole, devised a mathematical theory which was later to have great practical importance in computing. Boole showed how some logical problems could be expressed in symbols. These symbols could then be manipulated without destroying the sense of the original problem, provided that all the factors involved in the problem could be expressed by variables that have only two states, which Boole called **true** or **false**. Often this 'Boolean' approach clarified the original problem enough to aid its solution. In one step, Boole had transformed the study of logic from an art into a science. In 1849, despite his lack of formal education, Boole was made Professor of Mathematics at University College, Cork, Ireland, in recognition of his work.

Examples of logic

Once information has been compartmentalized into true and false, the deduction of facts from sufficient information is a mechanical process—as a reading of Sherlock Holmes indicates. In the nineteenth century, the American scientist Allan Marquand suggested making an electrical logic processor from switches and light bulbs. The machine's electrical state would be an analogue of the logical operations it performed, its switch positions representing the input conditions, and the result of the operation being signalled by the light being on or off.

Similarly, the electronics in computers is a system of mimicry of logical and arithmetical operations. Computer programs are written in a language that can be easily understood by humans, and then automatically translated into Boolean operations for the electronics of the computer to perform. Perhaps the most surprising concept in the whole field of computing is that 'intelligence' can be demonstrated by essentially trivial sequences of Boolean operations performed by a computer.

An example of Boolean logic

Boolean logic can extract sensible conclusions from known information. Consider the (rather optimistic) statement:

'Everyone who is both stupid and dishonest is a warmonger, and no one else is.'

This statement refers to a simple world, divided into two types of people—warmongers and peacemakers—and in Boolean systems everyone must belong to one group or the other. In addition every person is either honest or dishonest, and either intelligent or stupid. The statement can be expressed more simply as:

'If and only if you are both stupid and dishonest, you are a warmonger.'

Four statements that can be derived from the above statement are:

'If you are both stupid and dishonest, you are a warmonger.'

'If you are both stupid and honest, you are a peacemaker.'

'If you are both intelligent and dishonest, you are a peacemaker.'

'If you are both intelligent and honest, you are a peacemaker.'

Together these four statements contain the same information as the original statement. This divided the world into four groups of people—stupid and dishonest, intelligent and dishonest, stupid and honest, intelligent and honest—and went on to state that warmongers consist of the first group, and all three remaining groups consist exclusively of peacemakers.

An automatic logic machine would be able to transform the four statements into the original statement or vice versa. The original statement corresponds to an **AND** statement in Boole's logic. The two **inputs** to the AND statement are stupidity and dishonesty, and the **output** of warmonger is true only if both of the inputs are true. All other combinations of input produce peacemaker as an output. A system to mimic automatically this logic step can be constructed from only a few transistors, or indeed from any other switches. Hence, if we can translate complex ideas into Boolean logic, transistors can mimic that logic exactly.

The example given is simple, and hence the results that can be derived from it are equally simple. When a number of logic statements are linked together the results become difficult to evaluate, and we are soon lost. But the computer can easily track any number of logic steps.

Extensions to the logic chain may involve other Boolean logic operations, such as the **OR** function. In the OR operation, either (or both) of the two inputs being true is sufficient to make the output true, for example:

'Dishonest people are brought up badly or inherit dishonesty.'

This immediately extends the conclusions that can be drawn from the initial statement. We can work out that all warmongers are brought up badly or inherit dishonesty. Furthermore, we have the pleasure of knowing that if we are honest and bring up our children properly they will love peace.

Developments after 1871

Babbage's work on program control was almost forgotten after his death in 1871, but progress in the machine tool industry now allowed mass production of mechanical adding machines. Punched-card systems became popular, especially in offices, for storing information, with the added advantage that the information could then be analysed by special-purpose machines. The American engineer Herman Hollerith built electrically controlled machines that stored and analysed data on punched cards. Information was represented by the presence or absence of holes punched into the card. The machines had

Hollerith's punched-card machine

The Hollerith machine was developed in time to analyse the 1890 American census. Information about each person (age, sex, address, etc.) was punched on to a single card. The cards were then sorted electro-mechanically—the presence (or absence) of holes in the cards was detected by wire brushes. These brushes dipped through the holes in the card into pools of mercury, completing an electrical circuit and causing dials to rotate. Once set up, the machine could rapidly sort though a pile of cards in order to extract relevant information.

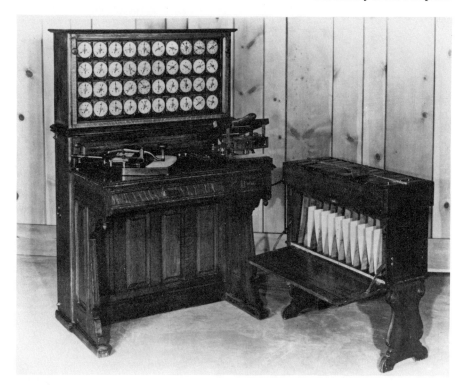

wire probes to detect the holes. Whenever a probe encountered a hole, it dipped through the card into a pool of mercury and completed an electrical circuit. This equipment was adaptable for many different purposes, and worked out the results of the 1890 American census as well as the mortality returns for New York City. There were complaints about the 1890 census because it cost twice as much to produce as in 1880, although the statistics were 'more accurate and produced more quickly'.

A flourishing business grew up in office equipment for accountancy, tabulation, and the handling of statistics—each task performed by a single-purpose machine, which employed punched cards to store and sort information. For example, a firm might keep its customer records on cards, and could automatically sort out who owed money. In 1913, Hollerith's company was absorbed into an industrial conglomerate that made office automation equipment, the Computer Tabulating and Recording Company (CTR); and in 1924, Thomas Watson, managing director of this firm, changed its name to International Business Machines (IBM).

Pre-war breakthroughs by Turing and Shannon

The long period of intellectual stagnation in computer theory came to an end in the decade before the Second World War. A disparate series of breakthroughs paved the way for practical computer systems. There was a rediscovery of the potential power of program control. Computers were also very much needed for weapon design, artillery calculations, and for code-breaking, and when war came, military money was made available to produce the first true computing machines.

Alan Turing—unquiet genius

The English mathematician Alan Turing paved the way for the computer. He was a friendly, pleasant person but his intellect, upbringing, and style tended to isolate him from other people. His particular genius was to understand the practical application of complicated mathematical theory. T. H. Flowers, who built Colossus, the first electronic computer, said 'If it was not original, he was not interested.' During the Second World War, Turing devised brilliant techniques for deciphering German codes, and was able to describe to engineers the computing machine that needed to be built for decryption. As a result, the UK was able to eavesdrop on the most secret German information. His efforts went unrecognized, however, for after the war the nation did not reward him with a prestigious job. He worked on computers at the National Physical Laboratory and at the University of Manchester, before committing suicide in 1954.

Turing's most important contribution to computing was to invent the concept of the general-purpose computer. He imagined a simple machine that could operate on any problem, once the program for it to follow had been provided.

His imaginary machine could perform only a few elementary instructions, using an infinitely long piece of paper tape marked into squares. Its operations were restricted to marking the tape, rubbing out the mark, moving one square to the left or right, and examining a square to see if was marked. Turing showed that the machine could process any problem expressed in algorithmic form. An algorithm is simply a set of instructions, or a 'recipe', for performing a calculation or solving a problem. Turing's simple machine could imitate any other machine, and no other machine, however complex, could solve any problem that his could not tackle. The little machine could always imitate a more complex machine, simply by using a program tape that mimicked it. Turing further showed that there was no way of deciding whether the machine could finish a computation, without actually trying the problem out.

The sole complication was that the Turing machine had a 'state of mind', determined by past events. However, Turing was able to show that this need not be complex, and if it was, that it could be stored on the tape and examined by the machine itself. Thus the program could be stored in the same way as the information being processed. Perhaps the most wonderful thing about Turing's work was that it demonstrated abstract principles through a simple mechanical metaphor. The simplicity of Turing's imagery proved an ideal stimulus for computer construction. The ultimate compliment to Alan Turing is that every programmer today takes his results for granted, never questioning that the computer can process a problem once the flow of the program logic has been developed.

Alan Turing   In 1936, Alan Turing, a young Cambridge mathematician, was able to show that one simple machine (the future computer, of course) could process any logical problem, providing there was a set sequence of steps (an **algorithm**) to solve the problem. Until then, mathematicians had thought that different computing machines would be required for different problems. After all, we need an assortment of equipment in order to perform a variety of mechanical tasks. It had seemed certain that the far wider range of intellectual problems would require a number of computing machines. Alan Turing showed otherwise, and became the first person to describe the modern computer.

Turing's ideas on artificial intelligence and computer languages and hardware seem balanced and rational even now. In the inertia that pervaded Britain after the war, Turing was never given the rewards he deserved, and his personal life was to collapse over a conviction for a homosexual offence. The man who breathed life into the computer, and who could well have lived into the twenty-first century, committed suicide in 1954.

Claude Shannon   In 1938, Claude Shannon, a research assistant at Massachusetts Institute of Technology, pointed out that **binary** devices, those with only two possible states, could completely emulate the logic that had been described by George Boole. This idea paved the way for practical computing machines built from reliable and inexpensive components, such as relays and valves (both binary devices). Shannon was later to be the author of a brilliant theory on the nature of information, which lead directly to the concept of error correction (p. 56).

Although no one realized it in 1938, the foundations of computing science were all in place. Turing had shown that the computer would be generally applicable, and Shannon told the world how it could be built. From this point on, the development of this automatic processor, or computer, was inevitable, although it turned out to be a halting, stumbling affair spread over three warring countries.

The Second World War

The Second World War was undoubtedly a stimulus to the development of the computer. In Germany, Britain, and the USA, special-purpose binary computing machines were developed for the aircraft industry, gun control, artillery calculations, and decoding enciphered enemy transmissions.

Germany   The most advanced design of all the wartime machines was produced by Konrad Zuse, a German working in almost total intellectual isolation. However, his machines were slow, using second-hand telephone relays to perform logic and arithmetic. These relays were merely mechanical switches which could be driven electrically into one of two different positions. In 1941, Zuse built the Z3 computer, a general-purpose machine that could store 64 numbers; this binary, program-controlled machine was effectively the world's first working computer. Such machines helped to design German aircraft (they suffered heavily from Allied bombing raids on the aircraft factories), yet Zuse was never allowed many resources, and towards the end of the war his efforts were surpassed in the UK and USA. The last of Zuse's wartime machines, the Z4, was rescued after the war, and clattered on into the 1950s in the Swiss Technical Institute at Zurich.

Konrad Zuse and his wartime computer

A reconstruction of Zuse's Z3 machine at the Deutsches Museum in Munich. Zuse's machines were far more advanced in concept than other wartime computers, but he was never allotted the resources that the UK and the USA devoted to computers. His 1941 proposals to build a computer from electronic valves were turned down when he admitted that the machine could not be completed in a year. As a result, his machines had to be built from second-hand telephone relays. Zuse's computers were used in the German aircraft industry and suffered heavily from wartime bombing. In 1985, the man who built the first computer was living in retirement in Germany.

Zuse's first machine, built in the mid-1930s in his parents' living-room, had been a mechanical monstrosity à la Babbage, designed to mimic the flow of a calculation—a naturally algorithmic process. After the war, deprived of his equipment, Zuse's fertile brain turned to the design of languages for computing machines. He produced Plankalkül, the first programming language, algorithmic in form, and capable of expressing complex types of information. Zuse's ideas on language design were absorbed by researchers at Zurich, and led to pioneering work there by Heinz Rutishauser, one of the architects of the Algol programming language. Zurich continued to be a fertile ground for language development, and the language Pascal was also invented there, by Niklaus Wirth in the 1960s. Pascal in turn led to the Ada programming language—completing the link between a solitary young man in pre-war Germany and the US Department of Defense language for the 1990s. In June 1985, I had the pleasure of talking to Professor Zuse. He built the first working computer, and has lived to see far more powerful machines made on a tiny piece of silicon.

Britain   If Zuse produced the most elegant design, the British Colossus computers were by far the most effective machines of the Second World War. They were built from electronic valves, which could switch on and off much quicker than

Zuse's relays, and so were generally much faster machines. The British constructed them at Bletchley Park for the specific purpose of decoding intercepted German radio signals. The Germans had a variety of encoding machines for scrambling the messages, the most important of which was *Geheimschreiber*—called 'Fish' by the Bletchley Park group. The British were very successful at decoding messages, but because they were careful about how the information

Colossus in action

Colossus in action at Bletchley Park decoding German radio messages during the war. The encrypted message was punched on to a paper tape, which can be seen on the right. The computer then compared possible settings of the German encoding machine with the patterns of the message tape. The racks of computing valves can be seen in the centre. In 1984, I talked to the man who, as a young engineer, destroyed Colossus 1: 'I took the valves out, returned them to Post Office stores, and threw the rest of the machine on to the rubbish heap.'

was used, the Germans never lost confidence in the security of their radio signals. Each Colossus machine compared the patterns of a message tape with the possible combinations that the encoder might have employed, looking for similarities that would indicate the settings of the encoding machine. Earlier in the war, Polish patriots had supplied the mechanical layout of German encoding machines, allowing the Bletchley engineers to develop computerized models of them. The Colossus computers provided Britain with a steady flow of the most secret German information.

Small programming changes could be entered into a Colossus through switches on the front panel, but major changes required rewiring. Each machine had a paper-tape reader capable of reading an amazing 5,000 characters per second. A prototype reader with a speed of 9,700 characters per second was tried, but the shock of travelling at 60 m.p.h. was too much for the paper tape, and it disintegrated.

After the war, Turing was involved in the design of computers at the National Physical Laboratory, but the impetus in computer manufacture was rapidly being lost to the USA. The UK continued to come up with ideas, and produced the first machine with electronic storage for its program (the Mk. 1 at Manchester), and the first office computer (Leo), but Britain faded away as

T. H. Flowers—the man who built the first eleven electronic computers

Tommy Flowers had considerable experience in the use of valves in his work for the Post Office during the 1930s. By 1939, he realized that any processing done by relays or mechanics could also be performed by valves, usually very much faster. 'It seems so obvious now, but few people understood it then', he said during a conversation in May 1984. (Mervin Kelly, Director of Bell Laboratories in the USA, had come to the same conclusion by 1936.)

In 1943 Flowers was asked to design a machine to decipher German radio transmissions, and at once he recognized that the necessary equipment was best built from valves. Flowers did not (he says) understand the mathematics of decryption, but was a practical engineer down to his fingertips. Working ninety hours a week with fellow engineers Sidney Broadhurst and William Chandler (and later Allan Coombs), Flowers set about designing a machine to implement Alan Turing's ideas on decryption. The machines were built and tested at the Post Office research laboratories in north London, and then taken to Bletchley Park. The basic design and construction of Colossus 1 took only ten months between February and December 1943, and the 1,500-valve machine worked almost immediately, decoding many messages. Eleven Colossus machines were made and performed valiantly in decoding enemy radio signals; none of them is known to have survived to the present day.

a commercial competitor. American computing supremacy remained unchallenged until the first half of the 1980s, by which time the Japanese industry had grown sufficiently.

The USA In the USA, the first developments in computing came from engineers, who were primarily interested in machines that would take over the laborious calculations then done by hand. The Bell Telephone Laboratories had been building relay-based calculators before the war. With the collaboration of IBM, Professor Howard Aiken, of Harvard University, organized the construction of a relay-based computer between 1939 and 1946. The machine program was controlled by paper tape, and although rapidly made obsolete by valve-based computers, this Automatic Sequence Controlled Calculator was the foundation of IBM's computing empire. Like Zuse's machines, the machine had no conditional branching, and so the sequence of a program was totally predetermined before it started to run.

The pioneering ENIAC (Electronic Numerical Integrator And Computer) was completed after the end of the war by Eckert and Mauchly, at the Moore School of the University of Pennsylvania. This was designed for the calculation of ballistic tables for the US Army. ENIAC contained 19,000 valves, was 100 feet long, weighed 30 tons, and needed 2,000 kilowatts of electricity to run. This was the first large electronic computer to become functional. Data was input and output through IBM punched cards.

Stored program control

The wartime computers had to be rewired or their switches altered in order to make them perform a different calculation, and indeed had been constructed with only one particular task in mind. They usually performed the same repetitive calculation on different numbers. Although they were computers, the alteration of a program was a time-consuming task. Towards the end of the war, the realization grew that the program itself could be stored and altered as easily as the information that was being processed. In a stored program machine, the controlling program is kept in the memory of the computer, rather than in an outside storage mechanism. The computer finds out which operation (such as addition or comparison) it has to perform next by examining its own memory. In Babbage's Engines, the program and information had been stored on two separate paper tapes, but it was now realized that both could be stored together in the memory—the numbers close to the instructions that were to operate on them.

In 1945, during his involvement in the ENIAC project, the brilliant mathematician John von Neumann drafted a report containing the first clear description of both the stored program and the modern computer. This document is often regarded as the birth certificate of the computer.

The 'stored program' concept was the final philosophical development of computer hardware, and critical for several reasons. Stored program control allows the program (and hence the function of the computer) to be altered in a simple fashion. A new program can be loaded into the computer memory from an outside memory, such as a floppy disc, and the computer set to work on this new function. This idea of the computer preparing and processing its own program seems to have been understood by Babbage, and is clear in the original description of the Turing machine. It also seems that Eckert and Mauchly at the Moore School understood the idea of the stored program by 1944.

If its program can be easily altered, the computer itself can assist in the preparation of programs. Complicated tasks can be written in fairly intelligible programming languages, and the computer can perform the painstaking work of translating the program into the language of the operations that it directly performs. The translated program can then be loaded into the computer memory and run. The whole process takes place under the supervision and control of the computer itself.

The abstract machine

Von Neumann's report meant that the outline of the abstract computer was complete, although the concept of a generally applicable machine was still little understood. Computers were initially so difficult to operate and so complicated to understand that computer scientists were more occupied with machine complexity than the philosophy of the machine. But the notion that a computer could be defined abstractly as a few thousand binary switches did gradually grow clearer. It was understood that the switches of the computer could equally well be valves, relays, or transistors—the function of the machine would be unchanged, although the speed and cost would be vastly different. Engineers could now concentrate on making the individual elements—and hence the whole computer—much smaller.

The commercial revolution

After the Second World War, the emphasis switched from theoretical analysis to construction. Government subsidy had developed the computer to a practical stage, even as far back in time as Hero, who worked in the State-subsidized Museum of Alexandria. Commercial companies were now ready to exploit the new technology, and from the early 1950s they have led the field, developing computers primarily for business, rather than defence, use. Eckert and Mauchly, the builders of ENIAC, left university life to build the Univac 1 computer, the progenitor of the first commercially successful series of computing machines, built by the firm Sperry-Rand.

In the mid-1950s, IBM swept past Sperry-Rand to become the world's leading computer company, initially due to the success of its 701 scientific computer. With superb salesmanship, shrewd financial control, and a series of reliable machines, IBM steadily gained dominance over the profitable market for business computers.

America's civil and defence industries, with a high incentive to cut labour costs, and a willingness to apply new technology, generated a market that fed finance back to the growing computer industry. The resulting technical and financial advantage of the USA was sufficient to stifle growth in Europe's computer industry, which has remained stunted. By the early 1980s both Japan and Europe were well aware that continued American dominance of this increasingly important industry would be economically disastrous for them. It became obvious that any serious attempt to challenge this dominance would have to be co-ordinated at national level.

The computer disappears into silicon

At the end of the Second World War, computer pioneers were convinced of the large market potential for computers, but no one foresaw the astonishing series of developments which were to shrink the individual elements of a computer from valves the size of cigars into transistors only $\frac{1}{4,000}$ inch square. Integrated-circuit technology has enabled the whole of a computing machine to disappear into a $\frac{1}{4}$-inch square of silicon—the microprocessor—costing only a few pennies to manufacture.

Three Binary, Digital, and Logical

Binary, digital, and logical—the computer is all three of these. To programmers writing programs in a high-level programming language (such as BASIC), these aspects may be invisible, because the language can hide the machine's internal complexity, but each needs to be understood in order to comprehend the essential nature of the computer.

Number systems

People are even more conservative in their use of numbers than they are in their use of words, and as a result our number system carries a great deal of historical baggage. Clock-faces still have Roman numerals, and pre-Babylonian divisions of the circle into 60 and 360 degrees are convenient enough to have been retained for the clock and the compass. Some people might scoff at the idea of primitive tribes having different sets of numbers when counting different objects, without thinking of the range of words we associate with a single number, such as duo, double, duet, binary, twin, brace, pair, and couple. These older systems act as an overlay to the decimal system, which came to us from India, disseminated westwards by the ninth-century Arab mathematician al-Khwarizimi. Despite its manifest superiority—try multiplication in Roman numerals—the decimal system took hundreds of years to displace the old Roman system. In England, decimals supplanted the Roman system in Elizabethan times, although the seventeenth-century writer John Aubrey describes people who were still unable to make the transition.

There are so many different types of information in the world, that whatever number system a computer uses, most data types would need to be converted into that system in order to be operated on. Decimally based computers, for example, are certainly fine for numeric calculation; indeed in their early days computers were often organized around the decimal system, because of the heavy emphasis on number crunching. But such machines are unsuitable for the straightforward manipulation of other types of data, such as text or drawings.

The binary system

The system employed inside the computer is the **binary** number system. All information is handled and manipulated in binary form, though it is usually

Binary representation of integers

The binary number system can represent all possible integers, and here we show how to represent the integers from 0 upwards. The first two numbers, zero and one, are the same in binary as in the decimal system, but then decimal two is represented as 10 (pronounced 'one zero' not 'ten'), because only the symbols 0 and 1 can appear in a binary number. The 1 in the left column indicates that a two is needed. The presence or absence of 1 in a binary column indicates whether that column number is contained in the total number to be represented. The following table shows the conversion process from decimal to binary.

Decimal	Binary
$0 = 0$	0
$1 = 1$	1
$2 = 2+0$	10
$3 = 2+1$	11
$4 = 4+0+0$	100
$5 = 4+0+1$	101
$12 = 8+4+0+0$	1100
$98 = 64+32+0+0+0+2+0$	1100010

The process can be continued to represent increasingly large numbers, and we can see that with enough columns every possible positive integer can be represented in binary. This binary series of numbers occurs continually in computer work and so grows familiar to anyone working in the field. Because the value represented by a column increases by a factor of two instead of ten, any binary number above one is longer than its equivalent decimal number.

A set of four binary digits has sixteen possible values, and so can represent 16 different values. The figure of sixteen can be easily obtained by multiplying four 2s. Similarly the number of values possible from eight digits can be found by multiplying 2 eight times to give 256.

We have concentrated on how to represent positive integers (the whole numbers from zero upwards) in a binary system. However, we should always remember that many different types of information can be represented by binary numbers. Eight digits can store 256 different values: we could use them to represent the numbers between 0 and 255, but with equal validity they could represent those between 1 and 256, or −127 and 128—one extra digit on the front of a number could indicate whether it is positive or negative, for example

110 might represent 2 in decimal, and 010 −2. We could also use the eight digits to count 256 different types of trees, cars, or nations.

Sequence for the addition of two binary numbers

The sequence (or algorithm) for adding two binary numbers is

1. Add the two right-hand columns.
2. If the result is less than two put the answer at the foot of the column.
3. Otherwise, subtract two from the result, put the remainder at the foot of the column and put a one into the next left column, to represent the 'carry'.
4. Perform the same set of operations on the next column towards the left, and stop when you reach the leftmost column.

This sequence is the same as in the decimal system, except that the number two has replaced ten, reflecting the use of only two number symbols (1 and 0). Consider the addition of two binary numbers such as 1101 and 0110. These two numbers are 13 and 6 in the decimal system, and so we should expect the binary calculation to give the answer 19. The first step is to add the numbers in the right-hand column. In binary arithmetic $1+0=1$:

```
1101
0110
----
   1
```

Then add the numbers in the next column to the left—exactly the same sum needs to be performed:

```
1101
0110
----
  11
```

The next column has the sum $1+1=10$ (2 in decimal) giving a 0 and carrying a 1 over to the fourth column from the left:

```
1101
0110
1
----
 011
```

Again this is $1 + 1 = 10$, with a 1 being carried to the next column left:

```
  1101
  0110
  1
 ─────
  0011
```

The last carry forms a new, fifth column, because the answer is too large to be expressed by 4 digits:

```
  1101
  0110
 ─────
 10011
```

Thus the binary answer 10011 is obtained. To check that it is correct, we can translate it into decimal. There are 1s in the columns that represent 16, 2, and 1, and so the final answer is the sum of those three numbers, that is 19.

Binary multiplication

Multiplying two decimal numbers is quite a difficult process for humans, and so we simplify it to a routine sequence of steps (an algorithm), which we learn by rote. The process is so familiar that we rarely think of the complicated algorithm we employ. If we have to multiply two large integral numbers, we split the problem by first multiplying one number by each column of the second number, and then adding the results, a column at a time. This method forces us to to learn all the multiplications up to 9×9, but having done that can we multiply indefinitely large numbers. The decimal multiplication of two large numbers is thus reduced to a set of multiplications of two single decimal numbers less than ten, followed by a sequence of additions.

Binary multiplication is similar to decimal multiplication, but since only two symbols are involved, there are only four possible multiplications (0×0, 1×0, 0×1, and 1×1) to be learnt. As three of these (the first three) yield the answer 0, and the other gives the answer 1, the process is very simple.

In order to multiply binary numbers by 2, 4, etc., we need only add the correct number of zeros to the right of the number concerned, just as when we multiply decimal numbers by ten, one hundred, etc. For example, to multiply the binary number 1 by a factor of 2 (10 in binary) we change 1 to 10 (2 in decimal). So to multiply any binary number by two, all that needs to be done is to add a zero to the end of the number.

Multiplying by the binary number 11 (3 in decimal) consists of multiplying by 10 and 1, and adding the two results. So on multiplying 1101 by 11 (13 times 3) we obtain the two numbers 11010 and 1101, which then need to be added

```
  11010
   1101
   1
 ──────
 100111
```

giving 100111 or 39. Hence binary multiplication has also been transformed into a series of additions.

Binary subtraction and division

Binary addition and multiplication have been dealt with in detail, and the processes of subtraction and division employ similar principles. Division could be performed by a process of repetitive subtraction—to find out how many twelves there are in 192 we could just count how many times we could subtract twelve. In practice, however, a computer program is cleverer than this and the process is much quicker.

presented to the user in a more accessible form. This system is as good as any other for representing various types of information: almost all information can be represented satisfactorily by combinations of the two binary symbols, 1 and 0. But the primary advantage of the binary system is that computers can be cheaply and easily made from devices with two stable states—switches—such as transistors, valves, or relays. The two states of each switch can be a physical representation of the two binary symbols. Thus information is represented in the computer by combinations of 1s and 0s, which in turn are represented physically by the positions of switches.

A short examination of the decimal system illuminates properties which we often only understand intuitively. The ten number symbols from 0 to 9 are a common code that transcends many national boundaries—the total at the bottom of a restaurant bill can be read by a monoglot in Florence, Paris, and New York. A number, such as 3,427, is a code that we learn to interpret as we grow up. The far right-hand column indicates the number of units, while the next left column represents the number of tens, the next hundreds, and so on. Each column represents a number ten times greater than the column on its right. As we see from a calculator, a vast array of numbers can be made with combinations of only the ten different symbols from 0 to 9.

The beauty of the binary number system is that combinations of just two symbols—0 and 1—are sufficient to represent all these numbers. The columns in the binary system represent numbers in the sequence 1, 2, 4, 8, etc., rather than the 1, 10, 100, etc. of the decimal system. For example, the 1s in the binary number 101 (5 in decimal) represent the presence of a 4 and a 1 (adding up to 5), and the 0 signifies the absence of 2. If a column contains a 1, then the number that that column represents is included in the total; if it contains a 0 then the column number is not. As in the decimal system, the largest number is represented by the column on the left.

Binary numbers can be added, subtracted, multiplied, and divided in similar fashion to decimal numbers, and because only two symbols are involved, the details are simpler. The results of the same sum in binary and decimal arithmetic should, of course, be the same!

Representation of information in the computer

Information, such as text or numbers, is represented in the computer by electrical signals. Because the computer is a binary machine, such a representation must necessarily be symbolic, rather than direct. A number, for example, must somehow be symbolized by a sequence of **on** and **off** states of the computer's transistors. We can be as flexible as we wish in encoding and processing information in its symbolic form, as long as logical consistency is maintained with the reality behind the information. The computer should therefore be thought of as a processor of symbols, and not simply of numbers. The symbols can be made to represent almost anything we can imagine; numbers happen to be particularly simple to represent because they are already symbols.

Data types and programming languages

Most types of computer data, such as text or lists of names, are not inherently decimal. However, this information could obviously be represented in a program or programming language by numbers, either decimal or binary. For example, we could encode A as 0, B as 1, C as 2, and so on, providing the programmer remembers what the numbers symbolize. Indeed some programming languages, such as BASIC and FORTRAN, are so numerically oriented that programmers have to go in for this type of distortion in order to represent non-numeric types of information. Ideally, this internal representation should be invisible to programmers, who can then ignore it when they work with natural types of data, and leave the computer to sort out how to organize them internally. Some programming languages (such as Pascal) are flexible enough to allow the programmer to define and work with complex types of information. The underlying representation within the computer is still binary, of course, but that this is so need not be obvious to the programmer.

Even apparently simple programming tasks can lead to relatively complicated data types. For example, imagine that you wish to write a small program to remind you to send Christmas cards to your friends. The characteristics stored for each 'friend' might include name, sex, address, the kind of relationship, its current condition, and the last date for posting cards. All of these factors together define the data type 'friend' in the program, but none of them are decimal, and only one (sex) could be thought of as binary. Most information is far more complicated than numbers, and so it is a great advantage to be able to represent different data types directly in a programming language.

Binary numbers can satisfactorily simulate many different data types to any required level of accuracy, provided that enough **bits** (**binary digits**) of storage are allocated for the task. A bit is a binary digit of storage, a 1 or a 0, and so can be represented by the on and off states of a switch. Of course, there are some types of information which naturally have binary states—such as whether a light is on or off, or the result of tossing a coin. These have a simple and direct representation in binary computers. Whereas such naturally binary information can be encoded with only one bit (heads or tails becomes 1 or 0), an integer usually requires either 16 or 32 bits of storage, depending on how large the number is. If 16 bits are used, they are enough to represent 65,536 different values, and 32 bits are enough, for about 4,000,000,000.

In order to represent the days of the week we need seven different states. Three bits are sufficient to represent these, with one number left unused because there are eight possible values for the three bits. We might encode Sunday as 000, Monday as 001, and so on, with Saturday as 110. Such a binary code would be meaningless to us, unless we know the system of representation being used. If a programming language restricts our ability to work with data types such as 'Sunday', we would be forced to represent days of the week by numbers (usually decimal if the language has these), and remember what these refer to. The programming language will then organize the necessary transformations to and from the internal binary system.

The computer, and the way it represents information about the world, is structured around the properties of **transistors**, small switches of electrical current. Each individual transistor inside a computer can either allow a current to pass, or, when switched off, block the current flow. These two states can symbolically represent 1 and 0. We have seen that any number, or other type of information, can be represented by binary numbers. These binary numbers can in turn be perfectly mimicked by a set of transistors.

Conversion to and from binary

Although binary numbers are awkward for us to handle, the conversion between external types of information and the binary numbers inside the computer is a routine process, performed by short computer programs built into each programming language. The whole cycle employed by the computer in dealing with non-binary information is:

1. The computer takes information in from the outside world.
2. It transforms this information into an appropriate binary representation.
3. It carries out the necessary processing on the binary form of the data.
4. When the computer processing is complete, it transforms the binary data back into a form easily understood by the computer user.

Step 3, the processing of information, may involve many thousands of processing steps in an average program, whereas the transformation to and from binary is a relatively simple operation. Hence in considering the overall efficiency of using the binary system, the work involved in the transformation stages is almost irrelevant. The processing, rather than the transformation, takes up most of the time.

Processing information in a binary computer

Information can take a large variety of forms—numbers, text, lists—and all of these need to be represented satisfactorily in the binary computer. To process information the computer must first convert it into a binary format. The data manipulation then takes place. Once the processing is finished the information can be transformed back into its original form. The transformation stages require a small, fixed number of steps whereas the processing steps often involve thousands of operations.

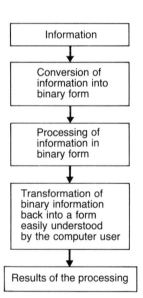

Continuous and discrete—or is it analog and digital?

Two types of measurement occur in our daily life—continuous and discrete—and their properties are different in important ways. The former measures smoothly varying quantities, while the latter is used when counting of any sort is required. The words 'continuous' and 'discrete' have been replaced in the computer world by the less specific terms **analog** (the American spelling is now universal in computing) and **digital**.

For convenience, we often mix continuous and discrete numbers, and sub-consciously sort out their small incompatibilities. Yet the two measures have distinct properties, and really should not be mixed without proper awareness of their differences. For example, an analog number (except zero) can always be divided to produce another analog number, but this is not necessarily true for digital numbers. For convenience, we normally treat a sum of money as analog, but actually it is a digital count, exact to the smallest value of the currency. For example, we cannot divide 7p evenly between three people; the correct value does not exist in the digital system of money.

Digital (discrete) numbers

Digital numbers are exact rather than approximate, being always 'quantized' into small steps, each one the size of the smallest unit being measured. The number of cows in a herd is an exact, and not an approximate, figure; if it changes, it does so by a minimum of one cow (the 'quantum step'). Similarly, money is measured in digital terms, exact to the smallest unit of the particular currency. Pascal's calculator and Babbage's Engine were digital rather than analog machines, because the information they manipulated was quantized by the individual teeth on the cog-wheels.

Analog (continuous) numbers

Some other values are naturally analog or continuous, and these can be varied smoothly, without the necessity to jump to the next largest or smallest number. These are measures, rather than counts. For example, the speed of a car or the height of a building has a continuous value. There are no steps with forbidden numbers in between—$\frac{7}{3}$ is such a number in our currency. Therefore an analog value will always have a small error. A car speed might be measured as 33 m.p.h. or 33.03 m.p.h., but each of these values is still only a close approximation—the real speed is unlikely to match these exactly. Indeed the very term analog implies that such measurements are only analogous to the reality.

The digital computer

The computer is a counting machine, based on the binary system, and so all information inside it must necessarily be digital. If an analog number is to be represented, it must be converted to the nearest step of some digital system—just as we have to convert $\frac{7}{3}$ to 2p, or perhaps 2.5p. However, with enough bits in the computer, we can reduce these steps to as small a value as we wish, so that adjacent numbers are as close as is necessary to give the desired accuracy. During the process of conversion from an analog to a digital value, there is usually an error, because the analog number is allocated to the nearest 'step' of the digital system. Thus we might have to convert the car speed from $33\frac{1}{3}$ m.p.h. to 33 m.p.h. If more bits represented the number, it could be 33.3 m.p.h.

Perfect copying in digital systems

A digital system has great advantages over an analog system for computing. In particular, digital information can be compared, copied, or transmitted without error. For example, we can copy a telephone number precisely (it is a digital quantity), but the sound and image of a telephone are analog, and we can only copy them approximately with a tape recorder or camera. As information in the computer is digital, it can be copied to another digital system absolutely perfectly. The results of a series of calculations are always the same, and indeed can be performed to any reasonable accuracy. Unfortunately for software producers, pirated copies of a program are indistinguishable from the original.

Examples of the perfect preservation of digital information are common. The letters of the alphabet are digital, rather than analog, symbols; there is no letter midway between A and B. Consequently letters, or sets of letters, can in principle be copied without any error and preserved indefinitely through time— unlike, say, the visual experience of a painting. Because they are digital, the words of Shakespeare in a modern edition may well be identical to the words that he originally wrote.

For several hundred million years, another digital code has preserved information that would otherwise be degraded through constant copying. DNA, which is the construction program for earthly life, consists of a 4-bit binary code. Genetic information is stored by a sequence of four possible nucleic acids wrapped around the helix of a DNA molecule. Stored digitally, this information can be protected against the ravages of time. If analog storage were to be used, the genetic information would degenerate every time it was copied into the next generation.

High accuracy

In a digital system, more accurate representation of information merely requires a few more bits of storage, and more processing time when that information is manipulated in the computer. Only 8 bits are needed to describe information correctly to 1 part in 256 (about 0.4 per cent), 16 bits to describe it to 1 part in 65,536 (about 0.001 per cent), and 32 bits to describe it to 1 part in 4,000,000,000 (about 0.00000002 per cent).

The nature of analog displays is such that they are only approximate representations of what they are measuring. It can be very costly and difficult to provide a small increase in accuracy. For example, a car speedometer, which is an analog device, produces a reading accurate to a few miles per hour, quite sufficient for the task. If there was a need to make a more accurate speedometer display, say correct to within $\frac{1}{100}$ of a mile per hour, the equipment would become much more expensive and complex. However, if the speedometer has a digital read-out, then to provide an extra digit on the output display would be very simple, although the device that puts the speed into the meter might have to be upgraded. Making an analog display device with an accuracy of more than, say, one part in a thousand is very difficult, but of course in many areas of life there is no need for such a degree of accuracy.

Analog machines   Analog computers are still employed for a few tasks, especially for simulation purposes, where they are literally an analog of the process being replicated, and can often process the data faster than a digital machine. In many ways the term 'computer' is a misnomer for such analog machines, because they lack the flexibility and accuracy of digital machines. Analog electronics technology is still common, for example in radios, televisions, and video recorders, but it is now controlled digitally.

Floating-point representation of analog numbers

A computer program may need to represent digital or analog numbers, both positive and negative, covering a range from the very large to the very small. Some numbers may be simply too large or too small to be represented exactly by integers. To illustrate the kind of numbers we may need to represent, there are about 10,000 million million million atoms in one cubic centimetre of material. On the other hand, the diameter of a single atom is one-hundredth of one-millionth of a centimetre across.

A particular program may need to represent both values, and hence a programming language (and thus the computer) must be able to express each with sufficient accuracy. However, neither can be represented satisfactorily by integers. One number is too large, the other too small. The awkwardness of the words describing these numbers is a reflection of how difficult they are to represent.

If we were to represent these numbers with integers, we would need an enormous number of bits for the large number, and still not be able to represent directly the smaller number. The crucial point is that such numbers usually do no need to be represented exactly, but only accurately enough for the particular problem being processed. Measuring things more accurately than necessary is simply a waste of effort. In the two examples above, we may not care if we are inaccurate by a few million atoms, and we might be satisfied if the atomic diameter is accurate to within a few per cent of the correct value.

Mathematicians have developed a standard format, **floating-point representation,** to represent analog or digital numbers that range from the very large to the very small. The number is split into two parts; one represents a standard factor, like a thousand or a million. The other part, which actually comes first, tells us how much we have to multiply the standard factor by.

A number like 1.5 million is an analogous representation in common use. This format immediately indicates that we are dealing with a scale of millions. The 1.5 tells us how many millions are involved, and we usually do not care whether it is 1,500,001 or 1,500,002. The computer splits floating-point numbers internally in this way, in a format modified to make some calculations quicker.

To compare crudely two numbers with the same factor, such as 1.5 and 2.5 million, we never need to deal with complicated numbers like 2,500,000.54, only the small, easily comprehensible numbers 1.5 and 2.5. If this level of accuracy is not sufficient, we can increase the number of decimal columns and write, say, 1.56 million.

In floating-point representation, the first part of the number, the **fractional** part, is usually between 1 and 10. The second, called the **exponent,** indicates how many factors of ten we have to multiply the fractional part by. The number 1.5 million would become

$$1.5 \times 10^6 \qquad (1.5 \times 1,000,000)$$

and the number six is in the exponent because there are six zeros in the multiplication factor of a million. The designation 'floating-point' is derived from the fact that the decimal point always 'floats' to keep the fractional part between 1 and 10. This floating-point system is very flexible: if we were to change the number from 1.5 million to 1.5 thousand the representation would become

$$1.5 \times 10^3 \qquad (1.5 \times 1,000)$$

Floating-point numbers have been expressed here in a decimal form. The computer uses similar floating-point techniques, but because it uses binary storage, the format is modified.

Analog and digital information

Analog and digital numbers have been discussed, but it should be made clear that the distinction is really between analog and digital information. Entities like colours, the weight of a fish, a piece of gold, pictures, conversation, and music are naturally analog, whereas letters, words, fish fingers, sums of money, or the number of children are digital. Counts are exact rather than approximate—we expect to return from an outing with exactly the right number of children, rather than an approximation to the number we started with. When we see a car, we have an analog experience: our image of it can rapidly fade. But when we can apply the word 'car', or 'green', or 'Ford' to what we have seen, we then possess a small amount of knowledge which may be retained indefinitely, because it is now encoded digitally.

Logical operations in the computer

Boolean logic is based around a system of **true** and **false** information, and so fits rather simply into a computer system built from binary elements. Each simple logical operation can be easily mimicked by a few transistors (a **logic gate**). Logic gates come in six primitive varieties, each of which is able to perform one of six logical functions described by George Boole. All computers have such instructions available as some of their most basic instructions, and

Circuit symbols for sets of transistors that perform Boolean operations

A drawing of a complex electronic circuit showing the transistors that make it up is very difficult to understand, and so a slightly more abstract viewpoint is often given, displaying the circuit in terms of the logic functions performed by groups of transistors. These functions are the Boolean operations, each of which is made up from a few transistors. Each has its own symbol, and the symbols for the six basic Boolean operations are shown here.

In each case, there are two binary inputs to the circuit (except in the case of the NOT operation, which has only one input). The output of the circuit (also 1 and 0) depends on the inputs. The values 1 and 0 correspond to Boolean true and false, and the transistor set mimics the Boolean operation involved.

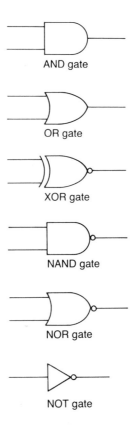

AND gate

OR gate

XOR gate

NAND gate

NOR gate

NOT gate

The logic functions

The six elementary logic functions have shorthand names—AND, NAND, OR, XOR, NOR, and NOT. Imagine each of them as a trivial logic function that a computer can perform relentlessly. They are discussed in order to illustrate their extreme simplicity, rather than to pretend that they are individually important. The computer is able to mimic each function perfectly with transistor switches, and each logic step corresponds to a single computer instruction, except that true and false are replaced by 5 volts and 0 volts. A program written in a powerful programming language can be broken down into a long sequence of these simple functions, which can in turn be replicated perfectly with transistors.

AND

The AND logical function is different from the arithmetical operation ADD. The output of an AND function is not the addition of the two inputs, but a measure of whether both of the inputs are true. The AND functions is true only if both of the two inputs to the gate are true, that is both are 1. All other three input combinations (0,0; 1,0; 0,1) have 0 as their output. Where two conditions both have to be true before a third is true, you are able to mimic the logic of that situation with an AND gate. 'If I can get the time off and Jill will come, we'll go to see the play'—both input conditions must be true for the output (going to the play) to be true.

NAND

The NAND (Not AND) operation is the opposite of AND, true only if both of the inputs are false. Both the NAND and NOR operations are important in computing because they are particularly simple to mimic with transistors. The other logic functions can be simulated directly with sets of NAND and NOR operations. 'I'm only going so long as Paul and Phil don't both come' is a simple example of a NAND statement. In this case

(unlike NOR) I will still come if one of the pair come. The output (me going) is true only if both of the inputs are false (both of them don't go).

OR

The OR function is a logical function that is true if either input is true. 'If it is either too hot or it rains, we will stay indoors to play chess' is an OR logical statement. Either or both input conditions will cause the output condition (playing chess) to be true.

XOR

The XOR (always pronounced 'exclusive or') logic function is similar to the OR, but is true if one and only one of the input conditions is true. Unlike the OR operation, both input conditions being true does not cause the output to be true. 'Either Tim or Bruce must drive the car to the garage' is an XOR rather than an OR operation; the action of one, and only one, of the two people can make the output (taking the car to the garage) true.

NOR

The NOR logic function is true if either or both of the input conditions are not true. 'If neither Paul nor Phil comes to the party, I will come.' The output (going to the party) is true only if neither of the other two is coming. Otherwise, the output is false. This function always produces the opposite result to the OR function—hence its name (Not OR).

NOT

The NOT Boolean function is the simplest of all, because it has only one input and one output, which are always logically opposite to one another, so that if one is true, the other is false. 'I'm not coming if you are' is a simple example of a NOT statement.

so the process of logical deduction of results from complicated sets of facts can be performed automatically by a machine. The words true and false refer to the mathematical validity of a statement, and do not carry any pejorative overtones. For example, the statement 'If the book is long, it is not short' is logically true (or valid), regardless of the actual length of the book.

In the computer, the concepts of true and false are represented by 5 volts and 0 volts respectively. The information being analysed is symbolized as the input voltages to an electronic logic circuit, and the conclusions are represented by the output voltage of that circuit. The particular operation (AND, OR, etc.) performed by a gate is determined by patterns of electrical connections between its transistors. All inputs and outputs to such circuits must be either one of the two possible voltages. Each individual gate has two binary inputs and one binary output (except the NOT gate). In practice, the computer doesn't process these operations one at a time, but several at once. For example, a microprocessor might operate eight logic gates simultaneously; in such a machine, eight AND operations might simultaneously process sixteen inputs and give eight logic outputs.

The individual operations are trivial; for example, the AND operation has two inputs and produces a high (5 volt) output only if both inputs are high. If either or both of the two inputs are at 0 volts, then the output of an AND gate will also be 0 volts. Different logical functions give different outputs for the same information. For example, while the two inputs of 5 volts will give an output of 5 volts for an AND gate and an OR gate, they will give an output of 0 volts for an XOR (exclusive OR) or a NOR gate. In digital electronics the high-voltage state is standardized at 5 volts, and the low state at 0 volts, so that different kinds of circuit can work together.

Each line of a computer program in a high-level language, a small step in such a complex process, is translated by the computer into at least one (but usually between two and fifty) primitive instructions. A computer program consists of perhaps ten thousand program lines, which are automatically translated into a few hundred trivial logical and arithmetical operations. Computer programs are founded on Boolean logic, but we should never imagine that logical operations are specific to computers. We use them continually in normal conversation—indeed they are so important in computing because they are such a part of everyday situations.

The computer operates on information using the two stable positions of simple switches. These switches, now invariably transistors, can store information of all types, and can also perform operations on that information. The simplicity of this internal binary system in no way restricts the types of information that can be manipulated. An incredible range of information can be stored and then operated on by a computer.

Four Hardware

Processor, memory, and input/output

Hardware is the name given to the physical parts of the computer, contrasting with **software**, the programs that control the function of the machine. A computer system is so complicated that both hardware and software have to be analysed and understood at many different levels of abstraction. All of these can be equally valid; they allow us to understand the computer at the right level of detail, whether we are programming, using, or perhaps repairing the machine. The simplest view of a computer's hardware is as a set of linked boxes, each performing a separate task. One box contains the central processing unit, another the memory of the computer system, and a third communicates with the outside world.

The processor, memory, and peripherals

The central processing unit (CPU) manipulates the data (following the instructions of a program).

The memory stores the instructions and also the information processed, both before and after it has been manipulated.

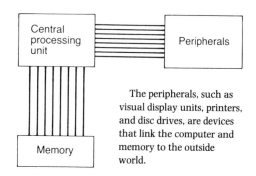

The peripherals, such as visual display units, printers, and disc drives, are devices that link the computer and memory to the outside world.

The central processing unit (CPU) manipulates the information that a program is actually working on. In order to do this, it copies the program and data from the memory. The CPU may be a single integrated circuit, as in a microprocessor, or be built from many circuit boards, as in a mainframe computer. The **memory** is made up of cells, which store both the program and the information that the program works on. The **input/output** (I/O) section of the computer connects the CPU to the **peripherals**, equipment that is not an integral part of the computer. For example, it enables the computer to print or display information, and receive data from discs or sensors. These sensors might be measuring the time, a temperature, or a pressure, providing information for the computer to manipulate. The same elements of the computer are used for both input and output, hence the term input/output. The **computer bus** is the set of control lines that connect the various parts of the computer, enabling them to transfer information to, and keep in time with, one another. The **interface boards** are circuit boards that interpret the electrical signals on the bus, and link the computer to the peripherals.

The central processing unit (CPU)

The engine of the computer is the CPU (examined in fuller detail in the next chapter), which can perform a variety of simple operations. These operations are performed one at a time, each applied to a single piece of data; a sequence of instructions that performs a task forms a computer program. The particular instruction chosen is dictated by the contents of a memory cell, and another cell contains the data to be operated on by that instruction. The CPU fetches both instructions and data from its memory cells and links them together. In single-chip microprocessor systems, the three hardware aspects of processing, memory, and communication are combined on to the same chip of silicon. More often in computers, the three are physically separate chips, with the advantage that peripheral equipment can be linked more easily to the relevant CPU control signals.

The three most important determinants of the processing power of the CPU, and hence of the computer, are its data width, address range, and clock speed.

Data width   The **data width** of a computer is the number of bits of data that it can manipulate at the same time. The set of bits as large as the data width of a machine is often called a **word**. Computers are usually referred to in terms of their data width, an 8-bit system processes 8 bits at once, a 16-bit machine 16 bits, and so on.

In order to be processed, information often requires more bits than a machine's data width. Such information must be split up, stored in more than one memory location, and manipulated with more than one instruction. To store some types of numbers, such as large integers or floating-point numbers, we need 32 or 64 bits per number, depending on the accuracy required. On an 8-bit computer, therefore, these numbers have to be split into four or eight separate blocks (each put into a separate memory cell), only one of which can be operated on at a time. To add two of these numbers on such a small machine would require four or eight instructions, and probably more to check for a 'carry' over between each part of the addition (this is like the need to check for a carry when decimals are added). On a machine with a 64-bit data width, like the Cray supercomputer, manipulating each of these numbers would take only a single instruction.

The processing of information can be an unnecessarily slow and unwieldy operation if a machine with too small a data width is used. For example, imagine a computer is storing figures for attendances at local football games, which may attract crowds of up to 10,000. A number this size requires 14 bits of storage, enough to cope with any number between 0 and 16,383. More sensibly, 16 bits would be used, and the computer could then cope with numbers up to 65,535. In an 8-bit computer, 16 bits of data would have to be split into two 8-bit memory cells. If two crowd totals were then to be added, this would have to be done in two parts, and an extra instruction would be needed to check whether there was a 'carry'. Hence the machine would perform the calculation three times slower than an equivalent 16-bit machine.

However, there is little point in the data width being greater than is needed for the type of information being processed. For example, for the manipulation of text, where each letter requires only 8 bits of storage, an 8-bit machine is as good as a much more complicated machine with a 64-bit data width. When a computer is processing text, the main factor determining its speed is the time taken to process a single instruction. Although computers are usually referred to by their data width, this is not the most critical measure of processing power.

Address range The 'directly addressable memory range' is the amount of memory that can be directly **read** (examined) or **written** (changed) by a computer's CPU. This memory is a line of cells, each one of which contains a small amount of information. In an 8-bit machine, every cell contains 8 bits, or a **byte**, of data. The **address range** is the number of bits that the CPU uses to reach these cells. Each combination of 1s and 0s on the addressing pins of the CPU reaches a different cell of the memory, and can either examine or alter that cell. A 16-bit addressing CPU has sixteen pins for addressing memory cells; the sixteen pins can have 65,536 combinations of 1s and 0s, and so the computer can access this many different memory cells.

A computer stores information not only in its directly addressable memory, but also on mechanical disc drives. Any information that must be retrieved from a disc, rather than from the memory chips, will take thousands of times longer to find, because of the wait while the right part of the computer disc is located. Whereas the access time from a single cell of a memory chip is less than 1 microsecond, it is 20 milliseconds or more from disc storage. Obviously if information can be kept inside the directly addressable, **semiconductor**, memory, it can be read or written much more quickly. The limiting factor for the speed of many programs is the time taken to read and write information held on computer discs, and so a large amount of semiconductor memory can make these programs much faster.

A large memory addressing range is also important in reducing programming effort, because information on discs is usually accessed by programs in a completely different way from information in the semiconductor memory. Disc information is stored and accessed in large blocks, which is a far less flexible arrangement than semiconductor storage, where every cell is directly accessible to the CPU. Even if a programmer wants to change just a single bit stored on a disc, a whole block of perhaps 512 bytes may have to be taken out, modified, and then returned to the disc; and in order to access this information, the programmer must specifically write the appropriate programming instructions.

Suppose we wish to add some new names to a list of customers that is kept, in alphabetical order, on a disc. If all the names on the list can be copied into the semiconductor memory, then each new name can be added, and the updated list copied back to the disc store, the whole updating process being simple and rapid. In comparison, if only a fraction of the list can be addressed directly, the list must be brought out in parts, each of which is sorted out and then restored to the disc. Disc storage is more difficult to program than semiconductor memory, as well as being much slower.

As programs become more complex they need more memory (up to several hundred thousand bytes), and the limitation imposed by a small directly addressable memory becomes a strait-jacket. Programs have to be partly stored on disc, the appropriate sections of the program being brought into the memory when required. Not only is this **overlaying** process slower, but it also needs more organization than if the whole program is contained in the semiconductor memory. A computer with 24 address bits, however, has the capability to address over 16,000,000 bytes of memory, presently sufficient for most programs.

The addressing range of a computer is probably more important than its data width in determining its power. Since the advent of microcomputers able to address more than 16 bits of memory, we have seen a flowering of more complex programs. These programs would have been difficult to cram into the 64 kbytes of the older, 16-bit microprocessors.

One of the main problems with single-chip microprocessors is the number of electrical connections needed. Each bit used, both for data and addressing, must have an electrical connection pin on the integrated-circuit package in order to link its signal to other chips. A 32-bit microprocessor, with thirty-two pins each for providing addressing and data signals to other chips, also needs perhaps another twenty to forty pins for other functions. The resulting package is rather larger and more complicated than it might be. Some microprocessors are therefore built without the full set of thirty-two data lines and thirty-two address lines connected to the integrated-circuit package. For example, the Motorola 68008 microprocessor is essentially a 32-bit chip internally, but only twenty addressing pins and eight data pins are connected to the pins of the chip package, thereby saving on thirty-six connection pins. Transfer of data to and from the chip is slower, but processing inside the chip takes the same time.

The clock speed   When an instruction is being performed in a computer, thousands of transistors are being switched from 'on' to 'off', and vice versa. The sets of transistors may be on separate circuit boards or on one integrated circuit. The switching time of each transistor is slightly different, because of variations in manufacture, and so the transistors would soon become out of sequence with each other without some sort of central timing reference. The central **clock** provides this: it ticks at a fixed rate (usually between 1 million and 100 million times every second), each tick being the signal to start an instruction, or part of an instruction (most instructions take more than one **clock cycle** of the system). Thus the faster the clock rate, the higher the processing power of a given microprocessor.

The power of a computer

It is not possible to define the overall processing power of a computer with a single number, in order to say that one is invariably faster than another. Some computers are better than others for specific tasks, and the speed and capacity of the discs used may also be critical.

Sometime the number of floating-point (normally 64-bit) operations that a computer can perform per second is used as an overall measure of computer power, giving a result in MIPS (Millions of Instructions per Second). However, the MIPS figure is very malleable, particularly in the hands of computer manufacturers. Large variations can be produced by subtle changes, and so computer manufacturers' advertisements should be viewed extremely sceptically. Not for nothing has the acronym been re-christened Meaningless Instructions per Second. For example, if a particular test program needs to manipulate a great deal of information, the speed of the disc drives at transferring information is likely to be a more important part of the overall speed than the processor speed. On such disc-limited operations, the process usually becomes slower if the disc is nearly full up with information—the mechanical parts of the disc drive have further to move to find the data. The time taken by a computer to process such a program might vary by a factor of three, depending on how full the disc is. Unethical manufacturers might be tempted to take advantage of this fact when drawing up comparisons between their own machines and the competition.

Memory

The memory (further discussed in Chapter 8) stores both the program and the data that the program operates on. The CPU interacts directly with the primary, semiconductor, memory, but secondary, disc-based storage is used for all long-term storage. Information is copied between the disc and the semiconductor memory when necessary.

The semiconductor memory, often referred to as the **random access memory (RAM),** is strictly organized, with its various parts allocated to different tasks. For example, the operating system—the software which controls many basic functions of the computer—will occupy a specific part of the memory. An operating system might take between 20 and 100,000 bytes of the memory storage, with extra functions stored on disc, to be brought in when required. One part of the memory which cannot be altered by the CPU is the **bootstrap read-only memory (ROM),** which copies the operating system into the memory from a disc when the computer is switched on. This bootstrap program occupies only a small part of the address range, but because it cannot be changed, other programs must avoid putting information into this area.

A small amount of memory, the **stack,** is reserved by the CPU for the temporary storage of information during calculations. Applications programs (those that give the computer its function) have to fit into the space that is left; the allocation of memory space is co-ordinated by the operating system,

Use of the semiconductor memory in a 16-bit addressing system

This shows how the random access memory is used in a 16-bit addressing microcomputer for two typical applications: firstly when a word-processing package is running, and secondly when a small program is being written in the BASIC language. Elements of the operating system are retained, and used, in both cases. The microcomputer has a 16-bit addressing range and so can access only 64 kbytes (65,536 bytes) of memory. Any good word-processing program will take up more than the 20 kbytes of memory space allowed here, and so elements of the program will be brought in from the disc only when needed. This overlaying process is complicated to organize. Such an example illustrates the restrictions imposed on programmers by 16-bit addressing systems.

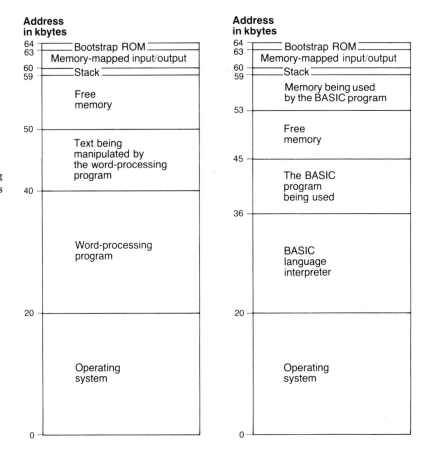

which monitors how the memory is currently employed. In a computer system that is looking after many users, the rest of the memory is shared out between their applications programs under the control of the operating system software.

The computer bus

The computer bus is the highway along which information travels to and from the CPU; it consists of electrical lines that link the CPU to connectors into which extra computer boards can be plugged. Each of these bus connectors usually has all the electrical signals needed to control the computer, so that a circuit board, which might link the CPU to a tape, disc, or printer, can fit into any one of them. Signals are transmitted along wires in synchronism with signals of the computer clock, and each board analyses the signals to see if any action is required. Some small computer systems are built on to a single circuit board, without standard connector slots. Important control signals then have to be routed over the whole board to where they are specifically needed. It is much more difficult to extend the facilities of such a single-board system.

Manufacturers of peripheral equipment usually build interfaces to link their own equipment to the bus of a popular computer, and existing computers can therefore take advantage of any new equipment. For computers like the IBM PC, customers have a choice of hundreds of boards. Even unusual peripherals can be plugged into standard computer systems. For example, when computers are used to process pictures, the picture has first to be put into the computer. This operation requires a scanning device that looks at the brightness of hundreds of thousands of points in the picture and transforms them into numbers. Only one in a thousand computer customers might require such a peripheral, but the manufacturer of a picture-scanner can build a special board, a 'bus interface', to link its equipment up to the customer's, or perhaps write software that enables a standard board to be used.

The computer bus with a circuit board plugged in

The bus of the computer links electrically various computer sections to the central processor in a standardized way. All appropriate signals are brought to every connector, and so a circuit board for a peripheral can be plugged into any of them. Standardized buses allow different companies to build boards for a computer system.

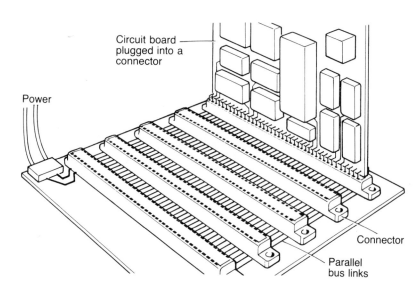

Circuit board plugged into a connector

Power

Connector

Parallel bus links

The bus may be more important and long-lived than the CPU itself. The circuit boards of the CPU represent only a small fraction of the total cost of a computer, and when they become outdated they can be replaced with newer, faster versions, which will link up to the old bus. Computer manufacturers can also make CPU boards of different powers to fit into the same bus. Existing

Tristate devices

Most digital electronic devices can be in one of two states, with their outputs set at either 5 volts or at 0 volts. When two or more circuit boards must work together on a computer bus, they might clash with one another—one might be trying to drive the bus with an output of 0 volts, while the output of the other might have been left at 5 volts. Such boards need to be made from chips with a third possible state, that of appearing to be disconnected from the bus. Devices which have these three states, 5 volts, 0 volts, and 'high impedance', are called **tristate**.

The S-100 bus

One of the simpler computer buses is the S-100 system, which has both a dubious parentage and a rather chequered history, but now seems to have attained respectability. The bus consists of a set of 100 electrical lines, including all the electrical control signals for a CPU. It first appeared in 1975 on the Altair, the first personal computer (see Chapter 9), and initially there was no real standardization. Manufacturers blithely claimed to make boards to the S-100 standard, undisturbed by the fact that no standard had been defined or agreed. When plugged into a computer with the S-100 bus, circuit boards would often not work with others from different companies.

Fortunately, the US Institute of Electrical and Electronic Engineers (the IEEE) adopted this orphan, and the S-100 bus became the IEEE-696/S100 standard. The twenty-four addressing lines on the bus connector enable 16 megabytes of semiconductor memory to be addressed directly, and there are sixteen bus lines for transmitting data. Originally the S-100 bus was designed for the 8-bit Intel 8080 microprocessor, but can now be used by 16-bit machines, since for some strange reason the designers decided to have two different data paths, depending on whether data is being read or written to the CPU. In most other types of bus, the same lines both read and write the data, whilst another bus line indicates which of the two processes is currently occurring. This quirk of having extra lines has been turned to advantage for 16-bit processors, by using the same lines both to read and write 16 bits of data; 8-bit processors transmit and receive in the original way. The S-100 bus can cope with clock speeds of up to 6 megahertz (1 megahertz = 1,000,000 cycles per second), has the connections for between four and twenty-two peripheral boards, and has the control signals to allow up to sixteen other processors to be plugged in and take over control of the bus.

The S-100 is perhaps the world's most popular computer bus, and unlike many others is not tied to the products of a single manufacturer. More than 200 manufacturers make over 1,000 different circuit boards to the S-100 standard, and for small-scale work the bus is satisfactory. Every new microprocessor chip seems to appear first on a board that can plug into the S-100 bus (usually long before there is enough software to do anything practical with the new chip).

However, the S-100 standard has disadvantages compared to other, less arbitrary standards. Perhaps its worst fault is the poor design of the connector that links the board into the computer. About half of the faults that occur in a computer are due to poor connections. Good-quality plugs and sockets, like those used on the more advanced VME bus, reduce this problem, but the S-100 bus will also not be able to take full advantage of the 32-bit processing capabilities of the new generation of microprocessors, and its memory speed is low compared to better buses. Nevertheless, the IEEE standard shows how sensible effort can make a useful product out of a bus that was designed in haste. One of the most surprising things in the changing world of microelectronics is that the obsolete Altair boards still conform to the IEEE-696 standard.

peripherals, which represent the major part of the cost of a system, need not be replaced, for the new processors will still be able to use them. The 'Unibus', the standard bus of the Digital Equipment Corporation (DEC), is a good example of buses' longevity; it has survived since the early 1970s, and hundreds of manufacturers still supply Unibus-compatible boards. Even when DEC introduced its new range of VAX computers in 1977, the equipment had two buses, a new, fast bus and the old Unibus, so that customers could plug their old peripheral equipment into the new system.

Reading from the computer's semiconductor memory

When a CPU (with a data width of 8 bits, in this example) needs to read a byte of data stored in the computer's semiconductor memory, it generates the address that corresponds to the wanted byte. For example, on a 16-bit addressing system, the CPU generates a pattern of voltages on its sixteen address pins, each either 5 volts (1 in binary) or 0 volts (0). This is then sent down the bus to access the contents of one word of the memory. The CPU finds the right information in the memory because the location of the particular memory cell is 'known' to the program. The data has in fact been positioned in the right place in the memory for the particular instruction.

The voltage pattern is applied to the address lines of the bus. One more line of the bus (the read line) is used to signal that a read operation is about to occur. The CPU drives this line (either to 5 or 0 volts) to signal that a read operation is imminent. The CPU generates the address of the byte, and transmits the voltage pattern. This is received by every circuit board plugged into the bus, but only the memory board with the wanted information actually responds. The memories containing the address of the wanted byte are activated and the byte is copied on to the bus and thus transferred to the CPU. This information transfer takes place along lines of the bus reserved for data transmission. On an 8-bit system, eight data lines are used for data transfer. The whole sequence has read only 8 bits of data, but fortunately the process is so fast that the computer can perform several million of these operations every second.

The bus connections

The bus lines are electrical connections that address the memory, carry the data, pass the control signals, and supply the electrical power. This might involve between 50 and 200 wires, which link to a set of connectors, into which circuit boards are plugged. Rather than supply the specific signals needed for a disc drive, for example, at just one particular point, the connections are usually made the same in each connector, enabling boards to be plugged into any available socket. Sometimes techniques of **multiplexing** allow the same lines to send both address and data information after one another. This reduces the number of connections and wires, at the cost of more circuit complexity.

Time and microelectronics

The terms describing time and frequency that are applied to computers are a little unfamiliar, although the usual measuring units of the second and the hertz (1 hertz = one cycle per second) can be used. The **millisecond** (one-thousandth of a second) is convenient for measuring access times to a disc. Because a disc rotates about fifty times a second, each of its revolutions takes about 20 milliseconds. The **microsecond** (μS), one-millionth of a second, is more suitable for the measurement of semiconductor speeds. A computer instruction takes about one microsecond to perform. The **nanosecond** (one-thousand-millionth of a second) describes even faster processes. A fast memory chip might be able to access a single bit in 25 nanoseconds (25 nS). Lest we become blasé about these times, we might remember that a beam of light, moving at 186,000 miles a second, travels only one foot in a nanosecond.

Frequency measurements contain the same information as those for time, but in a different form. A process that happens one thousand times a second has a frequency of 1 **kilohertz** (shortened to 1 kHz). If the event happens one million times a second then the rate is 1 **megahertz** (MHz). A typical use of this measurement might be for the clock speeds of a microprocessor, which are about 10 MHz. Note the use of capital and lower-case letters here: the capital letter M is always the shorthand for 'mega' or million, m for 'milli' or one-thousandth, k for 'kilo' or thousand.

The CPU addresses the semiconductor memory directly, and between sixteen and sixty-four lines of the bus are reserved for this task. The computer might manipulate between 8 and 64 bits of data at once, which are normally transmitted in parallel up and down the bus.

The computer is a synchronous machine, i.e. most of its operations are performed in time with the central clock. The clock's signal is therefore distributed along the bus. Only one peripheral device can send data down the appropriate bus lines at any one time, and so there must be bus connections for the CPU to control data transmission. One bus line transmits signals that indicate that a peripheral wishes to communicate, and another pair of lines indicates whether a memory read or write is required. Many bus systems allow a number of CPUs to be plugged in, and a set of bus connections is then needed to organize the control of the bus between them.

Electrical power may be distributed to the circuit boards through the bus lines. Many boards need only a 5-volt and a 0-volt (earth) line to power their chips, but a few devices do require other voltage levels as well. For example, the serial connection that takes data to and from the VDU needs $+12$ and -12 volts, and so these voltages are usually provided. Otherwise the interface board itself has a voltage converter to generate the necessary voltages.

Input and output

There are two main techniques of communication between the central processing unit and the outside world—**memory mapping** and **port addressing**. Memory-mapped input/output is the simpler type: whenever information is sent to a specific address in the memory, special-purpose hardware automatically organizes the transfer of that information from the position in the memory to the peripherals. The hardware also organizes the transfer when a peripheral sends data to that memory address from the outside world. The whole process is therefore one of addressing a particular part of the memory. In port-addressed computers, there are specific computer instructions for the transfer of information to and from ports, and hence the peripherals.

Serial transfer

The technique of **serial transfer** sends information from one computing device to another one bit at a time, along a single line. For example, the letter A is usually stored using 8 bits, and these 8 bits would be sent one after another. They would be re-formed at the receiver in order to make up the single character. Serial transfer is the normal method of communication between a terminal (VDU) and the CPU. It is suitable for devices connected only by a single channel of communication, such as a cable, or a telephone or radio link, for instance. We are familiar with an old form of serial transfer – the transmission of Morse code, a binary code for letters, along telegraph wires.

There is, fortunately, a well-defined and accepted standard, covering both hardware and software, concerning communication along a serial line—RS-

232C. A letter is converted into the ASCII (American Standard for the Computer Interchange of Information) code, and then transmitted down the serial line, accompanied by a few other bits that control the transfer. The device at the other end of the connection link converts the string of bits back to the original character.

Serial transfer can take place along a pair of wires, a radio link, or an optical fibre. There is even a standard plug (the 25-pin D-type) for serial connections, although this has been taken over for other applications in computers. Most home computers will have one or two D-type sockets with RS-232C standard interfaces. Both the transmitter and the receiver must be switched to the same **baud** rate—they must transfer the same number of bits every second—to be able to interact. VDUs usually operate at 9,600 baud, transferring 9,600 bits per second between the terminal and the CPU. As many as 10 bits are needed in order to transmit a single character, as some are needed for organizing the transfer. Serial transfers between devices take place at predefined rates (such as 300, 1,200, or 9,600 baud), regulated by crystal-controlled clocks in both the transmitter and the receiver. Serial transfer can link computers with different clocks and therefore needs to be an asynchronous process, controlled by an absolute time reference, rather than the uncoordinated clock pulses controlling the computers.

Parallel transfer

Parallel transfer is a rather faster technique for transferring information between the CPU and devices attached to the computer. Like serial transfer, it can use either memory-mapping or port-addressing hardware in the CPU. Instead of using a single electrical connection, information is sent along a large number of electrical connections. A few others control the transfer. Often 8 or 16 bits of information are sent or received at the same time.

The sequence of operations involved in the parallel transfer of a byte of information from a parallel port to a printer is as follows. The CPU must find the byte of information in the memory, read the data, check the parallel port to ensure that it is ready to receive the data, and output the byte from the memory address to the port. The printer receives the byte from the port, and normally prints a single character. Each step of this sequence requires at least one CPU instruction, and hence many clock cycles, for every word of data transferred. Nevertheless, the data rate is sufficiently fast to be suitable for medium- and slow-speed attachments, such as printers or floppy discs.

Direct memory access

Direct memory access (DMA) transfers information to and from the computer memory without it passing through the CPU. DMA is the fastest and most complicated transfer method, and is different on each computer. During the information transfer, DMA electronic hardware takes over control of the whole computer bus and performs the operation without reference to the CPU. The most common use of DMA is for computer disc drives, as it is a quick means of transferring large blocks of data from a disc to the memory of the computer. The DMA controller itself generates the address of the memory position and

Error detection and correction

One of the most powerful features of computer systems is their ability to correct errors in information being stored or processed. In any computer, errors will necessarily creep in, perhaps because a small area of the magnetic disc is badly made, or because an electrical surge in the mains has caused a semiconductor bit to change from 1 to 0. Computer systems can detect and then correct such faults, without the user even being aware that the process is occurring. At first this seems an unlikely function, yet as so often is the case with computers, there is an analogous process that we already use ourselves.

As we have seen, the letters of the alphabet are digital, and so we can use them to illustrate the principles behind error correction. Consider the sentence

Mr Smith went hxme for his dinner.

The average reader has no difficulty in spotting and automatically correcting the error in the sentence. There may be a small delay as the brain checks the faulty word and searches for the correction, but then we would read the sentence as

Mr Smith went home for his dinner.

An error has been spotted and automatically corrected. We are able to perform this correction because we know that the word 'hxme' is not permissible here. We know that it does not exist in the English language. We insert the closest sensible word in our vocabulary, on the assumption that there has only been a small error.

Several important aspects of error correction are illustrated by this process. For example, if the error forms a word that is legitimate in the context, it cannot be corrected. If every combination of the letters in the alphabet were to form a legitimate English word, and every combination of words a legitimate sentence, then such correction would never be possible. The longer the message, the easier it is to correct an error, since there is more contextual information. Furthermore, if there are too many errors, it is too difficult to correct the sentence.

The technique of error correction works because there is redundancy in the language—not every combination of letters has a meaning. Human languages also use apparently unnecessary words to reduce errors in speech or text; consider, for example, the word 'his' in the sentence 'he had a twinkle in his eye'—it conveys no extra information, but serves to protect the meaning of the sentence from distortion.

The process of error detection and correction in computers uses an exactly analogous technique, separating out possible interpretations of information from one another so that they will not be confused even if an error occurs. Consider sending an 8-bit message along a telephone wire. The normal condition is that all combinations of the 8 bits are permissible. A single error would normally produce a value which (unlike 'hxme') could be misinterpreted. But if the technique of error correction is used, extra bits are added to those original 8 bits in such a way that if any one bit is incorrect, then the incorrect information is still closer to the original information than any other possibility, just as hxme was the closest word to home. If a small error occurs, this extra information prevents the erroneous 'word' from becoming too similar to another, incorrect data value, and enables the error to be spotted and corrected.

Error detection is rather simpler to demonstrate than error correction. Imagine that we have 8 bits representing the letter C:

01000011

A ninth 'check' bit (the **checksum**) is added to make the total of all the bits added together into an even number. The bit code representing C has three 1s, and so the 'check bit' must be a 1 to make the total into four. Thus the nine-bit sequence, with the error detecting bit, becomes

01000011 1

If an error occurs in any single bit in this sequence, then it is immediately apparent, because the bits would add up to an odd number. No matter where a single error is, even in the check bit itself, we are able to detect that it is there. The IBM personal computer has this simple 'parity checking' scheme to check for any memory faults. Special-purpose error-detecting hardware checks the memory when the computer is switched on.

The technique of error detection can be extended so as to correct errors automatically. Imagine that we have two bits of information,

1 0

A checksum bit indicates whether the total of the first two is odd or even:

1 0 1

If we have a block of 4 bits

    1 0
    1 1

then the 'check bits' form

    1 0 1
    1 1 0

But we can also use check bits for the vertical pairs

    1 0 1
    1 1 0
    0 1

Whenever an error occurs in one of our 4 data bits, it can now be discovered by examining the checksums for both the rows and the columns. Both the row and the column concerned will add up to give an odd number. We will then know that there is an error, and also where it is, and so be able to correct it automatically. If there is first a problem with one of the check bits, there will only be a single checksum error, in the particular row or column.

If the 8 bits are transmitted one by one (for example over a telephone), and reassembled into the square, then any one error in the data bits can be corrected. But in order to correct any one error that has crept into 4 bits, an extra 4 bits are needed. Fortunately more efficient codes are available, and, in any case, the larger the block of data, the more efficient is the correction technique. The demonstration technique will fail if there is more than one error, but there are better error correction techniques available. For example, the error correction technique used in compact disc players for music can correct 1,500 successive wrong bits, enabling discs to play perfectly even when they are scratched.

Error correction is particularly valuable in computers with large amounts of semiconductor memory. Such machines have millions of bits of memory information, and errors do occasionally appear. The use of error detection can warn the user of faults, and faulty boards can then be replaced, while error correction can actually rectify such faults without the user being aware that they exist, or problems being generated. For example, the Cray 64-bit computer employs an extra 8 bits for these two tasks. These enable a warning to be given if one or two of the 64 bits are wrong, and can automatically correct one wrong bit. If 3 bits are incorrect the hardware cannot cope, but this situation is unlikely, and so such computers run for years without a single memory error.

then injects the data values into the memory. The process of reading information from the computer memory works along similar lines. DMA is a faster process than either serial or parallel transfer because data is transferred at the maximum rate that the memory can cope with, and is not slowed down by being routed via the CPU.

Naturally this whole sequence of events must be performed under the control of the CPU, in order to avoid spoiling information in the memory that may be required for another task. When a block of information is to be transferred from the main memory to a disc, the CPU tells the DMA controller the starting address in the memory, and the size of the block to be transferred. This data is usually to be copied from the disc into an unbroken sequence of semiconductor memory. Prompted by the program that is running, the DMA controller asks the CPU for permission to take over control of the bus by sending a signal down the bus request line. The CPU signifies that permission has been granted by returning a signal down the **bus acknowledge** line. Control of the bus is then temporarily given up by the CPU. When the data transfer is complete, the DMA controller passes control back to the CPU.

Five Inside the Central Processing Unit

From the earliest days of computers, their complexity has forced designers into dividing them into discrete elements. Each modular part of the computer is perfected separately and then linked to another section. Even the single chip of a microprocessor has to be designed in modules, so that each of them can be tested individually, and this segmentation is clearly visible in the physical arrangement of its transistors. As computers grow more complex, this modular approach becomes more important. A microprocessor can contain half a million transistors, and a powerful mainframe computer will have thousands of chips spread out over a large number of circuit boards. One wrong, or broken, connection between any pair of transistors could be sufficient to prevent the whole computer from working correctly. Such problems can only be diagnosed if we are able to isolate the problem area, and test it independently. Modularization also has the advantage that it enables us to analyse the component parts of the CPU on an individual basis.

Operations inside the central processing unit

The central processing unit is the heart of the computer. Element by element, the program and the information to be processed by the program are transferred from the memory for processing by the CPU. Physically the CPU is made from many thousands of interlinked transistors, each of which can be switched to either the 'on' state (conducting electricity) or the 'off' state (not conducting). The various instructions of the CPU correspond to small groups of transistors at different places on the chip; each group is able to perform a single fixed instruction on data supplied to its input. The **arithmetic and logic unit (ALU)** of the CPU performs the actual arithmetical or logical operations on the information. All instructions may be formed out of smaller subinstructions (**microprogramming instructions**), linked together automatically inside the computer. Individual CPU instructions take at least one, and usually several, cycles of the computer clock, and a microprocessor can perform about one million such operations every second.

Both instructions and data are kept in the memory, and in order to perform an instruction the CPU first copies the content of the first memory cell of the program, and determines what operation is specified. If data is to be operated on by that instruction, the CPU copies this from the memory as well, and then links the data and the instruction by switching transistors, rather like railway points, so that there is a continuous electrical path between the data and the group of instructions that are to process it. The operation is performed on the data, and then the result sent to its destination, using another continuous path created by the same switching techniques. The destination of the processed data is selected by the computer program itself. The parts of this instruction cycle are usually referred to as **fetch, decode**, and **execute**.

Together a set of instructions perform a single task, and so form a program. The sequence of **machine instructions** which make up a program have been directly selected either by the programmer or by the compiler within the computer, which translates a program in a high-level language into the machine's instructions.

The serial processor

The computer is called a **serial processor** because it follows instructions one at a time. The machine knows only to perform the current instruction that it has taken from its memory, a single operation in a program containing many thousands.

The sequence for a serial operation

Imagine that a computer is running a program to calculate your income tax. This program would have originally been specified in a programming language, and then translated into the machine instructions of the computer you are using. The translation of the program is stored on disc until you need it, at which time it is transferred into the fast, semiconductor memory of the computer. The sequence of instructions for the computer to perform now lies in the individual cells of the semiconductor memory. Here are the questions about how much you earn and what your allowances are, as well as the routines which will actually work out how much you need to pay, and then display the results for you. Some of the cells contain information (such as tax allowances), and others contain instructions to operate on that information (such as subtractions). All the computer can do is to copy the memory cells of the program, and perform the specified operations. Depending on your answers to questions about your tax, different parts of the program will be activated, other sections perhaps not being used at all.

In human terms, computer behaviour is very strange—the CPU 'knows' nothing about what it is going to do in the future. It is as if we were opening an envelope every few minutes and obeying the enclosed instruction. The envelope is one of a large pile of similar envelopes. As well as giving us the single instruction, the contents of the envelope will tell us which envelope to open next. This would normally be the next one in the pile; however, the envelope could ask us a question and, given the appropriate answer, then direct us to a completely different envelope. There is no past or future for the CPU, only the monotonous processing of one instruction after another.

A computer instruction can also tell the machine to go back to a memory cell it has already examined. This is called **looping**, and we can see that unless there is a way of breaking out, the machine could continue to cycle indefinitely through the same set of operations. Hence programmers always make certain that somewhere inside a loop there is an instruction that will allow the cycle to be broken—for example, an instruction like 'if it is dark, go to memory cell number 567, otherwise read this memory cell again'. The program continues processing the same instructions until eventually dusk falls and the cycle is broken by an instruction to open memory cell number 567. Branching instructions are important because they make the course of a computer program unpredictable. The program path will vary depending on intermediate results.

Before a program in a high-level language, such as BASIC, can be run in a machine, it has first to be translated into the instructions that are available on the particular computer. A typical computer has a repertoire of between 50 and 500 different basic operations, which together form its **instruction set**. The instruction set available on a CPU will vary with the manufacturer, unless a number of CPUs have been specifically designed to be compatible.

An **assembly language** is a symbolic representation of the machine instructions of a computer, designed in order to make programs easier to write. Each instruction is represented by a mnemonic (such as ADD for addition or SUB for subtraction) that is supposed to indicate the action of that instruction. These mnemonics are translated by a computer program into their respective machine instructions. Normally assembly language programs cannot be used on a different machine.

The low-level instructions performed by the CPU are always hidden from a programmer using high-level languages such as BASIC or FORTRAN, who is able to call on more abstract functions provided by such languages. Using these languages, the programmer writes a specification of what he or she wants the program to do, and this is then translated by a compiling program into the particular instructions that the individual CPU can perform. If a computer language is commonly used and standardized, then many manufacturers

A small part of a program in a computer memory

Each of the memory cells of a computer contains a number, and this can represent either an instruction to be performed or a data value. On the left is a column of eleven memory cells, and the central column describes what the number in each cell means. Together the numbers form a small part of a computer program. On the right, the CPU is shown reading a memory cell containing the number 107, which represents an instruction. The CPU has already processed the first three instructions of the subprogram; it has also read three data values, and written a new one back into the memory. Normally the computer processes the memory cells one after the other, but the comparison instruction could lead to the CPU jumping to some other part of the memory for instructions.

The diagram illustrates the need for registers in the CPU for temporary storage, for example, the value 179 needs to be retained while several instructions are being performed.

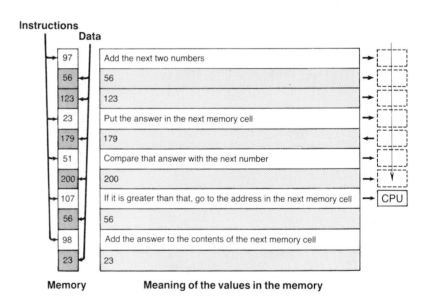

Instructions

Data

97	Add the next two numbers
56	56
123	123
23	Put the answer in the next memory cell
179	179
51	Compare that answer with the next number
200	200
107	If it is greater than that, go to the address in the next memory cell
56	56
98	Add the answer to the contents of the next memory cell
23	23

Memory   Meaning of the values in the memory

CPU

will provide compilers for the same language, and the same computer program can be translated for a number of machines. The high-level program will produce the same results on each machine, even though the machine instructions used will be different.

CPU instruction types

Most CPU instructions fall into the few general classes outlined here. In a sense these individual operations are not important, because each is so simple. Yet all programs, from the most simple to the most complex, are formed out of sequences of these individual operations, and so we should have some idea of the instructions that underlie the performance of the machine.

Logical operations

The six basic logical operations are NOT, AND, OR, XOR, NAND, and NOR (see p. 42), each of which is able to perform a single step of Boolean logic on between 8 and 64 bits of data at the same time, depending on the data width of the computer. These Boolean operations are directly replicated by transistors, with the true and false of Boolean logic becoming 5 and 0 volts respectively.

Arithmetical operations

The arithmetical operations available as basic machine instructions always include addition and subtraction. Multiplication and division by a factor of two are also simple to provide. These instructions operate on the data width of the computer, adding two 16-bit numbers on a 16-bit computer, for example. If the numbers to be manipulated require more storage than the data width, then they must be put into several memory cells and the calculation must be performed in more than one operation. A few other arithmetical functions, such as adding or subtracting one from a number (**incrementing** and **decrementing**), are also available as machine instructions.

Specific instructions to perform multiplication and division are not usually provided on small computers, because they would require a large number of transistors. These operations have to be built up from a series of addition and subtraction instructions. Floating-point arithmetic requires the ability to process two numbers with at least 64-bit (and possibly 80-bit) accuracy. Each floating-point instruction has to be made up from hundreds of simple instructions, and so they are very slow on a computer without the necessary hardware.

Comparison and branching operations

Comparison instructions enable the CPU to check data values and then access different parts of the program depending on the result of the comparison. This process is called **conditional branching**. For example, the result of a calculation may be checked to see if it is negative, and depending on the result the computer will branch to different parts of the program. Conditional branching instructions might be part of a computer program to check the balances of a bank's clients in order to send out notices to all customers who are overdrawn. 'If the bank balance is negative, then send a rude letter; otherwise offer the customer a free piggy bank.' The computer examines each customer's account, and if the balance is negative, the program moves to the part of the program that sends out the rude letter. Of course, if the computer sends out a letter only if the balance is not positive, then it commits the cardinal error of being rude to a customer with precisely nothing in his or her account.

Conditional branching instructions are needed for the structure of **loops** in programs—for example where an operation has to be performed a set number of times, or until a certain condition has been met. A program might repeat a set of instructions until a printer is ready to print more text, or it might follow a loop whilst it subtracts the same amount of money from a series of bank accounts.

Data transfer

The largest group of computer instructions do not actually alter any information, but simply move it around. Information may need to be transferred between different registers or addresses in the memory. A range of different types of **move** instructions are available for this. The simplest is one that will transfer a word of information between the memory and a register.

Many complicated types of move instructions are available in order to simplify the programmer's work. With 'indirect' addressing, the computer finds out from a memory cell where to put the data. 'Autoincrementing' addressing is used for moving large blocks of information around. After every instruction, the computer moves to the next memory cell and performs the same operation again. Such instructions make it easy to move large blocks of data and also shorten assembly language programs. Flexibility in move operations is vital in speeding up computer programs, because such instructions form a large part of many computer programs.

A typical instruction for data movement might involve transferring data from a CPU register into a particular memory position. In an assembly language, this would be written as a single line of a program, and might be something like:

MOVE A, (2000)

where A is the register holding the data, and 2000 is the memory address. The syntax of this line depends on the **assembler**, the program that translates it into a machine instruction. In order to move the contents of one register of the CPU (register B) into another (register A), the instruction might be:

MOVE B,A

Subroutines, calls, returns, and jumps

In the course of performing a program, the same set of instructions may be used several times; but the programmer only need write such **subroutines** or **calls** once. The computer spends a considerable amount of its time using subroutines stored in some part of its memory, and then returning to the mainstream of the program. These calls or subroutines are invoked in an assembly program by a standard name, which the assembler recognizes. For example, the instruction to load data from the memory to a disc might be,

CALL DISKLOAD

which would cause the program to move to the part of the memory containing the DISKLOAD **procedure** or **subroutine**. This elemental piece of software might already exist as part of the computer **operating system**, which is the program supplied by the computer manufacturer that enables the computer to perform many basic functions. At the end of the DISKLOAD subroutine there is a **return** instruction, which automatically returns the CPU to the instruction after the original call.

Jump instructions simply move the program to operations which are stored as a set of instructions in a different area of the memory. Such an instruction can be unconditional, i.e. the program will always perform it, or it can be dependent on the result of a previous operation, turning it into a type of branch instruction.

Other types of instruction

Computers usually have a variety of other instructions, such as for setting individual bits in memory cells and registers to 0 or 1, or checking to see whether bits in a memory cell are 1 or 0. This type of instruction could be used to check whether a number is odd or even, for instance. Input or output of data by the computer may be performed either by specific instructions or by hardware at specific parts of the memory.

Registers

The CPU has several types of register, in which it stores intermediate results or any data it may require frequently. Instructions that use this internal memory are faster than those which need to go to the external, semiconductor memory for information, for there is not the delay while information is read or written between the CPU and the memory. Most registers are available for the programmer to use, but the program counter and stack pointer registers are normally changed automatically by the computer or the operating system. The programmer can examine values in these registers to diagnose problems, but cannot alter them.

Program counter

The **program counter** register monitors the current position of the program. Remember that the program is stored in the computer memory, and that an instruction is usually stored next to the data that it operates on. Therefore both instructions and information are mixed up in the computer memory. To complicate matters, different instructions may occupy a different amount of memory—usually either two or three cells. Furthermore, the computer program does not necessarily proceed sequentially, but may loop a number of times, or leave out parts of the program, depending on the results of calculations. It is the program counter that 'knows' the length of each instruction, and so can track the progress of a program and make sure that the CPU does not confuse instructions and data.

Stack pointer   As well as its own internal memory the CPU reserves a small amount of semiconductor memory for storing excess information that it cannot itself retain. The **stack** is monitored by a special-purpose register, the **stack pointer**. The CPU deposits or retrieves information in the stack memory on a 'first-in last-out' basis. This means that information is retrieved from the stack in inverse order to the way it was entered. The CPU may use the stack memory to store the data from its registers when it is forced to interrupt a current task, and attend to a different one. The stack pointer indicates how much semiconductor memory is being employed for this purpose. Whenever more information is 'pushed' into the stack memory, or 'popped' from it, the stack pointer changes to indicate the new position of the top of the stack in the memory.

Flag register   Each single bit of the **flag** register (a 'flag') signals a binary conclusion about the last instruction that the computer has performed. For instance, an 8-bit flag register signals eight different conclusions about an operation. The flags are automatically set by the CPU, but can be read by computer instructions available to the programmer. A good example of a flag is the zero flag in the flag register of the Zilog Z80 microprocessor, which indicates whether or not the result of the previous instruction was zero. If two equal numbers have just been subtracted, then the zero flag is automatically set at 1, but otherwise it is fixed at 0.

Other types of flag can indicate whether there has been a carry after an addition or subtraction, or whether the answer is negative or positive. Many computer instructions can, in one operation, check a flag register and then, depending on the result, jump to one of two specified parts of a program.

Interrupts

Interrupts enable the computer to control several programs at once. A good analogy for the interrupt is a telephone call. We do not wait around in case there is a call; the bell on the telephone rings, and we then stop what we are doing. If we are in the middle of something really important, we ignore the phone call.

The computer will similarly attend to long-term jobs, while still being able to respond to interruptions, whether they are emergencies or trivia. The CPU may be working its way through a one-hour-long job, when suddenly another device calls on its attention. This interrupting device sends a signal to the CPU, and the computer checks to find out whether the request has a higher priority than the job currently being undertaken. This 'interrupt priority' determines

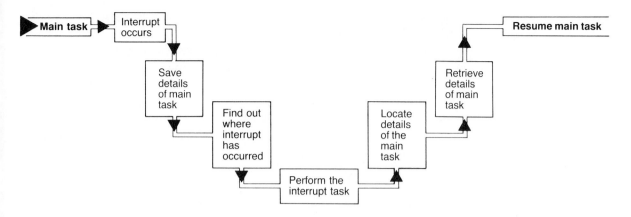

An interrupt

Interrupts allow a single computer to control several programs. Take the following (rather extreme) example. A steel-factory computer might be processing details of the factory payroll, and also adjusting the rollers in the steel mill from time to time. The interrupt breaks the flow of the main job—processing the payroll—and makes the computer perform the more urgent task—adjusting the rollers. While the new job is being dealt with, details of the original task must be retained (either in a protected area of the semiconductor memory or on disc) to enable it to be picked up again properly after the interrupt. When the new task has been performed, the old one is retrieved. Of course, the interrupt itself may be interrupted . . .

whether or not the present job is disturbed. If the new task is sufficiently important to allow the present task to be interrupted, the information in the registers and memory is transferred and preserved elsewhere, either being stored on disc or in the stack. The new task is dealt with next, and then the CPU returns to the previous task, restoring the original values to the registers and memory, after finding them on disc or in the stack.

There are two types of interrupt: **non-maskable** and **maskable**, controlled by hardware and software respectively. The non-maskable interrupt consists of a physical connection between the CPU and the peripheral device which needs to interrupt. When a signal comes down this line the computer always attends to it. A typical example is the **reset** button used on many home computers. When things have gone awry, rather than switching off and starting again, the computer may be restarted by pressing the reset button. This might be used when the paper jams whilst text is being output from a printer. The use of the reset interrupt forces the computer to jump to the bootstrap routine, which loads the operating system of the computer, just as if it is being switched on again.

The maskable interrupt is usually more flexible than its hardware counter-part. A variety of possible tasks (the interrupts) can be stored in different parts of the computer's memory, and the task that the computer must perform next can be chosen by the device that wants use of the computer. This device supplies the 'jump address' to the CPU, i.e. the position in the memory of the program that it wants activated. Maskable interrupts can be switched off (hence the name) or given a relatively low level of priority, so that the computer will not be disturbed while attending to a critical task. For example, the computer might be waiting to receive a radio signal from a satellite passing overhead, and so needs to be able to suppress other, less critical calculations while this radio signal is being dealt with. Computer instructions are provided both to suppress, and allow, maskable interrupts. Even a simple 8-bit micro-processor, like the Zilog Z80, has a specific instruction to disable non-maskable interrupts while it is in the crucial stages of a program. However, the Z80 does not have a very sophisticated system for allocating priorities to different tasks.

Newer microprocessors are more powerful and have special-purpose control chips for complex interrupt operations.

Interrupts enable computers to be shared between many tasks, and yet still be able to respond quickly to a crisis, major or minor. For example, a microprocessor in a greenhouse may be controlling the temperature and humidity, while the interrupt line could be connected to automatic devices which detect the formation of frost. Interrupts will be very rare, but in the event of one the computer must respond quickly to prevent greenhouse crops being ruined. The interrupt therefore has total priority over any other program.

Interrupts are essential for the sensible operation of multi-user computer systems. Where many users are typing in computer programs, each individual user sitting at a terminal may be entering perhaps one letter every second or so. If the whole computer were to be devoted to just one person, only a small fraction of its potential power would be used. Instead, the computer attends to other tasks, and is awakened to the fact that it is needed by an interrupt, even when this is only to deal with the entry of a single letter.

Computers vary greatly in how their interrupts are organized. It is difficult for interrupts to be encapsulated within a high-level language, and so they are normally dealt with at the level of the operating system. Although this means that they are hidden from programmers who use only high-level languages, they are still a vital element in computer efficiency, especially for multi-user computers or systems that have to respond to events in the world external to the computer.

Speeding up the CPU

The basic serial structure of a computer that has been explained here is valid for almost all computers. It was first clearly described by John von Neumann in 1945, and so is often referred to as the **von Neumann architecture**. There are many modifications of this serial approach which are able to squeeze out more performance. All add complexity and expense, and some produce problems for computer software, but in particular circumstances they may be worthwhile options.

Prefetch of instructions

The instructions that the computer is to perform are stored as a sequence in the memory of the machine, and time must be spent fetching them one by one into the CPU. The technique of prefetching brings both the next few instructions and the relevant data into the CPU before they are actually required, so as not to waste time. Because the program may branch to any other part of the memory, it is pointless loading long sequences of instructions into the CPU. Instructions that have been brought in may have to be abandoned. However, the instruction most likely to be performed is actually the next one in the memory, and so it does save time to fetch in the next few instructions. Most modern 16- and 32-bit microprocessors have this prefetch capability built into their chips. Prefetching is done entirely in the computer hardware, and requires no action from the programmer.

Cache memory

A small amount (typically 1–10 kbytes) of **cache** memory installed in, or close to, the CPU can speed up its operations by rapidly providing data which would otherwise have to be fetched from the main semiconductor memory. Data fetched from the cache memory arrives perhaps ten times as fast as that from the normal semiconductor memory. Attached to the cache memory is hardware that continuously monitors the CPU's interaction with the semiconductor memory. The cache takes over the process of writing information to the memory from the CPU, which can then attend to the next instruction (which may not require memory access). When the CPU requires data from the memory that is already duplicated in the cache, the cache automatically intervenes and provides it. The cache is able to provide the required information more than 95 per cent of the time, because many types of programs use information in a predictable fashion.

The success of cache memory depends on the type of problem involved, but such hardware can usually speed up a computer system by perhaps 20 to 50 per cent, at relatively low extra cost. It has to be constructed specifically for the particular kind of computer, but has the great advantage that no programming effort is required. Again, the latest microprocessors have cache memory built into their chips.

Arithmetic coprocessors

Arithmetic, or 'floating-point', **coprocessors** are special-purpose chips that can perform numerical operations much more quickly than the basic CPU. These might be operations on floating-point numbers, such as dividing 1.541 million by 3.456 thousand. Rather than the CPU performing the several hundred operations necessary for such a floating-point division, the numbers are transmitted to the arithmetic processor, and then the CPU waits for the results. On a multi-user computer, the CPU might attend to some other task while it is waiting. Numerical processing is performed much faster by the arithmetic processor because it has been designed specifically for the task. Modern 32-bit microprocessors now have their own specific number-crunching chips in order to speed up numerical calculations.

The Intel 8087 integrated circuit is probably the best-known example of such a specialized processor, and is usually referred to as a numeric coprocessor, because it is attached alongside the microprocessor it was designed for, the Intel 8086. The 8087 monitors the instructions being sent to the microprocessor, and when it sees the specialist floating-point instructions it takes over automatically. In a program primarily processing numbers, the judicious use of the 8087 could speed up a program by a factor of a hundred, but in a general-purpose program the improvement factor would probably only be between two and ten. The 8087 takes only 27 clock cycles to perform a high-precision floating-point division, whereas the 8086 on its own would take 2,100. The IBM personal computer uses an 8088 microprocessor, compatible with the 8086, and has a vacant slot for the 8087 coprocessor. The 8087 is an expensive chip, however, being as complex as a large microprocessor and not produced in such large numbers.

The problem with numerically oriented chips lies in their software. Ideally, programs for a microprocessor should be written in a high-level language, regardless of whether or not floating-point hardware is also being used. The compiling program that translates programs for the particular machine therefore has to be designed to take advantage of the floating-point processor if it is available. This involves a great deal of effort, and is not often done: if the user then writes software for the coprocessor, it is specific to the particular chip, and cannot be used on another computer without the numeric hardware.

Graphics processing

More and more of the processing power of computers is being absorbed into the organization of graphics, the presentation of information to the user as colourful, high-resolution drawings on a VDU screen. If a computer system has a graphics coprocessor chip, the CPU can delegate this time-consuming task. Newer computers, such as the Commodore Amiga, incorporate these chips; the combination of 32-bit microprocessor, numeric coprocessor, and graphics chip provides enormous computing power to the single user.

Pipelining

In a computer program, calculations are often performed repetitively on whole sets of information. For instance, a computer program might be converting several hundred temperatures from Centigrade to Fahrenheit. The sequence

Pipelining in computers

Pipelining is rather like assembly-line manufacturing. Several CPUs are used for one task, with each performing a single step in the process, and then passing on the result to the next processor. A simple example of a three-stage pipelining process is shown: a table of Centigrade values is being converted into Fahrenheit by three CPUs.

Some of the advantages and disadvantages compared to using a single processor are readily apparent. Communication between and synchronization of the modules are more important than for a simple serial machine. Pipelining is worth while only for large numbers of repetitive calculations; if there are only a few values to be worked on, then setting up the calculation would lose more time than is saved. Furthermore, as on an assembly line, the slowest function determines the speed of the whole process.

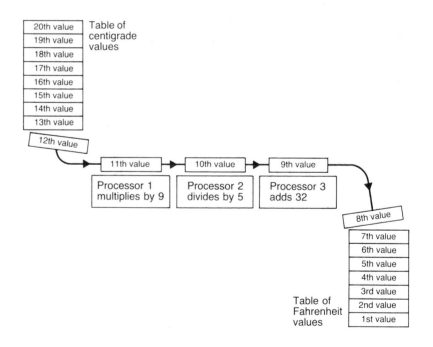

necessary for each number is to multiply by 9, divide by 5, and then add 32. If three separate CPUs were available within the same computer system, then each could perform one of the three parts of the calculation. Providing that the information transfer between the processors takes place rapidly enough, there is a net saving in time. This assembly-line division of the task into sequential elements is called **pipelining**, and is often used to speed up suitable tasks.

Pipelining is at the highest state of its art in supercomputers, such as the CDC supercomputers, which not only have special-purpose pipelining hardware, but also programs that direct tasks to the hardware able to process the particular function most quickly. High-level-language translators attempt to detect when this specialized hardware can be brought to bear on a problem. The so-called 'array processors', which are often linked up with minicomputers, do not normally operate on 'arrays' of data, but are high-speed pipelining machines.

Pipelining is suitable for repetitive tasks which can be split into separate elements, but it cannot be applied to less structured problems. The analysis of software that is necessary in order to detect whether such a division of labour is feasible is difficult to automate. Pipelining techniques are also different on different machines, and no one wants to write programs specific to a particular pipeline processor. Programmers want to write software in a standard language so that it can be used on other machines as well. Nevertheless, pipelining is the most common form of **parallel processing** (see Chapter 15), the technique of linking a number of CPUs to speed up a computer system.

Six The Microprocessor

The microprocessor is a computer that has been made on a single 'chip' of silicon about 4 to 6 millimetres square, and ½ millimetre thick. The smallest computer needs a minimum of a few thousand transistors, and this many were first put on a single chip in 1971. The first microprocessor (the Intel 4004) was a 4-bit chip (i.e. manipulated 4 bits of data at once), with a clock speed of 100,000 hertz. In the decade following the appearance of the 4004, the processing power of a single chip increased several hundred times. Microprocessors (usually referred to as 'micros') have now grown enormously complicated, and their design takes many years of effort by teams of engineers. The chips are so complicated that the various functional parts are designed and perfected separately, and then linked together.

The first microprocessor

Intel's 4004 processor was designed in 1971 under the direction of Ted Hoff, who realized that all the processing required for a new calculator could be put on to one chip. Hoff's previous mini-computer experience had shown him that electronic hardware could be simplified if it were controlled by software, i.e. complexity in hardware and software were interchangeable. The big advantage of software is that it is easier to alter. The functions provided by the calculator could then be altered by reprogramming two memory chips, without altering the design of the processor chip. The 4004 proved to be sufficiently general-purpose to be built into a range of equipment, including traffic-lights, video games, and cash registers. There are 2,300 transistors in the chip, which is long since obsolete.

Most of the chips called microprocessors are not in fact complete computers, but rather the central processing units of computers. The chips need additional memory, a clock, and input/output facilities in order to interact with the outside world. Self-contained single-chip microprocessors are produced—the first, the 8048, was produced by Intel in 1976—but such chips are normally to be found controlling simple, single-purpose machines, such as washing-machines, cameras, or calculators. Personal computer systems are usually built from CPU-only chips, because additional chips or circuit boards can be attached more easily to these than to totally self-contained chips. The term **microprocessor** is therefore applied to any chip that contains the whole of a CPU.

The early microprocessors were simple enough for their computer instructions to be designed ('hard-wired') directly into the chip as connections between transistors on the chip. Examination of such chips shows a complex web of wiring, seemingly connecting at random different sections of the chip. Today the machine instructions of most microprocessors are controlled by a built-in read-only memory (ROM—see Chapter 8). If there is a design fault, altering the ROM is a relatively simple operation and is unlikely to affect any other part of the microprocessor. Organizing the functions of a microprocessor with a ROM requires the use of an area of silicon about 20 per cent greater than if an equivalent 'hard-wired' microchip is used. But the design process is much simpler, and extra instructions can be added to the microprocessor later.

Because of its general applicability, the microprocessor is much slower, and the chip larger, than an integrated circuit designed for a specific task would be. However, it is quite fast enough for most purposes, and its flexibility usually compensates for the loss of speed. One chip can be programmed to perform many different tasks, instead of a new circuit design being needed for each problem.

Microprocessors have changed the role of electronics engineers, who previously spent their time designing and wiring up boards using a few dozen integrated circuits. Whenever a new circuit was required, it was designed and constructed from scratch. Instead of designing a circuit board for a specific problem, the engineer now writes a program to make a standard board perform the particular task—a demonstration of the fact that hardware and software are to a great extent interchangeable. Of course, microprocessors must be able to interact with the outside world; for example, if they are to control central heating, they have to be able to read thermometers, and switch water valves on and off. A small amount of new electronic circuitry might then need to be built, but the wide variety of standard boards available definitely reduces the requirement to design and build specific boards.

The Zilog Z80

The Z80 is one of the most popular microprocessors ever built, and is at the heart of many personal computer systems. The Z80 was originally developed by the Zilog Corporation of Cupertino, California, a company founded by a small group of engineers who left Intel in 1975. As well as still being produced by Zilog, the chip is now also made under licence by a dozen other companies, and illegally by several others.

The Microprocessor

The Zilog Z80

The Z80 microprocessor was developed by a group of Zilog engineers who had left the Intel Corporation. They produced a chip which could not only use all the software for Intel's 8080 chip, but also run it faster. The Z80 has been used extensively for personal computer systems: every letter of this book was processed by a Z80, because the text was written on a word-processing system using one.

Z80 pin connections

The Z80 is an 8-bit data, 16-bit addressing chip. This means that it performs all its basic instructions on 8 bits of data simultaneously, and has 16 bits available for addressing its random access memory (RAM). Each combination of 1s and 0s on the address lines reaches the information in one cell of the computer's memory, and so allows the chip to address 65,536 bytes of memory.

The forty pins on the outside of the Z80 microprocessor package are linked directly to the silicon chip by thin wires inside the package. Between them the **address** and **data** pins take up twenty-four of these forty pins. Two other pins (5 and 0 volts) supply electrical **power**, and a further two are used to signal that either a **read** or a **write** operation is being performed.

Two pins are used for the microprocessor **clock**—one to put clock pulses into the chip, and another for the micro to indicate to other chips which part of the clock cycle has been reached. Two more are used for **interrupt** control, one for a hardware interrupt, the other for a more flexible, software interrupt. There is also a **reset** pin, a specific kind of interrupt; this pin is normally at 5 volts, but when 0 volts are applied, the microcomputer abandons whatever it is doing and moves to a predefined part of the memory. A **wait** pin is used to suspend the program until a peripheral, such as a disc, is ready to respond, and a **halt** pin makes the microprocessor pause until an interrupt arrives. Another pin (the **input/output ready** pin) is used to signal that the Z80 has the address of

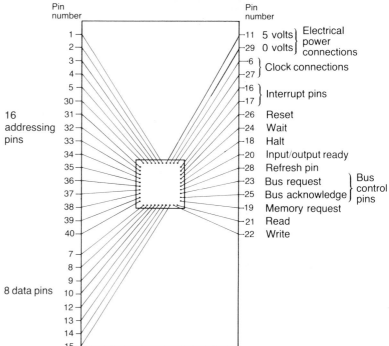

an input or output port on part of the address lines.

The Z80 has circuitry built on to the chip to co-ordinate the process of refeshing any attached dynamic memory (see Chapter 6), and the **refresh** pin signals to those chips that the sequence can begin. **Memory**

request pins allow the Z80 to indicate to the memory chips whether an instruction is examining or altering the contents of the memory. **Bus request** and **bus acknowledge pins** are used to ask the CPU for control of the computer bus, and for the CPU to grant this request, to a disc controller for example.

Zilog made the sensible decision to build a microprocessor that could do everything the already popular Intel 8080 microprocessor could do, and more. The Z80 is software-compatible with the 8080: the 158 instructions of the Z80 include all 78 instructions of the 8080. This means that a Z80 can run all the software written for the 8080, but the Z80 chip cannot be plugged into the same circuit board as the 8080, because the pin connections are different. Zilog recognized that compatibility in software is more important than compatibility in hardware. A considerable amount of software already existed for personal computers using the 8080 chip. The natural way to improve the performance of these computers was to upgrade the processor chip to the Z80, which could still run all of the old software.

Initially, the highest clock speed of the Z80 was more than twice that of the 8080, 2.5 MHz ($2\frac{1}{2}$ million cycles per second) compared with 1 MHz. Apart from this increase in speed, existing applications could be speeded up by taking advantage of the extra instructions and improved interrupt features of the Z80. Unlike the 8080, the Z80 can be programmed to move large blocks of data with a single instruction. Another of its advantages is that it requires only one voltage supply (5 volts) compared to the three (5, -5, and 12 volts) necessary for the Intel chip. New software written to take advantage of these extended features cannot be used with the Intel chip. Although the Z80 is now technically obsolete, faster versions (Z80A and Z80B), as well as the investment in existing software, will ensure that its basic design will be with us for many years. In 1983, Zilog announced the Z800 family of chips, which will be able to use Z80 software, but has increased performance. The Z800 can address 1 megabyte of memory, has extended arithmetic instructions, and a higher clock speed.

'Upwards compatibility'

Zilog's trick of making the Z80 perform all the 8080's functions and more ('upwards compatibility') is used time and time again in the electronics industry. As soon as a product becomes an established success, a host of 'compatible' rivals appear. Often the original firm is so busy producing its popular product that it doesn't keep an eye on the competition until it is too late. The newcomers must offer more facilities at a lower cost, in order to gain a slice of the market. Because customers have written software for the standard model, they can use the new equipment immediately, providing it is software-compatible. The customer gets more performance, at the risk that the 'look-alike' product will not run some particular piece of software.

The new product might well be made by a group of engineers who had left their old firm after their suggestions for improvements had been turned down by the management. Writs and counter-writs are issued, making the lawyers rich although usually no one wins a cent in court. In Silicon Valley, California, the heartland of the microelectronics industry, this process has become so institutionalized that venture capitalists can judge the quality of a project by the number of writs issued by the engineers' old company. If it's not worth suing, then the idea can't be very good. After the dust settles, the natural response of the firm producing the standard model is to come up with a better product, compatible with their own original equipment, but incompatible with the extra features offered by the new firm. Intel did this with the 8085 microprocessor chip, which was compatible with the 8080, but not with the Z80.

Support chips

Each different microprocessor needs a set of support chips so that it can link up with terminals, printers, disc drives, and other peripheral equipment. These chips are tailored to the particular microprocessor, and the Z80 needs only a few other integrated circuits in order to control, for example, a washing-machine or a greenhouse.

Developments of the Z80

The clock speed of the Z80 microprocessor has crept up from the original 2.5 MHz, and by 1983 had reached 8 MHz. Lower-power versions of the chip have become available which consume only 0.1 watts of power, sufficiently low for battery-operated equipment. National Semiconductor paid Zilog the somewhat dubious compliment of producing the NSC-800, a low-power microprocessor compatible with both the Z80 and the Intel 8-bit microprocessor, the 8085. Many other firms build Z80-family chips under licence from Zilog. 'Second-sourcing', as this is called, is popular with customers of integrated circuits, because they will not be left in the lurch if the original firm gives up making a particular chip, or the only factory burns down. Many times a firm has announced that a chip will be available, and designers have built equipment to the particular specification, only to find that the new chip has never been produced, and their work is wasted.

Z80 instructions

The Z80 operates on 8-bit-wide data, and therefore any individual data value stored in a memory cell can represent 256 (2^8) different values, for example any number from 0 to 255. Each individual instruction takes between 4 and 23 cycles of the clock, and so a Z80, with a clock speed of 4 MHz, will perform up to a million operations every second. Each individual instruction is like a brick in a building, unimportant in itself but essential to the overall construction—the program. The Z80 has only two flexible registers, the 8-bit A register (for data) and the 16-bit HL pair of registers (for addressing), and assembly language programs use these intensively, because the other registers are slower and more difficult to program in assembly language. There is, however, another set of registers in the Z80. They cannot be used at the same time as the primary set, but can be used as an alternative while information is preserved in the first set.

A typical Z80 instruction might add two 8-bit values together, and the assembly language instruction for this is

ADD A,B

This would be a single line (a **statement**) in an assembly language program, and correspond to an operation that can be performed in a single instruction by the Z80 CPU. This particular operation takes 4 clock cycles, and adds the two 8-bit values stored in the A and B registers, the result being stored in the A register. Hence the original value in A is destroyed. The maximum value that can be stored in an 8-bit register is 255, and so if the two numbers between them add up to more than this, the microprocessor stores the value over 255 (the 'remainder'), and signals this by setting a bit in the flag register (the carry bit) to 1 rather than 0. If this overflow is critical to a program, then the programmer will have to make sure that the next program instruction checks the flag register to see if the carry bit is set to 1.

Another of the Z80's instructions can add two numbers when one of them is in the A register and the other is at an address in the memory. However, the memory address must first be loaded into the HL register of the Z80. For example, suppose the value in A is to be added to the value stored at the memory address 2000. This instruction would be

ADD A, (VALUE STORED AT MEMORY LOCATION 2000)

or, in the code actually required in a line in the Z80 assembly language,

ADD A, (HL)

where the memory address (value 2000) has already been put into the HL register. Again the answer to the addition finishes up in the A register, destroying the original value.

The instructions described are arithmetical. Other arithmetical instructions on the Z80 include subtraction, and incrementing or decrementing data values by 1. The Z80 performs a range of logical operations, data movements, conditional branching, call and return operations to subroutines, as well as operations to send and receive data from input and output devices.

The input and output of information between the Z80 and peripheral devices are normally through ports. A typical Z80 instruction to output 8 bits (in the A register) through a port to a printer might be

OUT A, (PORT NUMBER)

where the printer is connected to that particular port. Note that the data must be put into the A register before being output to the printer.

Interrupts

The Z80 has both the non-maskable and maskable types of interrupt discussed in the last chapter. The hardware interrupt is directly connected to the Z80 chip through one pin on the package. When the device connected to this pin needs to signal an interrupt, it sets the interrupt connection line to 0 volts. Whatever the Z80 is doing at the time, it responds, and the program moves to a specific point in the memory, where the instructions that perform the function required by the interrupt are stored. The program to deal with the interrupt must already have been loaded at the particular memory position. This is called the non-maskable interrupt because it cannot be switched off by software.

Of course, the Z80 should eventually be able to return to the task it was performing originally, and so, before attending to details of the interrupt, the interrupt program must save the information on the current task, so that it can be retrieved later. The values in the registers should certainly be saved, because the registers are likely to be altered during the interrupt, but also the interrupt program should not be allowed to change any information that is still needed for the first program.

The Z80 has a maskable interrupt as well. Each interrupting device is able to direct the computer to a specific program, by supplying its address in the memory. Maskable interrupts can be switched on and off by software instructions, so that they have no effect when the Z80 is attending to a more important task.

16-bit and 32-bit microprocessors

The larger microelectronics firms, such as Motorola, National Semiconductor, and Fairchild, were largely caught unawares by the development of the 8-bit microprocessors. Hard lessons were learnt during the early struggle for supremacy in microprocessors. Motorola was the first large firm to respond to Intel's 8080, and in 1974 brought out the 6800 microprocessor. This chip turned out to be somewhat similar in performance to the Intel 8080 chip, but it was never able to wrest the mass market from Intel-compatible chips. Motorola was too late, because most customers had already committed themselves to Intel or Zilog, and changing was too expensive. Making a product using a particular microprocessor requires a large investment in both equipment and experience, and once a particular family of microprocessors is chosen, a company will tend to stick with it.

Despite the overwhelming commercial success of the 8-bit chips, deficiencies soon showed up. In particular, the limitation of 16-bit memory addressing proved to be a severe disadvantage as memory prices fell and programs grew longer. In 1984, 64 kbytes of memory, which had cost thousands of dollars in the mid-1970s, had fallen in price to $25. Furthermore the cost of the processor itself fell to a few dollars. Microprocessors became a small part of the total cost of the systems into which they were incorporated, and customers were willing to pay more for faster processing and, in particular, a greater memory addressing range. This was an exact rerun of what had happened in minicomputers in the mid-1960s. The first customer for DEC minicomputers had come back to DEC and explained that he wanted more direct memory addressing.

Intel was the first firm to produce a commercially successful 16-bit chip, the 8086, and this was incorporated into many new pieces of equipment. The 8086 and a slightly different version, the 8088, have both become commercial successes. Zilog came rather a cropper with their equivalent chip, the Z8000, which was never very popular. Both the 8086 and the Z8000 chips suffer from having memory addressing spaces divided into 64-kbyte blocks. Although they can access many such blocks, the software must be structured to cope with this compartmentalization of the memory. Motorola was later than either Intel or Zilog in producing a 16-bit microprocessor, perhaps too late again for the mass market, but it did manufacture a product superior to the first 16-bit offerings from the other firms—the Motorola 68000 family.

The Motorola 68000 family

The Motorola 68000 is a far more powerful microprocessor than the Z80. This in no way reflects upon the Zilog chip, but demonstrates the rapid progress in microelectronics in the five years or so between the design of the two chips. The 68000 has a (more or less) 32-bit internal structure, has 24 pins for memory addressing, but only manipulates 16 bits of data externally. So 32 bits of data are split into two for transmission to outside devices. The big advantage of restricting the external addressing and data ranges lies in reducing the number of pin connections on the chip. The 24-bit memory addressing means that the chip can directly address 16 megabytes of semiconductor memory, more than enough for most computer programs. However, the 68000 family of chips has been planned so that 'upwards compatible' 32-bit external addressing and data microprocessors can be developed.

The 68000 is an enormously complicated chip, built from 68,000 transistors (a coincidence). It has many advantages over the Z80. Firstly, its enlarged data width (from 8 to 32 bits) and addressing range (from 16 to 24 bits) make the chip both more powerful and easier to program. Its clock speed, presently up to 12.5 MHz, is also higher than that of the Z80, which has a current maximum of 8 MHz. It contains built-in features for detecting some standard types of program errors. For example, an attempt in a program to divide by zero (a classic program 'bug') provokes an automatic warning from the chip. This is treated by the processor as a type of interrupt. The 68000 contains pins to allow other devices (such as disc drives) to take temporary control of the computer bus using direct memory access (see p. 55).

A large range of instructions (about 1,000) are available in the 68000, including some instructions for division and multiplication. Although 32-bit, the chip instructions can operate on 16-bit and 8-bit data, decimals, and single bits of data, reflecting the range of data types typically needed in programs. The fastest instruction (moving information from one register to another) takes only 4 clock cycles, i.e. the chip can perform about two million of these per second. The slowest instruction (32-bit division) takes 170 clock cycles, and

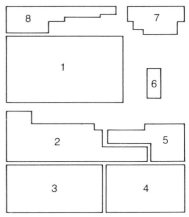

1   Read-only memory (ROM)
    for the instructions

2   Microprocessor control unit

3   Address execution area

4   Data execution area

5   Arithmetic and logic unit

6   Trap & illegal instructions

7   Bus control logic

8   Clock and timing

The Motorola 68000

It is easy to forget that there is a physical reality behind the microprocessor. The various functions of a microprocessor are produced by blocks of transistors on the chip. The photograph is an enlargement of the ¼-inch-square silicon chip that forms the 68000 microprocessor. Coincidentally the chip does contain 68,000 transistors.

The regularity of the design is apparent, and in the functional diagram the contributions of different areas of the chip can be seen. Large areas are dedicated to single functions, for instance the ROM microprogram area from which the individual computer instructions are formed. The

trap area deals with program faults, such as the appearance of non-existent or impossible instructions (for example, divide by zero). Around the edge of the chip are the 'buffers', which amplify the small electrical signals used inside the chip to make them powerful enough to interact with the outside world.

therefore the chip can perform about 50,000 such operations every second. The 68000 has eight registers for data, and seven for addressing information, all of them 32-bit. From the programmer's point of view, the registers are much more flexible than those in the Z80. Instead of always having to pass data in and out through only two (the A and HL) registers, all data registers function identically, making assembly language programming much easier.

The 68000 also 'prefetches' instructions, i.e. it fetches into the CPU the next part of the program, before it is due to be executed. This saves the fetch time from the memory and allows instructions to be carried out more quickly.

Developments of the 68000

The 68000 is the first of a family of compatible microprocessors and support chips, which can be combined to produce a variety of equipment. Motorola have signed deals with leading semiconductor firms for the joint development of these chips. The masks that are used to fabricate the various chips are exchanged between the partners, although not without squabbles and suspicion. This gives a choice of several suppliers to the customer, and shares the cost of research between many firms.

The 68010 microprocessor has virtual memory facilities (see Chapter 8), enabling programs to use disc storage as if it were semiconductor memory. Other compatible chips use less power, communicate with peripherals, perform floating-point instructions or memory management, or organize DMA interaction. The whole range of chips will be upwards compatible, and so software developed for the simpler chips will, in theory, run on a more complicated chip. Motorola have also produced the 68008, a version of the 68000 with 8-bit data output. This chip is used in both the Apple Macintosh and Sinclair QL micros. The 68020 microprocessor became available in 1984, with 32-bit addressing and data width, but still able to run 68000 software. Another interesting variant is a version of the 68000 able to emulate the IBM 370 mainframe computer instruction set; this enables an IBM personal computer (the IBM 3270/PC) to run programs originally written for the much larger 370 mainframe.

Other 32-bit micros

Motorola is not alone in attempting to provide a range of chips based on a 32-bit microprocessor, for National Semiconductor, NEC, Intel, Inmos, and Zilog have all announced similar families of chips. Other firms, such as Digital, Bell Laboratories, NCR, Hewlett-Packard, and Data General produce equivalents for use within the computers that they sell. The Hewlett-Packard chip used for the 9000 computer packs 450,000 transistors on to a single chip, which in 1985 was the most complex integrated circuit. However, the amount of investment needed to produce the most advanced chips is continually increasing, and so the weaker firms are ceasing to design and manufacture their own microprocessors.

Reduced Instruction Set Chip

The design effort for the 32-bit micros has been a terrible strain on the microelectronics companies, costing more, taking longer, and producing less income than they expected. The Intel 4004, the first microprocessor, took one person nine months to design; a 32-bit microprocessor can absorb up to 100 working years. To reduce the design effort, a research project at the University of California built a 32-bit microprocessor able to perform only a few simple instructions—the **Reduced Instruction Set Chip (RISC)**. Because the chip has fewer instructions, it is smaller, and more chips can be squeezed on to a single wafer during manufacture. Any given program in a high-level language will translate into more machine instructions than on, say, a 68000, because the instructions are simpler, but each instruction can be performed more quickly. The RISC was designed in one-tenth of the time that the 68000 took, and when tested, it ran at about the same processing speed as much more complex microprocessors. Although the 68000 is far better for assembly language programmers, because its individual machine instructions are much more powerful, many microprocessors now only run programs written in high-level languages. Once one programmer has written the translator from a high-level language for a particular chip, the machine instructions of the microprocessor chip are largely irrelevant, and only the overall speed and facilities of the chip really count. Subsequent programmers care only about how quickly the machine processes their high-level language programs.

The future

In the future, in order to reduce software costs microprocessors are likely to be designed with instruction sets that run high-level languages directly, or copy the instruction sets of existing computers. This will reduce the requirement to write programs in assembly languages, and also allow old software to be retained. Reducing the cost to customers of writing software is a major aim. Single-chip computers are also encroaching more and more upon the territory of larger computers, because the processing power of single-chip microprocessors is increasing by about 60 per cent each year, whereas that of larger computers, which are built from separate chips, is improving at only 25 per cent. In 1985, the fastest 32-bit microprocessors already had a processing speed of 5 MIPS, when coupled with an arithmetic processor. This was as fast as a larger, supermini computer costing far more. Computer manufacture used to be a matter of assembling large numbers of components, but now success is a matter of producing a good chip design. The future for computer manufacturers unable to afford the most advanced chip design and manufacturing facilities looks bleak.

Seven The Integrated Circuit

Open a computer and you will see rows of black plastic packages, linked together by the solder tracks of a circuit board. Each package contains a single chip, or integrated circuit. Integrated-circuit technology is the key to the microelectronics revolution. The same manufacturing process makes chips that are computers, memories, disc controllers, and thousands of other electronic circuits. The many components needed for a circuit, such as resistors, capacitors, and transistors, were once made individually, and then wired together to form the necessary circuit. Now hundreds of thousands of transistors, a whole circuit and its connections, are fabricated on a small piece of silicon.

The process that transforms sand into integrated circuits relies on decades of intensive research, as well as twenty-five years of applied development. The theory behind semiconductors was worked out during the 1920s and 1930s, and the first transistors were produced at the Bell Laboratories in 1947. Since the invention of integrated circuits in 1958, the techniques for producing many transistors on a small semiconductor chip have been developed enormously. Integrated circuits that sell for a few pence are the result of this research effort and thousands of millions of pounds of investment. At present, there seems to be no technological barrier to prevent integrated circuits with tens of millions of transistors being made. The global name for the technology is very large-scale integration (VLSI).

Producing integrated circuits—a summary

The process of producing a chip has three stages. In the first, the integrated circuit is designed and perfected using a computer as an intelligent drawing-board and notebook. A computer program then simulates the whole circuit to detect possible problems. When the design is satisfactory, the computer makes a set of photographic masks, which control the processing of the chips during the manufacturing stages.

In the second stage, very pure silicon is melted in an enclosed container, and a large crystal is grown from the liquid. This is sliced into thin wafers, which are then polished flat and smooth.

The last stage takes place in the silicon foundry, where the thin wafers of silicon are turned into chips through a series of chemical processes. Millions of transistors are formed simultaneously on the surface of each wafer, in patterns

The Integrated Circuit

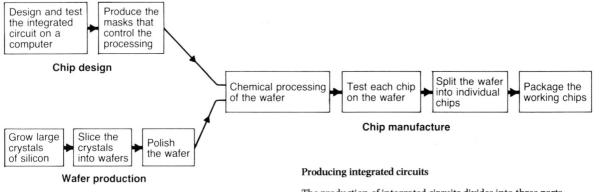

Producing integrated circuits

The production of integrated circuits divides into three parts. The first two are the separate processes of chip design and the manufacture of thin wafers of single-crystal silicon. The third stage of chip manufacture imprints the design several times over on each wafer, producing dozens of identical chips. The chips are then split up and packaged for sale.

controlled by masks. The manufactured chips are tested while they are on the wafer, which is then split into individual circuit chips. The successful circuits are packaged for sale.

Dozens of electronic circuits are formed when a wafer is processed, and each chip is able to perform the same function as the original computer simulation, but far faster. The sequence of steps to produce a chip is roughly the same for different kinds of chip, and also for an equivalent chip design with smaller transistors. A small factory employing a hundred or so people can turn out several million integrated circuits every year.

Producing millions of transistors on a silicon wafer is a complex, but now standard, process, each step involving tolerances of about 1 micron (1/25,000 inch). This degree of precision is higher than for any other mass-produced good. Meticulous attention to process control and cleanliness is necessary to keep up the yield of successful devices. At the end of the manufacturing process the majority of the chips won't work at all, and a 30 per cent success rate is considered reasonable. For an integrated circuit that is being mass-produced, the prime determinant of cost is its 'real estate', the area of silicon occupied by the chip. If the individual transistors in an integrated circuit can be made smaller, so can the dimensions of the chip, and more chips can be squeezed on to a wafer.

Not unnaturally, the industry uses advanced computer techniques for controlling and analysing the chip manufacturing process. Chips with hundreds of thousands of transistors regularly work first time out from the manufacturing process. The design process for powerful integrated circuits is becoming easier and cheaper. As a result, smaller electronics companies will be able to afford 'customized' chips, specially designed for their purposes, provided that several thousand of the same circuit are required.

Semiconductors

Semiconductors such as silicon, germanium, or gallium arsenide, are substances that have electrical properties between those of metals and insulators. Electrons are the usual means by which electrical current flows in materials, and in metals, for instance, the negatively charged electrons are free enough to move easily past metal atoms when an electrical voltage is applied to the material—resulting in an electrical current. In an insulator, on the other hand, the electrons are held tightly by the atoms and cannot be moved by a voltage. Consequently, while metals conduct electricity well, insulators do not allow electricity to flow. As their name implies, semiconductors lie between these two extremes. In a very pure semiconductor crystal, such as silicon, electrons are held rather more weakly than in insulators, but still strongly enough to prevent the flow of electricity. Transistors rely on the properties of crystalline semiconductors, and particularly on the ease with which the electrical conduction properties can be locally modified by small amounts of impurities.

Silicon   In silicon, we are fortunate to have a semiconductor possessing an almost ideal combination of properties necessary for making integrated circuits. To begin with, sand is largely composed of silicon dioxide, and so silicon is plentiful and cheap. Silicon can be grown into large, almost perfect crystals, and is more resistant to the high temperatures produced in chips by current flows than other semiconductors, especially compared to germanium, from which the early transistors were made. Heating silicon in the presence of oxygen converts a thin surface layer into silicon dioxide, making a superb insulating material

---

Gallium arsenide

Silicon will remain the mainstay of the microelectronics industry for a long time, but there is another semiconductor material gradually creeping into some specialized areas. Gallium arsenide (GaAs) is a compound of equal numbers of gallium and arsenic atoms, forming a crystal structure almost identical to silicon, but with one great advantage. The electrons in gallium arsenide move more quickly under the influence of an electric field than do electrons in silicon, and so transistors made from gallium arsenide can operate at a higher speed than equivalent silicon transistors.

However, chips are much more difficult to make from gallium arsenide than from silicon, and at present only small numbers of transistors can be formed on the chips produced. A particular problem is that there is no equi-

valent to the insulating surface oxide that can be formed by heating silicon.

Gallium arsenide integrated circuits are much more expensive than silicon chips but, even so, may well be suitable for parts of computers where their improved speed would really make a difference, such as cache memory, the very high-speed memory used intensively by the CPU. The addition of even a small amount of cache memory made from gallium arsenide may speed up a computer by perhaps 20 to 50 per cent, for a small fraction of the computer's overall cost. However, the continual improvements in the techniques for manufacturing silicon chips leave little room for gallium arsenide technology.

needed for several of a chip's processing stages. Integrated circuits, such as memory chips or microprocessors, use silicon's properties to the full.

Very pure silicon crystal is a poor conductor, but its electrical properties can be changed dramatically by the addition of small amounts of impurities, or **dopants**. To aid conduction, a small amount of dopant material (for example arsenic or phosphorus) is added to the silicon crystal. The dopant has an atomic structure similar to silicon but with an extra electron. The atoms of, say, phosphorus, fit easily into the lattice of atoms in silicon, and add a few spare electrons to the previously insulating material. These spare electrons become 'free' to carry electricity. The new material is called **n-type** silicon, because current is carried by electrons, which are negatively charged. Less than one part in a million of the dopant phosphorus is all that is needed to change dramatically the electrical properties of the semiconductor. Hence the original silicon crystal must be very pure before the process of 'doping' starts.

If a material similar to silicon, but with fewer electrons (like boron), is added to the crystal, again it fits easily into the array of silicon atoms. However, a crystal with a deficiency of electrons has now been made—there is a positive 'hole' where there should have been a negative electron. Current can in fact flow through this material by the movement of these holes. When a voltage is applied to the material, an electron will move to fill in such a hole, leaving another hole behind it. The current flow can be thought of as a movement of holes in the opposite direction to electrons. The movement of these sites is equivalent to a current flow carried by positive charges. This **p-type** material (positive carrier) allows electricity to flow almost as easily as in the n-type semiconductor. The ability of transistors to switch current on and off depends on the electrical properties of small areas of n- and p-type silicon formed in the wafer by the localized addition of dopants.

The transistor

The transistor, a small switch for electric current, is the basic element of the integrated circuit. The power of a digital integrated circuit depends on the ability of transistors to switch between their on and off states. The transistor has three electrical connections—one where the current enters the device, another where it leaves, and a third connection that controls the flow of current. These connections are referred to as the source, drain, and gate respectively. Sets of transistors linked together can perform arithmetic or logic, or move information around a computer.

The invention of the transistor

The transistor was invented in 1947 by John Bardeen, Walter Brattain, and William Schockley at the Bell Laboratories in the USA. For this 'discovery of the century' they were awarded a Nobel Prize in 1956. Their original transistor was a primitive point-contact transistor constructed out of germanium, a semi-

The invention of the century

The three inventors of the transistor, standing beside their apparatus in Bell Laboratories in 1947. Dr William Shockley is seated, Dr John Bardeen stands on the left, and Dr Walter Brattain on the right.

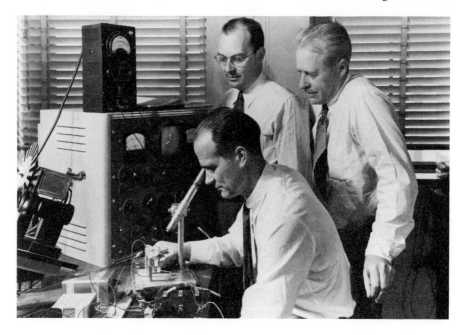

conductor similar to silicon. Although physically quite different, it performed the same function as the transistors in today's integrated circuits.

The transistor is called **solid-state** since it relies on the electronic properties of a solid, crystalline semiconductor. This contrasts with the older technology of electronic valves, which used a heated metal filament inside a gas. Such a valve has a minimum size of perhaps one cubic inch or so. Transistor switching

The first transistor

The first transistor worked at Bell Laboratories on 23 December 1947, amplifying a small electrical current. The inventors were not quite convinced, and the next day they rebuilt their apparatus just to prove that the effect was really there. Within a few years, transistors had been dramatically improved, and were manufactured by the million. The germanium semiconductor is at the tip of the triangular wedge, which acts as a support for the delicate connections to the transistor.

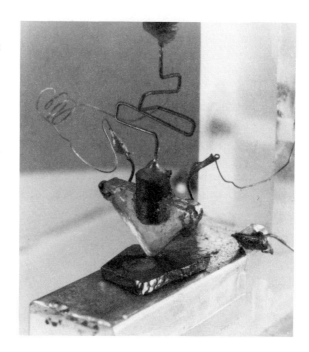

relies on the crystalline properties of silicon, and so transistors can be made smaller and smaller, and yet still be able to perform the same switching function. As it becomes smaller, each transistor uses less current, and so the chip as a whole consumes less power. The transistor operates faster because the electrons carrying the current have shorter distances to travel.

Once transistors had been introduced, they were rapidly improved, and better processing techniques produced smaller devices and faster switching speeds. In 1954, Texas Instruments produced and sold the first silicon transistors. At £20 each the main market was for military applications, and for amplifiers for hearing-aids. But prices fell rapidly as companies began to mass-produce them, and by the late 1950s the word transistor became the generic term for that contemporary status symbol, the transistor radio. By 1965 transistors were only 20p each—one hundred times cheaper than in 1951, even without taking inflation into account. Silicon gradually replaced germanium as the semiconducting material, primarily because it is cheaper, and also because its electrical properties are less affected by the heat that is inevitably generated in computers.

The integrated circuit

Within a few years of the invention of the transistor, scientists were discussing the prospect of making a whole electrical circuit on the surface of a piece of semiconductor. A number of transistors, together with other components of a circuit, such as resistors, could be formed on the same crystal, and then all linked together by thin aluminium tracks on the semiconductor surface. Rather than having to link a set of electrical components together with external wires, the components and their connections would be built on to the same piece of semiconductor. This would save the price of those other components, and avoid the unreliability of external connections. The semiconductors would carry a miniature version of a circuit board, which was already familiar inside radios and TVs. What the scientists foresaw was the **integrated circuit**, so called because an electronic function, such as a calculator or a temperature controller, can be integrated on to (and slightly inside) the surface of the semiconductor.

Texas Instruments led the way by making the first integrated circuit, containing a few transistors, in 1958. Since then, the production process for integrated circuits has been continuously improved. In the 1960s, Texas Instruments produced the 7400 series, a range of chips capable of performing simple logical functions like the AND operation. These chips were the first popular integrated circuits. Larger electronic circuits can be constructed by linking different logic chips together. Scientists have been able to make a few, then dozens, thousands, and now millions of transistors on a single chip. The process uses cheap raw materials, and has repeatedly produced smaller and better devices. Transistors are made as small as the lines on the surface of the silicon that define them during manufacture. The minimum **line-width** that can be formed has shrunk to about 1 micron (a human hair has a diameter of about 50 microns), leading to a transistor with an area of a few square microns. To show how small this line-width is, if the lines on the most advanced integrated circuits were to be expanded to the size of roads, an advanced chip would cover an area the size of Greater London—and the area would be expanding by a square mile every week.

Planar technology

An essential element in modern integrated-circuit production is the ability to make transistors when only having access to one side of the silicon wafer—**planar technology**. Planar technology was invented in 1960 by a team of scientists working for Fairchild, and it quickly displaced Texas Instruments' integrated-circuit technology. Planar technology allows transistor manufacture to be highly automated. The first integrated circuits were produced by a laborious process that involved a delicate etching technique from both sides of the semiconductor. Now each transistor is formed by a series of chemical processes on just one surface of the wafer. The areas affected by each of these processes are determined by a set of photographic masks, glass negatives which help

The first planar integrated circuit

Although beaten by Texas Instruments in the race to produce the first integrated circuit, it was Fairchild that developed planar technology, which allows chips to be mass-produced. This was the result in 1961—the world's first planar integrated circuit—a simple circuit that would previously have been made from half-a-dozen transistors and a few other components. Because the elements in the chip are larger than today's integrated circuits, it provides us with a much clearer picture of planar technology. We can see the aluminium tracks, and the results of different diffusions of dopant impurities into the semiconductor. Chips are now made with a hundred thousand times as many transistors.

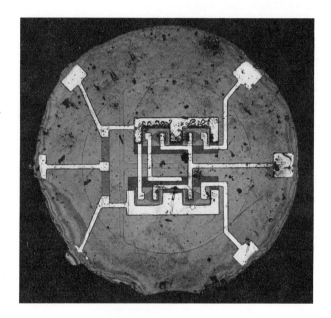

produce thin protective patterns on the wafer. These patterns protect parts of the silicon surface from the different chemical processes that form the transistors. Individual transistors can be made smaller simply by shrinking the dimensions of the patterns. Large numbers of transistors are made on the same surface, and then linked together by metal tracks to form a complete circuit.

Logic processing using transistors

Transistors are the building blocks from which a whole computer can be made. When sufficient numbers of them are connected in the right pattern, they can perform complicated logical and arithmetical functions. The particular operation performed (such as subtraction or addition) is determined by the connection pattern between the set of transistors. Sets of transistors can also be used as switches to direct data from one part of the chip to another, just as railway points switch trains from track to track. A few transistors together mimic a logic function or switch data from one part of the chip to another; two or three thousand transistors make a small computer, and a million make a very powerful computer system.

The MOS transistor

The most common transistor type used for integrated circuits is the **metal oxide semiconductor (MOS)** transistor, which relies on an electrical field to control current flow. The MOS transistor is also one of the simplest types of transistor. Other transistors rely on the electrical properties of junctions of n- and p-type semiconducting materials.

The structure of one type of MOS transistor is shown in simplified form in the accompanying diagram. The current flow is caused by the flow of electrical

How the MOS transistor works

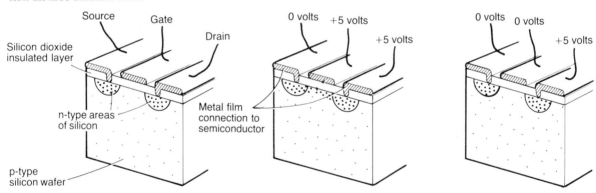

A cross-section through the transistor, showing the three connections of source, gate, and drain. Current can flow from the source to the drain, switched on and off by the electric field from the gate, even though this is electrically isolated from the rest of the transistor by a layer of silicon dioxide. The source and drain are two identical areas of n-type material formed in a body of p-type material.

When the gate is at 5 volts, its positive charge attracts electrons, which form a thin layer underneath it. This channel links the electrons in the n-type areas underneath the source and the drain. The transistor is switched on and electricity can flow from the source to the drain.

When the gate is at 0 volts, the channel reverts to p-type. Current cannot flow from the source to the drain—the transistor is switched off.

charge from one contact (the **source**) to another (the **drain**); because electrons are negative charges, they flow from the lower to the higher voltage. The current flow can be switched on or off by a third contact—the **gate**—and this switching action forms the basis of the whole computer. When a voltage is applied to the gate, an electrical charge is formed, in turn producing an electric field that interferes with the current flow. The gate acts as a small reservoir of electrical charge, capable of attracting and repelling electrons underneath it, just as an electrically charged comb can attract or repel small pieces of paper. These electrical charges on the gate can switch relatively large currents between the source and the drain on and off.

If the gate voltage is 'high' (5 volts), then this positive voltage attracts negative electrons into a thin layer underneath the gate capacitor and these are available to carry current from the source to the drain. Current flows between the source and the drain, and a high voltage is generated across a resistor placed in the current flow. This voltage—the 'output' of the switch—can be fed as information into other transistors, which are linked together to make up a set that performs a single computer instruction.

When the gate voltage is 'low' (0 volts), electrons are repelled from underneath the gate area. Current cannot flow from the source to the drain because

Other transistor types

One variety of MOS transistor has been discussed, but this is only one of many types of transistors found in digital integrated circuits. For low-power work the **complementary metal oxide semiconductor (CMOS)** transistor is better. The basic element of the CMOS chip is not a single transistor, but a pair of transistors across the supply voltage. They are electrically connected so that when one of the pair is switched on, the other is switched off—hence the name complementary. Depending on which one is on, the centre of the pair is at either 5 or 0 volts. Thus the current flow through the two transistors is always low because one of the pair always blocks it. However, the pair consume more power during the switch-over from one transistor to the other. Current consumption therefore rises dramatically as the CMOS processor speeds up, because the transistor pairs spend more time in the transition state between on and off.

CMOS chips are harder to make than their MOS equivalents, because more transistors are needed and the manufacturing process is more complicated. If an MOS chip becomes popular, a low-power CMOS version often appears a few years later. As the manufacturing processes for CMOS transistors are mastered, they are steadily displacing MOS technology, and most new microprocessors are made using CMOS.

MOS and CMOS transistors are both **field-effect** devices. The current flowing between the input and the output terminals is controlled by an electric field produced by the third gate terminal. The **bipolar** transistor relies on the properties of p–n junctions. Adjacent areas of n-type (with electrons) and p-type material (with holes) are formed. The electrical charges that control the current flow are formed at the junction between two such areas. By altering the external voltage, these charges are altered, and current flow can be manipulated. The bipolar transistor is faster than the MOS transistor, but has a more complicated structure, and also consumes far more power. It tends to be used in chips that are designed to be fast, and have fewer than average transistors.

Many other types of transistor are used to make integrated circuits. Some of them are specific to one manufacturer, while others are minor variations on the main types. In general, individual transistors are becoming more complex, and require more processing stages during manufacture.

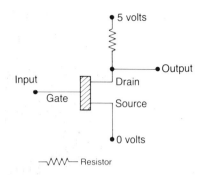

—/\/\/\— Resistor

The NOT gate

This is a diagrammatic representation of a single MOS transistor—the gate is the input, switching current between the source and the drain on and off. If the input is high (5 volts), then the output is low (0 volts), and vice versa. The output is always the negation of the input, and so the device replicates the Boolean function NOT. All other logical and arithmetical functions can be constructed by suitably connecting up a number of transistors. The gate current controls a much higher flow of current between the source and the drain. The output current must be strong enough to be used as input to other transistors.

A **resistor** is a device which controls the flow of current between two points.

An AND gate made from three transistors

The logical function AND (a comparison rather than an addition) can easily be made from a small set of transistors, which together are called an AND gate. As a result this function is always available as a machine-level instruction on any computer or microprocessor. In an AND gate there are two inputs and one output. Only if both the inputs are high (5 volts) is the output also high. The other three combinations of inputs produce a low output (0 volts).

to see whether a 1 or a 0 should go in the right-hand column of the answer to the overall adition. It gives a high output (1) only if one of the two inputs is high; if both are 0 or both are 1, then it gives the answer 0. The AND gate operates on the numbers to see what should go in the left-hand column; it gives the answer 1 only if both of the inputs being added are 1. Hence the output of the two gates simulates the addition of two binary numbers for all the four combinations of input. The table shows the output of the circuit for each possible input.

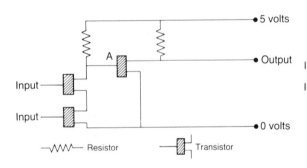

—/\/\/\— Resistor   Transistor

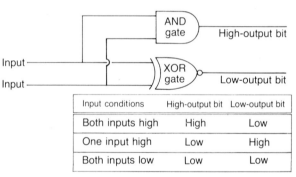

Input conditions	High-output bit	Low-output bit
Both inputs high	High	Low
One input high	Low	High
Both inputs low	Low	Low

First look at the pair of transistors on the left-hand side of the diagram. If either of these is switched off, then the pair of transistors doesn't carry any current, and the point A is high (5 volts). If A is high then the output of the right-hand transistor is low.

Current can flow through the pair of transistors only if both are switched on (both of their inputs are high). A is then low, and the final output is high.

The ADD circuit

The circuit takes two bits as its input, and its output is the addition of those two bits. It is drawn as two gates (see Chapter 3), each of which performs a Boolean operation, rather than as individual transistors, thus showing it at a slightly more abstract level. The two gates needed to perform the function are the exclusive OR gate and the AND gate. The exclusive OR operates on the two single-digit binary numbers

The simplified ADD gate shown in the diagram would not be of much use in a computer because it does not have an input for a carry bit—it adds only a single column of two binary numbers. The computer needs to add many (typically 8 to 64) bits of information simultaneously. Each bit is like a single column for a binary number, and, as with the addition of two decimal numbers, the second column from the right cannot be added up until the first column has been checked to see if there is a carry. Doing it one column at a time would be a very slow process—adding two 32-bit numbers would take 32 clock cycles of the computer, because the carry bits need to be passed on from each ADD circuit to the next. Similarly the third column has to wait for the second column. By using a more complicated arrangement of transistors, the 'full-adder', the computer is able to add all the bits simultaneously; the carry bits are taken account of automatically.

electrons are not available to move through the area of p-type material be-tween them. Only a few holes are available to carry a minute current in the area between the source and the drain. Thus a small gate current can control a large current flow between the source and the drain. On its own, a single MOS transistor can simulate directly the simplest Boolean logical function— the NOT gate. Whichever voltage (5 or 0 volts) appears at the gate, the opposite voltage appears at the drain. In practice, an individual MOS transistor is more complicated than this description, and contains many more layers. Designs have had to be extensively modified as the dimensions of transistors become smaller.

Designing the chips

An integrated circuit, such as a microprocessor, can be designed and tested in abstract before ever being made. It is designed with the help of a computer system, which simulates the operation of the chip and thereby puts the design through its paces before the chip is manufactured.

Computerized design has many advantages. When designers create a new chip, they need not start completely afresh, but can instead make improve-ments to an old design. Many designers can work on the same chip: each works on a separate element, but all can use the computer to see how the overall design is progressing. Much of the design work for a large chip is repetitive, and therefore the computer is used as a 'library' to store the details of parts of chips that are known to work successfully. These can be called up by the circuit designer and used for a new design. Because the whole design has been specified on the computer, the computer can also produce the masks that are used in manufacturing the chips.

Using these advanced techniques of **computer-aided engineering**, most errors in design can be spotted and eliminated before any major manufacturing ex-pense has been incurred, and the design process is also speeded up enormously. During 1983–4, Bell Laboratories took less than twelve months to design and produce working prototypes of a microprocessor with 180,000 transistors. Automated design techniques are changing chip design from an art into a science. Many chips are still designed with pencil and paper, but firms persist-ing with such practices will not survive much longer. The use of computerized techniques is essential for the design of more complex chips, which will soon contain tens of millions of transistors.

Semi-custom design

The net cost of designing a chip specially for a task can sometimes compare favourably with that of programming a general-purpose chip. Providing that a firm needs more than about 10,000 such chips, and that the design is unlikely to change, it may well be cheaper to have a special chip made.

Completely new designs are called **custom** chips; but it is more common to link together existing design modules. Such a **semi-custom** chip can replace

The Integrated Circuit

From design to finished product

The chip held in the tweezers is the 32-bit Bellmac A microprocessor in a new kind of package (**leadless**). The chip contains 150,000 transistors. Behind is a silicon wafer covered in the same kind of chips before they are separated. In the background is a very small part of the electrical circuit diagram of the chip, which was itself designed on a computer.

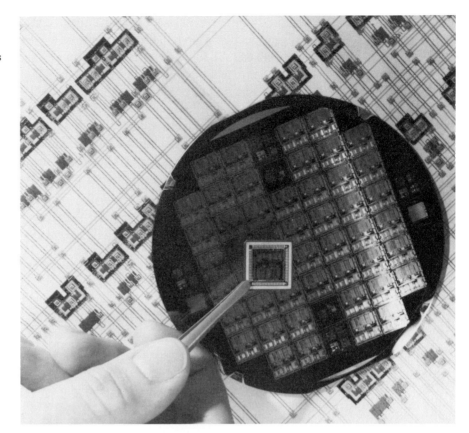

Silicon compilation

New techniques allow designers of integrated circuits to work at a more abstract level than before. They can describe the chip in a computer program written in a high-level language, and allow a silicon **compiler** program to sort out where to put individual transistors. Instead of being bogged down in detail, chip designers can concentrate on the structure of their design. Silicon compilation is only now starting to be successful commercially. As chips become more complicated, such design methods will be essential. Here is one of the chips in the DEC microVAX computer, designed in only eight months using silicon compilation techniques.

many simple logic chips. For example, the Apple Macintosh and Sinclair QL personal computers contain several semi-custom chips. These reduce the chip count and also make the computer systems more difficult to copy, since more of their design is in the hardware.

Masks
The design sequence eventually produces photographic masks, which will be used as optical stencils to make certain patterns on silicon wafers. The mask patterns generated by the computer are drawn at about 500 times the size of the mask used to make the integrated circuit. Enlarged this much, they can be checked by the human eye for imperfections. The mask patterns are then photographically reduced to the final size of the chip. Special care is taken to avoid distortions of the masks, or contamination by dust, because these would spoil the images which will shape the transistors. The mask for an individual chip is only $\frac{1}{4}$ inch square, but the silicon wafer may be 5 or 6 inches in diameter, and so dozens of copies of the chip pattern are made on a single mask the size of a whole wafer. A device such as an MOS transistor may need a set of eight to ten different masks to control the various stages of its fabrication, one for when dopant is added, one for the metal film, etc.

In each microlithographic stage, the silicon wafer is coated with a thin film of light-sensitive photoresist, and the mask allows parts of the film to be exposed to ultraviolet light. This produces a hardened plastic pattern in the shape of the chip design; and this pattern controls the areas affected by a subsequent chemical reaction.

Electron beam masks
The line-widths used on the final masks are so small that they are comparable to the wavelength of light. The quality of the shadowing produced by the masks during the exposure of the photoresist to light is consequently blurred, and the sharpness of the lines produced on the silicon is affected. To combat this problem, new techniques form the mask patterns using a sharply focused beam of electrons inside a vacuum. This technique produces much sharper detail, but is more costly and much slower than the older methods.

Projection technology
As might be expected, the delicate masks that cover the silicon wafer are easily damaged, and can only be used a few times before they need replacing. An alternative method of producing the required pattern on the silicon is to use a lens to project an image on to the photosensitive material. The expensive masks then last indefinitely—they act like photographic slides, rather than negatives, which have to touch the wafer surface. The lenses needed to produce sharply defined lines only a few microns across are both extremely difficult to design and expensive to produce. They cannot produce this level of detail over the whole area of a wafer, and so only project the image of one chip at a time on to the wafer. The machine holding the wafer then steps to the next chip position, and the process is repeated. A new projection machine is needed for each microlithographic step, because the process of setting up the mask in the projection equipment is very time-consuming.

Manufacturing the silicon wafers

Silicon can exist in a disordered form, without any repeated arrangement of its atoms, or in a more ordered, crystalline state—like a diamond. The ideal semiconductor is a very pure crystal, and silicon is one of the few materials that can be grown into almost perfect crystals. These crystals are several feet long, and up to 6 inches or more in diameter. The atoms are stacked in a regular pattern, a lattice which extends from one end of the crystal to the other.

The crystal growing stage involves fairly heavy engineering, unusual in microelectronics: large cylinders, or 'boules', of single-crystal silicon are produced from powdered silicon. Whilst the crystals are growing, a small amount of an impurity (about one part in a million) is added to the liquid silicon so that it will conduct electricity. There are two main methods of producing the large boules of silicon crystals from purified silicon powder—the Czochralski and the floating-zone processes. Both involve melting the powder, and then allowing the hot liquid (at 1,420 °C) to cool and solidify in a controlled fashion.

The Czochralski process

About three-quarters of the silicon used for integrated circuits is made by the process invented by Czochralski in 1917. A silicon crystal is dipped into a crucible containing molten silicon and slowly withdrawn, all the time being rotated. As the **seed crystal** is removed, silicon atoms from the crucible solidify

Growing the silicon crystal

A silicon crystal is seen here emerging from a glowing pool of liquid silicon heated to 1,420°C. The huge crystal grows as an extension of a small 'seed' crystal dipped into the liquid, and slowly removed. As the boule of silicon is pulled out, it is rotated in order to keep it circular. The process, named after its inventor Czochralski, takes place in an inert gas, to avoid the oxygen in air reacting with the silicon.

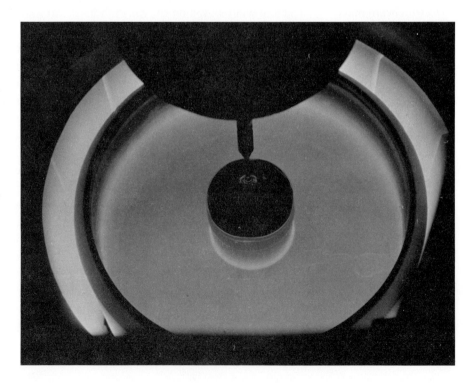

Silicon wafers

Silicon wafers lie scattered around a boule. The wafers have been polished to provide the surface required for their further processing in the silicon foundry. We can see from the seed crystal on the end of the boule that it was grown using the Czochralski process.

Silicon wafers

Silicon wafers lie scattered around a boule. The wafers have been polished to provide the surface required for their further processing in the silicon foundry. We can see from the seed crystal on the end of the boule that it was grown using the Czochralski process.

on to it. These atoms line up with the existing arrangement of atoms in the seed crystal, and so form a larger crystal. The crystal-growing process is carried out in a sealed container filled with an inert gas (argon) that does not contaminate the hot silicon. If the process was carried out in air, oxygen would react with the silicon. The end result is a boule of silicon, ready to be sliced into wafers and polished.

Floating-zone process

In the floating-zone process, a bar of silicon is held vertically, whilst a horizontal section at its centre is heated with radio waves. This creates a liquid pool of silicon between the two solid surfaces, which is retained by surface tension. The liquid zone can be moved up and down the bar, simply by changing the position of the heat source. As the zone travels up and down, silicon solidifies behind it into crystal form. The process also automatically purifies the silicon, because impurities do not fit easily into the atomic structure of the crystal as it solidifies, and therefore they become concentrated into the liquid section. We see the same effect when we freeze ice lollies—the pure water freezes first into a clear layer, and the colour is concentrated into the last liquid to freeze. When the crystallization process is complete, the liquid zone is moved to the end of the bar, and itself solidified so that the impurities are concentrated in one place. The contaminated end is then cut off and discarded. If necessary, the process can be repeated to remove more impurities. Any dopant is added the last time the silicon is liquid, taking into account its reluctance to fit into the silicon as the crystal solidifies.

This method produces silicon of very high quality, purer and with fewer faults in the crystal than the result of the Czochralski process. This is because the hot silicon is not contaminated by being in contact with a container, as must happen in the Czochralski process. But the floating-zone technique is more expensive, and tends to be used only when absolutely necessary, such as for experimental or very complex chips.

Slicing and polishing the silicon wafers

The next stage is for the crystalline silicon boule to be sliced into thin wafers by saws—thin metal blades covered in powdered industrial diamonds. One surface of each wafer is then polished with successively finer diamond pastes, which are hard enough to make the smooth flat surface on which chips can be formed. The manufacture of silicon wafers to this stage is a difficult process, and so many integrated-circuit manufacturers prefer not to make wafers themselves, but buy them from specialist firms. The wafer is a pure, almost insulating material, upon which transistors will be imprinted and then linked together.

Producing the integrated circuit

Any one dust particle falling on to a silicon wafer could prevent a small area of its surface being correctly processed, and cause a complete circuit to fail, for example by breaking a connection between two transistors. Circuits are therefore made within **clean rooms**, the inner sanctums of integrated-circuit manufacture. Special attention is paid to removing particles of dirt from the air. In an averagely dust-free room there are thousands of millions of such particles floating in the air. The problem dust particles are about 1–10 microns in diameter—about two to twenty times thinner than a human hair. Any dust particles larger than these tend to fall rapidly to the floor, where they can be easily dealt with. Obviously all surfaces in the clean room have to be kept meticulously clean, but this is a fairly easy task since very little dust actually enters the room.

Sophisticated techniques for removing dust particles from the air have been developed by the semiconductor industry over the last twenty years, and it is surprising that these have not become standard in hospital operating-theatres. In the latest design of clean room, the roof is turned into a large dust-extraction filter, and air is forced downwards through it under pressure, and out through the floor of the room. The continuous stream of air flowing downwards clears any dust generated by the work within the room. The filters reduce the level of dust by about a factor of a million, leaving perhaps only ten to one hundred particles floating in each cubic foot of air. The air pressure within the room is also kept slightly above that of the outside world, so that if there are any small leaks in the room, or if a door is opened, dirty air is not brought in from the outside world. Entry is through a room with a double-door airlock, where staff change into special clothes. The factory itself is normally situated in a location that is remote from industrial pollution, in order to reduce the amount of pollutants and grit brought into the room on clothes, in water, or by air leaks.

The clean room

As the transistors on the chip grow smaller and more numerous, faults become more likely. A clean manufacturing environment is essential to keep the yield of successful chips at a reasonable level.

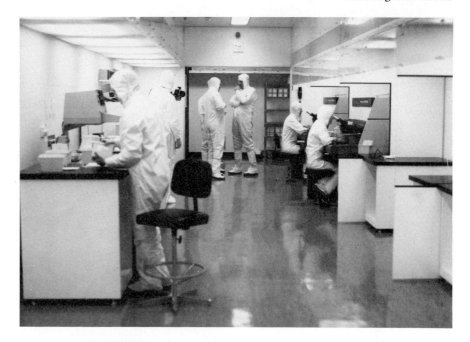

Is this the end of the clean room?

This dust-proof box holds a stack of silicon wafers in an atmosphere 100 times cleaner than in a clean room. The box has a standard trapdoor that links to the various machines used in wafer processing. Each processing machine automatically removes the wafers, processes them, replaces them in the box, and reseals it.

People are a major cause of contamination within clean rooms. Thus everyone working inside them has to wear a face-mask, and is clad from head to toe in clothing which does not shed dust. In future, the fabrication stages will become far more automated, with few human operators. However, total robotic control is difficult to imagine, because so much of the circuit manufacturing equipment is delicate, complicated, and needs continuous maintenance to be kept in good condition.

Microlithography

Microlithography, the technique which controls each stage of the processing of a wafer, is an extension of the printing process of photolithography. The silicon wafer is first covered with a thin layer of material (**photoresist**) which is sensitive to light. A mask is then put over the wafer surface, its black and clear areas respectively protecting areas from, and revealing them to, an ultra-

The Integrated Circuit

Microlithography

Microlithography is an extension of conventional photolithography, using photographic techniques to define fine patterns of hardened material on the silicon wafer. The patterns, which are determined by the masks produced by the chip design process, control the areas of the wafer affected by subsequent chemical steps.

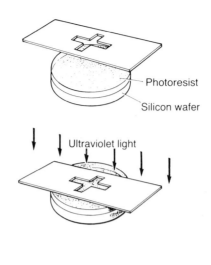

Photoresist

Silicon wafer

Ultraviolet light

The silicon wafer is completely covered with photoresist material.

The control mask is a glass photographic negative with the black-and-white pattern that needs to be reproduced on the wafer. The mask is placed in contact with the wafer and both are exposed to ultraviolet light. This hardens the photoresist except where it is protected by the dark areas of the mask. The unexposed areas are then dissolved away.

We are left with hardened areas of photoresist, which will resist the next chemical process applied to the wafer. Thus when it is dipped into acid, for example, only those areas without photoresist will be affected. The thinnest lines of hardened photoresist that can be formed are about 1 micron wide.

violet light. Where the photoresist material is exposed, it hardens to an impervious plastic layer, but any unexposed areas of photoresist can be dissolved away. This photoresist pattern controls the areas which subsequent chemical processes affect. About eight to ten microlithographic stages are necessary to produce an integrated circuit.

An example of a microlithographic step—forming electrical connections on a transistor

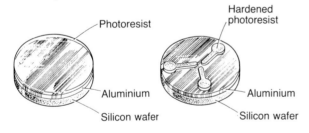

Photoresist

Hardened photoresist

Aluminium

Silicon wafer

Aluminium

Silicon wafer

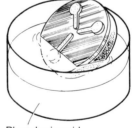

Phosphoric acid

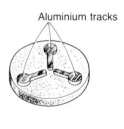

Aluminium tracks

The source, drain, and gate of the transistor have already been formed in the silicon, but now they need to be electrically linked to, for example, other transistors on the chip. Metal connection tracks are needed. The wafer is covered first with a layer of evaporated aluminium, and then with a layer of photoresist.

The pattern of the tracks is formed out of photoresist. A photographic mask is placed over the wafer, exposed to ultraviolet light, and the photoresist under clear areas of the mask is hardened. The rest is then dissolved away.

The wafer is placed into phosphoric acid, which strips away the aluminium, except where the hardened photoresist protects it.

The aluminium pattern is still covered by the hardened photoresist, but this can be easily removed by another chemical stage, revealing the connection tracks.

Electrical connections

Transistors in integrated circuits are electrically linked by thin aluminium tracks, directly equivalent to the connection tracks on a circuit board. The process of producing these lines illustrates one of the many microlithographic stages. The tracks are made by evaporating a thin layer of aluminium over all of a silicon wafer, and then removing unwanted areas through microlithography.

The aluminium is heated in a vacuum chamber until it melts then boils; its atoms fly off in straight lines in the form of a vapour, which then condenses into a thin layer of aluminium on the silicon wafer. Because the aluminium rests on an insulating layer of silicon dioxide, it does not electrically short-circuit the whole wafer.

The silicon wafer is then completely covered with photoresist, and exposed to ultraviolet light passed through a photographic mask with the required design of lines. Hardened photoresist forms in the exposed areas, but the areas under the clear parts of the mask remain soft, and are easily dissolved. The surface of the wafer is next bathed in phosphoric acid thereby removing the unprotected aluminium, but leaving the aluminium under the protective photoresist to form tracks. The hard photoresist is then removed with a different chemical.

The aluminium lines are so densely packed on a chip that there may be 60 feet of track on a $\frac{1}{4}$-inch-square silicon chip. The aluminium also forms the electrical connection tracks to the pads on the edge of the chip. These pads, often gold-plated for longer life, are in turn connected by thin wires to the legs of the integrated circuit.

Silicon oxidization

One fortunate property of silicon is that a glassy surface layer can easily be produced by heating a wafer in a gas containing oxygen (for example steam). This provides an almost perfect electrical insulator, and a protective layer for the silicon surface. The layer of silicon dioxide can be removed with a powerful acid (such as hydrofluoric acid). Using microlithographic technology, selected areas of the glassy layer can be protected when the chip is bathed with acid. The silicon dioxide pattern formed on the chip controls the addition of dopants.

Doping

Small amounts of material added to a silicon crystal alter its electrical properties enormously, making electrons or holes available for conduction. As we have seen, completely pure silicon scarcely conducts electricity at all. Arsenic atoms are similar to silicon atoms, except that they have one extra electron. If a little arsenic is added to a silicon crystal, then the resulting material contains surplus electrons, which can carry electrical currents. The silicon wafer is p-type material (electricity is conducted through holes) for the type of MOS transistor discussed, but small areas of the wafer are made n-type (electricity is conducted through electrons) by introducing a dopant, such as arsenic, on to the right places on the wafer. The MOS transistor is formed from two islands of n-type material, and so hundreds of thousands of these areas need to be formed on each chip—tens of millions on each wafer.

The Integrated Circuit

Making the MOS transistor

Each step of the chip-manufacturing process uses microlithography. These diagrams illustrate the formation of a single transistor, which would occupy only a few square microns on a wafer.

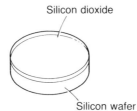

Silicon dioxide

Silicon wafer

A layer of silicon dioxide is formed by heating the silicon wafer in steam.

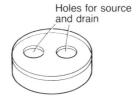

Holes for source and drain

Two holes are etched through to the silicon; these will form the source and drain of the transistor.

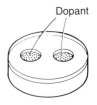

Dopant

Dopant material is applied to the silicon surface.

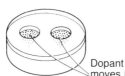

Dopant moves into the silicon

The dopant diffuses into the source and drain areas of the silicon when the wafer is heated, but other areas are protected by silicon dioxide.

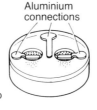

Aluminium connections

Aluminium connection tracks are laid down over the layer of silicon dioxide insulator. The middle track connects to the gate.

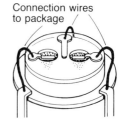

Connection wires to package

Thin wires link the connections of the transistor to the pins of the integrated circuit-package—in an integrated circuit the transistor would be linked to other transistors.

Diffusion

In this process, the silicon wafers are heated in quartz furnaces in order to make the dopants diffuse into the crystal. The furnaces can be seen glowing inside the cabinet; their temperatures are controlled to fractions of a degree.

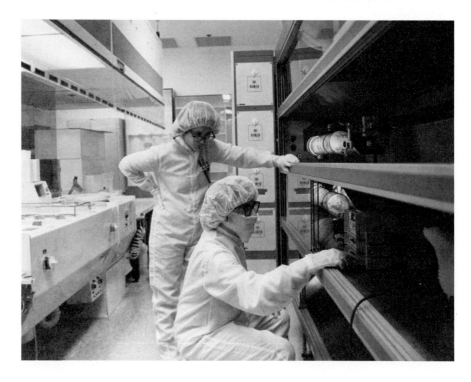

Diffusion and ion bombardment

There are two methods of introducing dopant materials into the silicon wafer. Firstly, if the wafer is heated in a gas containing some of the dopant material, a small amount of the dopant, say phosphorus, will stick to the silicon and then diffuse slowly into the silicon crystal. The areas affected by the phosphorus are those which are not protected by a layer of silicon dioxide. These small areas become n-type, providing electrons for current flow.

An alternative method is ion bombardment. Individual atoms of the dopant material are electrically charged in a vacuum, accelerated to a high speed, and then sent crashing through the surface of the silicon wafer. This method allows precise control of the amount of dopant material introduced. The impact causes some small-scale damage to the silicon crystal, but this can be repaired by gently heating the crystal.

Quality control

Quality control throughout the manufacturing process is essential if failure rates are to be prevented from creeping up. One method of doing this is to produce a few specially designed test transistors and other components on each wafer passing through the process. Each of these will indicate the quality of a particular stage of the process—for example, the thickness of the aluminium coating can be determined by checking a small electrical resistor made during the aluminium evaporation stage. These components are like the dots of colour produced at each stage of a printing process, examination of which is sufficient to check each individual process stage.

Chip testing

When the manufacturing stages are finished, the chips are tested to see if they perform the function for which they were designed. Each chip is checked individually while still on the silicon wafer. Fine, needle-like connectors are applied to the connection pads of the chip; these supply electrical power, inject test programs into the chip, and check its performance. Specially designed high-speed test equipment tries the circuit in much the same way as the user might. This is the moment of life or death for the chips, and most of them fail. The failures are immediately marked with a spot of ink, to be discarded when the wafer is broken up into separate chips. The greater the complexity of the chip, the more silicon it covers, the more vulnerable its transistors are to a processing problem, and hence the more likely it is to be discarded.

For very small circuits, the process of testing the chips on the wafer is both easy and comprehensive: all combinations (of 5 or 0 volts) of the inputs can be tried, and the outputs checked to see if they are correct for the particular inputs. With more complicated circuits, however, a totally comprehensive check is not possible, because there are simply too many combinations. Only a few sample inputs can be checked, and the chip is considered acceptable if it passes this test. The number of possible patterns of 1s and 0s in even a small memory chip is enormous; with only 64 bits there will be 2^{64} possible combinations, and even if we check one million of these combinations per second, testing just one chip would take hundreds of years. There is clearly no hope of thoroughly checking a 256k-bit chip. Unfortunately, some kinds of faults only

The Integrated Circuit

The chip tester

The fine needles are the connectors which reach down and test the chip while it is still part of the silicon wafer. The chip is put through its paces to see if it works properly. If it fails it is marked for scrap.

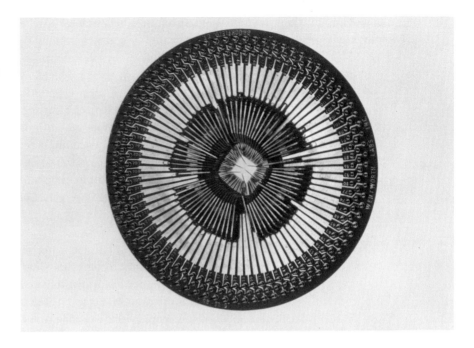

appear for a specific pattern of bits in a semiconductor memory. Since it is impossible to test all possible patterns, an untested combination could be the one used to prevent a stockpiled missile from exploding, or to control the last stages of a plane's landing.

In the latest chips (such as the Motorola 68000 family), the test process is extended even further. Circuitry is built into each chip specifically for the test stage; it is never used by the customer. The chips themselves help run a test which decides whether they will be packaged and sold, or destroyed when the wafer is split.

Yield of successful chips

On average, only one out of every three silicon chips passes all the tests. In a process with so many steps, there are many reasons for defects: small particles of dirt on the chip, faults in the silicon crystal, poor transistor formation, or a slight change in temperature during the diffusion. Paradoxically, a low success rate may be an indication of high profits. If there is a near 100 per cent yield, this probably means that the device is not at the forefront of the technology. This in turn means that the chip is 'mature' and low-priced, and that the company making it faces severe competition and low profits. A much more advanced device, with a relatively high unit profit, but a smaller yield, may be far more profitable.

Separating the chips

After the chips have been tested and marked, the wafer is scribed with a diamond between the individual chips, and split down these lines. Thin wires connect up the connection pads of the chips to the pins of the protective package of the integrated circuit. The wires are welded to the package pins and

Connections to the chip

This enlargement shows how the chip is linked to the legs of its plastic package. Thin wires are 'welded' to the connection pads on the edge of the chip. High-speed vibrations, applied through a small tip, create sufficient heat to weld the wire to the layer of metal on the chip surface. The two wires are about $\frac{1}{16}$ inch apart.

This photograph was taken with a microscope, using electrons instead of light to form an image. The chip was put into a vacuum chamber and a small beam of electrons scanned over its surface. The picture of the chip is then formed from the electrons reflected and emitted from its surface. The magnifying device is called a scanning electron microscope (SEM).

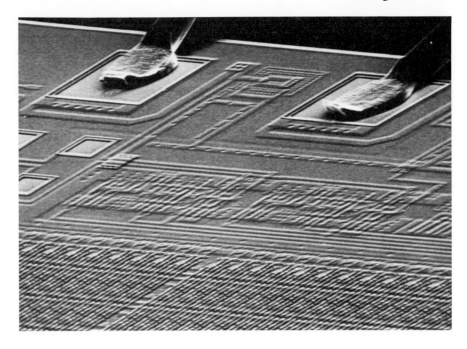

From wafer to final package

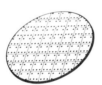  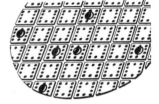

The silicon wafer after it has been processed; each rectangle contains a complete electronic circuit, but not all of them will work.

Electrical probes reach down to the connection pads of each circuit in turn (only five probes are shown here for the sake of clarity). The circuits are tested and the failures marked with dots of ink.

The wafer is scribed with a diamond, and split into separate chips; the failures are discarded.

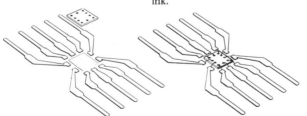 

The successful chips are mounted on to a metal web that will eventually be part of the plastic package of the integrated circuit.

The connection pads on each chip are connected by fine wires to the metal legs of the package.

The chip is hermetically sealed in a plastic package. Note the alignment notch on the package which indicates which way to insert the chip into a circuit board.

the contact pads on the chip by ultrasonic heating. A finely tipped rod vibrates each wire so powerfully that it becomes hot enough to weld to the surface it is in contact with. Normally the protective package is made of plastic, but some chips are packaged to 'military' standards, in sealed metal containers and tough ceramic holders, enabling them to withstand the combinations of extreme temperature, pressure, and humidity that they might be exposed to in a radio, aircraft, or rocket. After the device has been packaged, it may well be tested again, in conditions of high temperature and humidity, in order to try to eliminate 'infant mortality'—the tendency of a few chips to fail very quickly when used.

The process of checking and mounting the chips is highly automated, carried out by equipment which automatically orientates the chips on to their holders. The most common chip package is a black plastic rectangle, familiar on circuit boards. This package has two parallel rows of connection pins, from which it gets the name **dual-in-line (DIL)**. The DIL packages can be fitted into standard sockets on printed circuit boards. If a device fails, it can easily be removed from the socket and replaced. This package design is suitable for devices which require perhaps eight to eighty pins, but becomes very bulky for larger numbers of pins, and hence newer designs, like the leadless package (see illustration on p. 92) will eventually supplant it.

Eight Memory

Memory is an essential element of both human and machine intelligence. The CPU of a computer needs a large amount of memory for storing information before and after it is processed, as well as some for storing programs. Ideally, a memory device should be inexpensive, quickly accessible, retain information when the power is off, and allow information to be both read and altered.

No existing memory technology matches more than part of this specification, and consequently every computer system uses several types of storage. In particular, there is a severe trade-off between the speed of information retrieval and the cost of storage. Storing information in semiconductor memory chips is thousands of times more expensive per bit than doing so on magnetic discs or tapes. However, the process of retrieving or accessing data from magnetic storage is thousands of times slower than from semiconductor storage. The slow and fast memory must be linked so that information can be transferred between the two. This transfer process is complex, and forms a substantial part of the work of the computer operating system. It is performed only because of the requirement to store large amounts of information economically.

Memory that can be read or altered rapidly is made from silicon, and is often called directly addressable, since unlike disc memory the CPU can read or write each memory cell individually. This type of memory is organized into a large number of cells, each of which contains a single word of information, for example 8 bits on an 8-bit machine. Each cell can be read or written by some combination of the memory addressing pins of the computer, and each cell is reached by the CPU in approximately the same amount of time (hence this kind of memory is described as providing 'random access').

In a **disc drive**, information is stored by a magnetic process in tracks on flat circular plates (discs). A sensitive head can move to any one of the tracks, and read or alter the stored information as the disc rotates underneath. The information is stored in blocks, called **files**, each of which is given a separate name allowing it to be tracked down. A program written by a computer user would form a complete file on a disc, as would the editing program that was used to write it. The file might be a few bytes (a password or a date), or millions of bytes long (a **data base**). When a particular program is needed, it is brought into the semiconductor memory for processing.

The storage requirements of computers can be divided up into primary and secondary memory. Primary, semiconductor memory is fast and directly accessible by the CPU. Secondary memory, usually disc-based, is slower but cheaper, and is used for storing larger amounts of data. Whenever this needs to be manipulated, it is moved into the primary memory. Secondary memory is based on magnetic storage, which, unlike semiconducting memory retains data when the computer's power is turned off. There is a third kind of memory, digital magnetic tape, which is slower but cheaper still. This is ideal for large amounts of rarely used information, but is steadily becoming less important as a means of storage, and is not discussed in detail in this book.

Primary memory

Various types of semiconductor memory are made, each having a combination of speed, capacity, power consumption, and price suited to a particular application. They are all manufactured using similar techniques, as described in Chapter 7. The two basic kinds are **read-only memories (ROMs)**, and those that can be both read and written, **random access memories (RAMs)**. In purely economic terms, memory chips are more important than microprocessors, because a computer normally requires only one microprocessor, but many memory chips.

The number of transistors that can be put on a single silicon chip is about the same for any semiconductor memory chip at any given time. Hence the fewer transistors needed to make a cell to hold each individual bit, the larger the storage capacity of a chip. Designing the interconnecting structure of the cells on a memory chip is relatively simple, because of the large amount of repetition; the most design effort goes into structuring the cell that makes up an individual bit of data.

Memory chip capacity has increased somewhat more slowly than Moore's Law would have predicted, but the pace has still been very fast. In the early 1970s, with the advent of single chips holding 1,024 and then 4,096 bits of information, semiconductor storage displaced ferrite core storage, which had

---

Measurement of memory capacity

Because of the techniques used to address the cells on a memory chip, the number of elements along each side of the chip is usually a factor of 2 (32, 64, etc.). The total number of storage cells is therefore found by squaring this binary number, giving a series of storage capacities increasing by a factor of four each time (1,024, 4,096, 16,384, etc.).

In 1972 the 1,024-bit RAM was introduced and this was called the 1k RAM. It was formed from a 32-by-32 square of memory cells. The letter k had long been used by scientists as shorthand for a factor of 1,000 and was now taken over to be shorthand for 1,024. A few years later the 4,096-bit RAM was developed with a grid

of 64×64 cells. Naturally this was referred to as the 4k RAM. Next came the 128×128 memory—the 16k RAM, actually with 16,384 cells. Each step improves the capacity by a factor of four, and so the next contained 65,536 bits, but is always called a 64k memory! Subsequent 256k and experimental 1-megabit chips were available in 1985.

The most common measure of the size of memories or programs is the kbyte, or one thousand bytes (a byte is a set of 8 bits); one can never be sure whether the k represents 1,000 or 1,024. The megabyte (one million bytes) is the measure for larger programs and memories.

A memory chip

This photograph illustrates the regular structure of memory chips, especially compared to a microprocessor. Most of the area of this chip is taken up with the repetition of individual cells, each one of which holds a single bit of information. A computer can examine or alter cells several millions times a second. The rest of the circuit is occupied by address control functions which select the right cell for reading and writing, and amplification circuits which ensure that the signals provided by the chip are powerful enough.

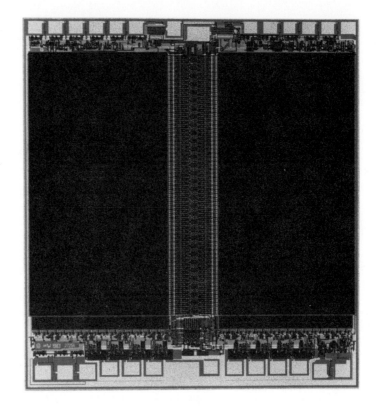

been used for the previous twenty years. By 1985, chips with 262,144 bits were commercially available, and research conferences were being shown prototypes with four times that storage.

Reading from and writing to a memory chip

Consider the sequence for examining the information in a single cell of a 64k-bit RAM to check whether it is a 1 or a 0. Only one bit of the memory chip can be examined at any one time, but about ten million reading or writing operations can be performed every second. A pattern of voltages corresponding to the binary address of the cell is applied by the CPU to the address pins of the memory chip. Sixteen pins are needed to be able to address every cell of the 64k chip. Each pin can be set at 5 volts or 0 volts, corresponding to 1 and 0 in the binary system. Each combination of 5 volts and 0 volts on the pins selects a different cell, and with sixteen pins there can be 2^{16} combinations, enabling the pins to address 65,536 cells. The **address decoder** electronics of the memory chip interprets the addressing combination and selects the relevant cell, which is then read to see whether it contains a 1 or a 0. The answer appears on the data pin of the memory chip. Normally the bus lines of the computer would be used for communicating the information between the CPU and the memory.

Writing information to the chip follows almost the same sequence. The address of a cell is placed on the sixteen pins, but this time the 'write' pin of the memory chip is set to 5 volts, telling the chip to write to, rather than read from, the selected cell. The 1 or 0 that will be stored in the cell is sent to the data pin of the memory chip by the CPU, and the address decoders of the chip work out which cell to put it into.

The connections on the 64k memory chip

The 64k memory chip stores 65,536 (2^{16}) bits. To reach a cell (containing a bit) in the chip, we must be able to select one particular combination of sixteen 1s and 0s—the address of the cell. To select an address with sixteen variable elements, we would expect to have sixteen addressing pins. Yet this 64k-bit memory chip has only sixteen pins altogether, including power and control pins. The technique of multiplexing uses the same pins more than once during the cycle of reading and writing. The 16 bits of the address are split into two 8-bit halves, which are then loaded one after the other on to the eight addressing pins of the chip. Two other pins indicate which particular 8 bits of the address are available on the pins.

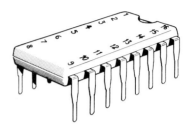

Two more are used for the power (5 volts and 0 volts), and another selects whether the data bit is being read or written. A further two are the data input and data output pins, and one pin is not used. Reducing the number of pins means the integrated-circuit package is smaller, and that more chips can be crammed on to a circuit board.

An 8-bit computer system manipulates not just one, but 8 bits (a byte) simultaneously. To read a byte of data stored in a memory cell, the central processing unit generates a single address, which obtains one bit each from eight memory chips at the same time. The CPU also indicates that it wishes to read (rather than write) that memory location, usually by switching a voltage line on the computer bus. The byte is disgorged from the eight memory chips on to eight data lines on the bus and transferred to the CPU for manipulation. Eight memory chips have been read simultaneously to provide the byte of information. The process of writing 8 bits follows a similar sequence, except that the CPU switches on the 'write' line, as well as supplying 8 bits of data. The timing of the whole sequence is regulated by the computer clock.

Random access memories

Unfortunately, there are two distinct usages of the acronym RAM. The first merely distinguishes directly addressable, semiconductor memory from disc memory. The second refers to semiconductor memory which can be read from and written to, as opposed to semiconductor memory which retains the same information permanently (read-only memories).

A CPU uses RAM chips in the latter sense for storing a program, program data, and, temporarily, blocks of data moving to and from discs. A large computer program may need many millions of bytes of semiconductor memory to run in a computer. The speed of the RAM chips is critical in determining the overall power of a computer. Because a large number of chips are required in a single computer system, the cost of the memory is usually a significant part of the total cost of a computer, especially of microcomputer systems, and there is constant pressure on manufacturers to reduce the cost of RAM chips.

The most common memory chip is the **dynamic RAM (DRAM,** pronounced d-ram), which stores information in the form of an electrical charge. The DRAM memory is the most integrated of all memory chips, containing more cells than any other. It has this larger storage capacity because its individual cell structure is very simple, requiring only one transistor and capacitor to retain one bit. Each capacitor is a miniature store of electrons, and the presence or absence of a charge on the capacitor changes the electrical characteristics of the single transistor that is used to store the bit. In 1985, DRAMs with 256k bits were available (costing only $4), and prototype chips for storing 1,000,000 bits were demonstrated.

Electrons stored by the capacitor linked to each DRAM cell quickly leak away, and have to be **refreshed** about a thousand times every second, or the data bit would be lost. Complicated circuitry is required for this refreshing process, which involves reading out the contents of cells before the charge has faded, and then writing them back into the memory. Fortunately, the same circuitry can be used to refresh large numbers of DRAM chips, cycling around each memory cell in turn. Refreshing does slow the computer down slightly, for if the machine needs to access cells currently being refreshed, which are consequently unavailable to be read or written, it has to stop operating.

The complicated circuitry needed for DRAMs is an extravagance for computers that only have a small amount of memory, and so for these it is better to use RAMs which do not need refreshing. The **static RAM (SRAM)** fulfils this criterion: it is able to retain information indefinitely without being refreshed as long as the power is switched on. It also consumes less power than a DRAM and so is often used for battery-operated equipment. But it does have a more complicated individual cell structure, typically requiring four to six transistors per bit—hence SRAMs usually have a smaller storage capacity than DRAMs. The cell structure of a SRAM often consists of two sets of three transistors, and at any one time one of these sets is switched on and conducting electricity, whilst the other is switched off. The processes of reading and altering an individual bit involves, respectively, detecting and changing which of the two sets is on.

Pseudo-static RAMs (PSRAMs) attempt to combine the advantages of dynamic and static RAMs. Potentially they are high-density chips that are easy to use. PSRAMs have complex 'refresh' circuitry actually built on to the memory chip itself, rather than merely attached to it (as is the case with DRAMs). By detecting the fleeting moments when the computer is not looking at the memory, the circuitry may be able to refresh the memory chips without needing to stop the computer. Unfortunately, different computers need different refreshing techniques, and so it is difficult to design a PSRAM suitable for many different computer systems.

Read-only memories

Read-only memories (ROMs) can be read, but not altered, by the computer. There are several different types. For example, the computer needs to access some information as soon as it is switched on. Computers are therefore built to run automatically a small program permanently stored in a particular kind of memory chip. This simple ROM-based program finds the operating system of the computer on a disc drive, and then loads the operating system into the RAM. It is usually called the bootstrap program—it allows the computer to pull itself into life by its own bootstraps! Obviously the fairly simple contents of the bootstrap memory must be retained after the computer has been switched off. A number of different ROM technologies are used, depending on the application. ROMs are also used whenever a normal computer program is fixed and will not need to be altered; an example would be a program controlling a washing-machine, a robot, or a computer terminal.

The **electrically programmable read-only memory (EPROM)** is a memory chip which can normally only be read, and not written, by a computer. However, information can be put into the EPROM (pronounced with a long *e*) using fairly simple equipment, affordable to small companies or electronics enthusiasts. The device retains this information when the electrical power is switched

A single storage cell in an EPROM

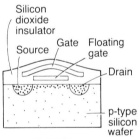

The cell reads 1

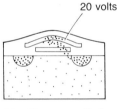

20 volts are applied to the gate

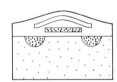

The cell reads 0

The EPROM storage cell is essentially an MOS transistor (see p. 88). Current can flow between the source and drain connections, and the flow is controlled by the voltage on the gate connection. The key to the EPROM is the **floating gate**—an electrically isolated gate standing between the source and the drain. This gate controls the current flow between them, depending on its own electrical charge. The EPROM is normally delivered without any charge on the gate, and so each of its cells reads as a 1. Current can flow between the source and the drain.

The user has to program some of the cells of the chip using a special EPROM programmer. The floating gate is normally insulated from the rest of the cell. To get charge into it, a high voltage (about 20 volts) is applied for a short period between the gate connection and the drain. The silicon dioxide in the cell, normally an insulator, starts to conduct electricity and current flows between the two. A small number of electrons remain on the floating gate after this process, and their negative charge repels electrons underneath—preventing the normal current flow between the source and drain.

Thus, with the floating gate charged, the transistor does not conduct, and the memory cell reads 0. The silicon dioxide is such a good insulator that the charge can remain for years. However, it can be removed by shining ultraviolet light on the chip. This makes the silicon dioxide conduct electricity and the floating-gate charge leaks away. The whole chip has been converted back to reading 1s.

The EPROM cell enlarged

Here we see an array of the cells used in an EPROM memory, each cell capable of storing a single bit, and separated by less than one-thousandth of an inch from its neighbours. An enlargement shows a single cell. Like the photograph of the pin connections in the previous chapter, this picture was taken with a scanning electron microscope (SEM).

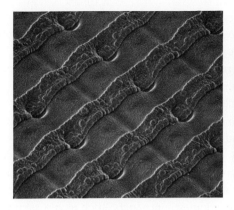
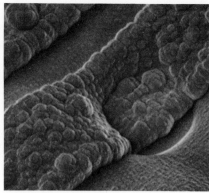

off. This reprogramming facility has made EPROMs very common devices compared to other ROM technologies. Most home computers have at least one EPROM, easily recognizable by the quartz plate on its package, enabling the silicon chip to be seen underneath.

When the EPROM is delivered to the user, all of its memory cells are set at 1, and special electronics equipment is needed to program in the 0s that are required. The user works out which cells need to be programmed, and stores this information in an EPROM programmer. The EPROM is plugged into this, and the address of each memory cell is selected in turn by generating the right combination of 1s and 0s on the address pins of the chip. A high voltage (typically between 12 and 18 volts) is then momentarily applied to the 'write' pin of the EPROM. This causes an avalanche of electrons to penetrate the normally insulating layer around the storage area of the memory cell. The charge is retained there almost indefinitely. Such a cell is thereafter always read as a binary 0—the electric field of the charge is sufficient to switch the cell transistor off, and cause it to be read as a 0.

The contents of the whole EPROM can be erased by an ultraviolet lamp. Ultraviolet light has enough energy to cause the storage charge to leak away. All the EPROM information is obliterated at the same time by this process; no parts of the memory can be saved. The $\frac{1}{4}$-inch-square quartz plate covering the top of the chip allows the ultraviolet light through—so don't leave the chip out in the sunlight!

The **electrically erasable read-only memory (EEROM)** is the ideal type of memory for the circuit designer. Information can be read from or written to the EEROM chip and also retained when the power is switched off. Unfortunately the technology to make these chips is complex, and so the size of memory available has lagged behind other RAM types. Small, specialist firms like Seeq Technology are the market leaders in this field. You might find an EEROM monitoring a car engine, or as part of the tuner control of a TV. Details of the particular channels can be stored, and retained if the set is taken from room to room. The name for this chip has not yet been fixed, and it might also be referred to as an EAROM or E²ROM.

Other types of ROM

Two other types of ROM are commonly in use, and both can only be programmed once, either by the chip manufacturer or by the person assembling the circuit board that uses the chip.

The contents of a **mask-programmable ROM** are permanently fixed by evaporating a thin metal pattern on to the memory chip. The pattern of miniature electrical links determines which cells are 1s and 0s, and this information has been worked out by the customer and supplied to the manufacturer. Chips can be mass-produced ready for this last stage of fabrication. This type of ROM is substantially cheaper than the EPROM when produced in large quantities, but is clearly less flexible and more expensive in small numbers. The most common application of a mask-programmable ROM is as the store for the control program of simple domestic products, such as a washing-machine or television, or for programs in home computers.

In the **fusible ROM**, the contents of the memory cells are initially all connected by thin metal links. The presence of these links makes every cell a 1. Specific links can be melted away, or 'fused', by the application of a high current for a short time, and particular cells can thus be converted into 0s. This process is performed with a special piece of equipment—a fusible ROM programmer. Once information has been entered into fusible ROMs, the chips cannot thereafter be reprogrammed.

Secondary memory

Magnetic discs form the secondary level of storage in computer systems, holding large amounts of data which can be brought into the faster semiconductor memory when needed. Data is retained in circular tracks which are formed in a thin magnetic layer on the surface of a rotating disc by a magnetic head. This surface layer is divided into millions of small bar magnets, which can be made to point in one of two directions, either towards or away from the centre of the disc. All information is stored on the disc in binary form, as with other forms of computer memory; one direction represents 0, and the other 1. Writing individual bits involves altering magnetic patterns, rather than any physical change in the magnetic layer.

By using the head, the computer can either examine (read) the data pattern or alter (write) the direction in which particular bar magnets point. Unlike when it is stored in RAMs, information stored on discs is retained when the computer is switched off, because the small magnets retain their magnetism without any electrical power. The manufacture of disc drives is complex, and computer manufacturers do not usually make their own, but rely on specialized firms to supply them.

Tracks and sectors

The magnetic patterns of bits of information are arranged on a disc in circular tracks, which are formed by the read/write head as the disc continuously rotates underneath. The tracks do not make up a spiral, as on a gramophone record, but are separate rings. Each track contains the same amount of data, and is subdivided into several standard-sized sectors of data (often 512 bytes). Information is both read and written by the disc drive's magnetic head, which can be moved over any track. The magnetic bit patterns in the tracks are parallel to the disc's surface; this technique is called **longitudinal** storage.

Moving the magnetic head to be over the right track takes a few hundredths of a second, and there is another delay while the disc rotates so that the correct sectors of the track are underneath the head. Because 'hard' discs rotate fifty times a second, compared to floppy discs, which rotate perhaps five times a second, their 'access time' for information is much shorter. On average, discs take about one-tenth of a second to find the first bit of information required, while the semiconductor memory could have been altered one hundred thousand times during this period. However, once the correct area of the disc has been located, the disc can read or write information at very high speeds, from tens of thousands to hundreds of thousands of bytes every second. The time taken to read the first bit of information is called the 'latency'.

Storing bits on a floppy disc

Storing bits on a floppy disc involves magnetic rather than physical changes in the surface layer of the disc. Each arc in the photograph is part of a circular track on a disc, and the individual magnetic bits lie across the tracks. The tracks are only one-hundredth of an inch apart. The bits have been made visible by an extension of the old trick of putting a magnet under a piece of a paper and sprinkling iron filings on top to show the magnetic field. A fluid containing minute magnetic particles has been applied to the surface of a disc. When the liquid dries, the particles show the magnetic patterns on the disc.

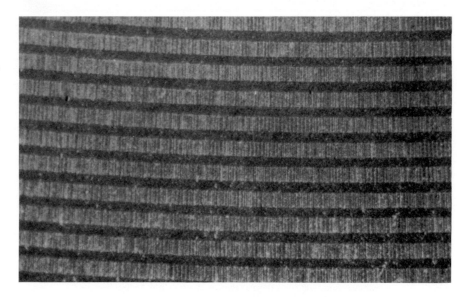

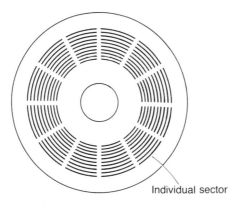

Individual sector

This diagram shows how the tracks on a disc are divided into sectors. Each sector contains a standard amount of information, usually 512 bytes. The disc shown has twelve sectors and ten tracks, and so would store about 60,000 bytes.

The magnetic head

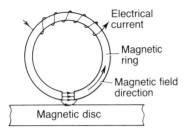

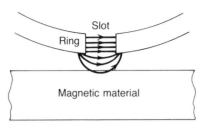

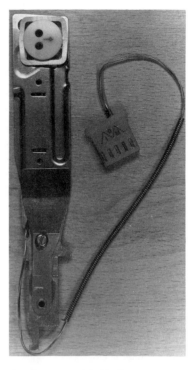

The magnetic fields that write data bits on to a disc are the 'fringe' fields produced by an electromagnet. No physical changes are made by these fields; they merely alter the magnetic patterns on the disc. When a current is passed through a wire coiled around a ring of magnetic material, the ring becomes intensely magnetized. If the ring were complete, the magnetic field would be confined inside it. But when the ring has a small break, as in the case of the magnetic head, the magnetic field spreads out of the ring around the fringes of this break.

The magnetic field around the break is very intense, but affects only small areas of the disc underneath the head, magnetizing them in one particular direction.

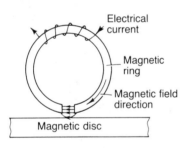

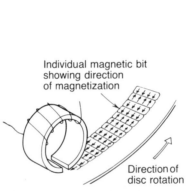

When the direction of the current is reversed, the direction of the magnetic field is also reversed, and the magnetic bit underneath the head is made to point in the opposite direction. The direction of the bit corresponds to whether it is a 1 or a 0.

The magnetic head is writing a single track of data on the disc as it rotates underneath. The same head is also able to read the direction of the magnetic patterns on the disc by detecting the small electrical impulse produced as each individual magnetic bit passes underneath the head.

A real magnetic head looks very different from its diagrammatic representation. The head has to be flat in order to skim over the magnetic surface rotating smoothly at 100 m.p.h. beneath it. The sensitive tip of the head is buried into the white teflon disc, with only the area near the break in the magnetic ring emerging through the teflon. Electrical signals are brought from the head to the disc controller by leads, which have to be flexible enough to accommodate the movement of the head across the magnetic disc. Because the signals from the head are so small, an amplifier is usually built into the head to enhance them.

Virtual memory On the more advanced computers, techniques of **virtual memory** allow information to be taken from disc drives and supplied automatically to the semiconductor memory without users being aware of the process. The virtual memory hardware and software make the disc storage appear to be an extension of the semiconductor memory. Programmers can write programs as if there is a very large amount of primary memory; this makes their work much easier because there is no need to provide the explicit instructions necessary to access disc information. Special hardware and software organize the interchange of information between the two sorts of memory, and programs can ignore the distinction. If the transfer process can be performed quickly enough, the process is completely invisible to the user.

Virtual memory

An example of virtual memory is shown; it enables a computer with only 1 megabyte of semiconductor memory to use programs requiring sixteen times as much. The difference is made up by disc storage, but the virtual memory hardware makes the disc simulate semiconductor memory. The major advantage of virtual memory is that programs written for a larger machine will run on a smaller computer. Retrieving data from discs is a slow process, but the virtual memory hardware will often be able to predict what information will be required and fetch it into the memory in advance, thus avoiding delays. Virtual memory creates the illusion for the CPU, the program, and the programmer that a large amount of semiconductor memory is available.

The real size of the semiconductor memory on the computer system is 1 megabyte.

Virtual memory (VM) techniques expand the apparent size to 16 megabytes, using disc memory to make up the difference. To the programmer the extra memory appears to be semiconductor memory.

When a program requests data that should be at 10 megabytes in the semiconductor memory, the virtual memory hardware determines where this data is stored on the disc.

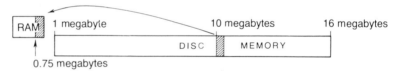

The virtual memory hardware moves the data from the disc into a slot in the semiconductor memory (for example at 0.75 megabytes). The hardware then alters the addressing of the computer to make it appear to the CPU that this slot is at 10 megabytes.

Software costs are reduced by virtual memory techniques, since programs that require large amounts of random access memory can be used on smaller machines that do not have this amount of RAM. Of course the process can never be as fast as manipulating data stored in the semiconductor memory, but often the virtual memory system is able to predict which data will be needed and have it available when required. Most programs tend to use information in a fairly predictable manner. The system keeps the main memory full of information, and so when a new block of information is needed its task becomes that of predicting which old block should be put back on the disc. When a program's use of data is unpredictable, virtual memory performs poorly, slowing down the computer system.

Large programs will run correctly on a computer with virtual memory, regardless of the memory size (within limits) of the computer. In the case of a multi-user system, the computer can always attend to another user while the information is being fetched. All of the main 32-bit microprocessor families provide virtual memory facilities, built into either the chip or a separate chip which can perform memory management as well.

Hard and floppy discs

Disc systems can be divided into two types, using either **hard** or **floppy** discs to store information. Hard discs have solid aluminium discs as their base, while the substrates of floppies are flexible sheets of plastic. In both cases the base is coated with a uniform hard-wearing layer of magnetic material, in which the data is stored. The disc drive is the whole unit that connects to the computer, while the disc inside the drive is called the disc **media**.

Writing and reading information

The magnetic head in the disc drive consists of a coil of wire wrapped around a ring of magnetic material. When a current is passed through the coil, a magnetic field is generated, and this field is intensified by the magnetic material. The magnetic material in the head is called 'soft', because it can be made strongly magnetic by external magnetic or electrical fields. Without this external field, the head has no overall magnetism. The ring of magnetic material forms a completely closed magnetic 'circuit', except for a small break which is filled in with glass. A completely closed ring of magnetic material would confine the magnetic field, but around the small break the ring exudes an extremely intense magnetic field. If this localized field is applied to one of the bar magnets that store a single bit, it can reverse the magnet's direction. If a current is passed through the coil in the opposite direction, then the magnet's direction is changed again. The head is then able to write information on to the disc.

Binary information can also be read from the disc. Whenever a bit passes rapidly by the head, its magnetism generates a small voltage in the head coil. The direction of the electrical pulse in the head indicates whether the bit is a 1 or a 0. The reading process does not affect the bit.

Magnetic materials on the disc surface

The magnetic layer of a disc, in which data is stored, is a mass of thin needles, made from iron oxide with some cobalt. Each needle is a miniature bar magnet, approximately 1 micron long and $\frac{1}{10}$ micron wide, and several hundred of these needles are necessary to store a single bit. Because of their shape, the needles can only be magnetized along their length, with a north pole at one end and a south pole at the other. This ensures that only two magnetic directions are possible for the needles.

The surface layer of the disc must have specific magnetic properties: the magnetism corresponding to each stored bit must be retained after the magnetic head has passed by, and it must be possible for the direction of the small bar magnets to be changed by the magnetic field of the head coil. These

Magnetic properties needed for the disc's surface

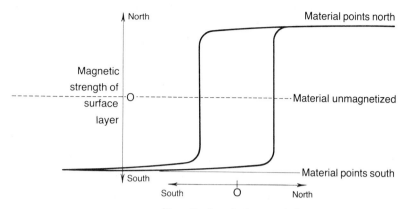

The surface of the computer disc must possess specific magnetic properties to be suitable for storing data. It must be able to be magnetized into one of two possible directions by a magnetic field. These directions are arbitrarily called north and south here. The magnetic strength must be retained for long periods without weakening, and the small bar magnets in the surface must always switch direction when the head applies the necessary magnetic field.

The magnetic direction in which the bits point depends not only upon the current magnetic field but also on the 'history' of the large magnetic fields that have been applied to them—they exhibit **hysteresis**. The graph shows how the magnetization of a single bit varies as a magnetic field is applied to it. A large enough magnetic field will always cause the bit to point in one direction, and this direction remains stable as the field is removed, and even when a small field is applied in the opposite direction. However, when the opposing field is large enough, the bit will switch direction. Note that when no field is being applied, the magnetic bit will point in one of two directions, depending on the direction of the last large field.

properties are summarized in the accompanying diagram, which shows how the magnetism of the layer varies with an external magnetic field. When no magnetic field is being applied to it, the magnetic material can be in one of two possible directions, depending on the direction of the last large magnetic field that was applied to it.

When a disc is manufactured, the needles are deposited on its rotating surface as a slurry. A strong magnetic field applied in a circle around the disc ensures that the needles point in that direction before their position becomes fixed. Needles can be magnetized either clockwise or anticlockwise around the disc, but not in other directions. Once the needles are settled the disc is gently polished, and a lubricant is added to reduce the damage caused by any contact between the magnetic head and the surface layer.

Organization of data on a disc

The software of the operating system of the computer organizes how data is stored on a disc, although disc drives are gradually taking over more of the detailed control, i.e. becoming more 'intelligent'. Each system works differently, so the following describes only a representative method of disc storage.

The operating system controlling the disc divides it into two parts: one stores the data, and a second, smaller area stores the **directory**, which is a map of where the data has been stored. The computer system normally only works on complete files of information. Each file is treated as a complete unit by the operating system, at least as far as the user is concerned. Because there is no standard way of organizing data on disc, discs for one computer system will almost certainly be incompatible with another system, even though both systems may use physically identical discs.

The computer keeps a record of the files on a disc by storing a directory of such details on the disc itself. The directory is usually located at a fixed place on the disc, so that it can always be easily located by the operating system. It consists of a list of the names of all the files stored on the disc, and details of the tracks and sectors the files are stored on. Any disc operation that needs to locate a file, or to find out if there is enough space to put a new file on to the disc, must first examine the directory. The directory is therefore a file itself, but with a different structure from other files. When a file is erased from the disc, the actual information on the disc is normally left untouched—erasing the entry for that file in the directory is quite sufficient.

In practice, rather than writing a file on to a disc as one unbroken unit, the operating system often splits it into standard-sized blocks of data, which are then written to separate parts of the disc. This technique enables the operating system to make use of even small areas of the disc for storing a long file. Unfortunately the smaller the size of the blocks, the bigger the directory needs to be, because of the need to point to each sector.

How a computer file is stored on a disc

A single computer file, such as a program, is often divided into discrete blocks so that it can be stored at several places on the disc. This technique allows the whole disc to be used. If a file was stored in a continuous block, there would be problems in trying to fit large files into the odd spaces left after other files have been erased off the disc. However, with files split up, more movements of the magnetic head are required for reading and writing a file. In the more 'intelligent' disc drives, the block positions are organized so that the least number of head movements are performed.

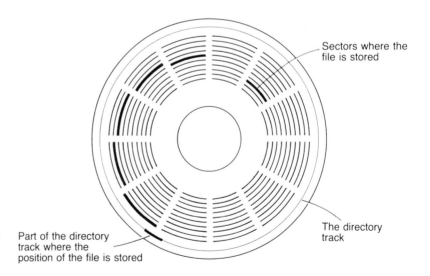

Sectors where the file is stored

The directory track

Part of the directory track where the position of the file is stored

When a file, such as a computer program, is needed by the computer, the first action of the operating system is to examine the directory to find the position of that file. The magnetic head of the disc drive is positioned over the directory track and reads its contents into the semiconductor memory.

The operating system can then find the position of the wanted file, move the magnetic head to the correct track, wait until the correct sectors of the track move underneath the head, and then read them into the RAM.

A file on a disc is a complete entity, such as a whole computer program, or a complete section of text. Imagine that some text has been stored on a magnetic disc under the name MAGDISC, and that a word-processing program is being used to modify the text. All the disc manipulation takes place under the overall control of the word-processing program, without the user being aware of the process. The program uses simple disc manipulation functions available in the operating system. First it examines the directory to find out where the text is stored. From the information in the directory, MAGDISC is found to be on track 23, sector 1, and to be ten sectors long. The magnetic head is moved out to track 23 where it copies the ten sectors into the semiconductor memory of the computer. The information on the disc remains unchanged by this process.

The word-processing program then starts to modify the text of the MAGDISC file stored in the RAM, until the file needs to be written back to the disc. The original MAGDISC file, which is still kept as a back-up in case something is wrong with the new text, is then renamed. The new version of MAGDISC is allocated a temporary name (such as MAGDISC.$$$) and the directory is examined to find where on the disc there is enough space for the new file to be put. Having been positioned over the right track, the head waits until the correct sector comes around, and writes the new file. Often the newly written file is read to check that it has been correctly entered, and only after this has been done is the directory entry updated from the temporary name to MAGDISC. If you have a home computer, you can follow this sequence of operations by listening to the movements of the magnetic head as it moves from track to track reading or writing information.

Safety of information

During the whole process of reading from and writing to a disc, there is great emphasis on ensuring the safety of the information being stored, so that an electrical power failure or a disc problem does not cause the loss of vital data. Old files are not deleted until the new ones have been read to make sure they are stored correctly. The preservation of the directory is particularly important, because if it cannot be read then the information on the disc is effectively lost, simply because it cannot be located. To ensure the safety of the directory, some operating systems duplicate the directory information.

Dust

Dust can have a devastating effect on disc drives, especially now that information is packed very tightly on to discs. In the case of hard discs, the disc surface is passing underneath the head at about 100 m.p.h. The head is kept at the right distance above the surface by aerodynamic forces, moving up and down over distortions of the disc. The gap between the head and the disc is as little as 1/50,000 inch (half a micron)—one-hundredth of the diameter of a human hair. The closer the information is packed together, the smaller this

Dust and the magnetic disc

The magnetic head glides only half a micron above the magnetic surface of the disc, kept at the right height by the flow of air passing underneath. The speed of the surface past the head can be as fast as 100 m.p.h; even a single dust particle could cause the head to crash.

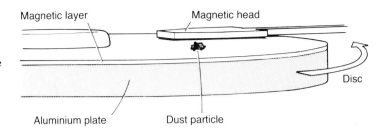

Magnetic layer   Magnetic head

Disc

Aluminium plate   Dust particle

head-to-surface gap must be, so that when the head writes magnetic patterns it does not affect neighbouring bits of information. Small dust particles on the surface of the disc can cause the head to crash, wrecking the head and the disc's surface. Three solutions to the problems of dust contamination have led to three kinds of magnetic discs being produced; these are the floppy disc, Winchester disc, and removable hard disc, each offering certain advantages for particular applications.

The floppy disc drive

The floppy disc drive is an inexpensive, slow-speed disc system. The floppy discs themselves (often called 'diskettes') are manufactured by applying a magnetic coating to both sides of a thin flexible sheet of plastic. In the drive, the magnetic head is actually in contact with the surface of the disc when reading from and writing to it. Compared to hard discs, the area used to store each bit of information is relatively large, and so small dust particles or scratches do not obliterate data. Inside the flexible cover of a floppy disc is a paper material which cleans the disc and traps dust as the disc rotates. Each floppy disc stores between 100,000 and 10,000,000 bytes of information. Floppy disc systems are now much more reliable than when they were first introduced, and if not maltreated can give years of service. This is primarily due to more stable plastics, better adhesion of the magnetic layer to the plastic, improved lubrication of the surface, and better control of the position of the magnetic head.

Floppy discs were invented in the early 1970s by Al Shugart of IBM, and were initially used for minor tasks on large mainframe computers, such as storing error messages. As with microprocessors and EPROMs, their eventual wide-ranging applications were not immediately apparent, even to the company that invented them. Shugart left IBM in 1973 and formed the first company to manufacture floppies for small computer systems. They became popular very quickly as an inexpensive storage medium for the early microcomputer systems. The first floppy was 8 inches in diameter, but this is now obsolescent, and subsequent versions have been $5\frac{1}{4}$, 3, and $3\frac{1}{2}$ inches. Japanese manufacturers such as Mitsubishi and Teac moved into the market in the late 1970s and have now usurped the American domination of this field.

Hard- and soft-sectored discs

If you can get hold of a floppy disc that has failed on a computer system, cut its case apart with a pair of scissors and examine the interior. Towards the centre of the disc there is either one or a series of holes. These holes are used by the disc drive to monitor the rotation of the disc. A small light inside the drive shines on to the disc's surface, its beam passing through the disc and striking a light detector when a hole rotates to the right position. On a 'hard-sectored' disc, the holes physically divide the data on each track into standard sectors. If the disc has a single hole, the sectors are defined by a pattern of bits laid down by the magnetic head itself. Such discs are called 'soft-sectored', and the single hole marks the start position for each track. A computer program (often called the formatter) writes the sectors on to new discs.

The soft-sectored floppy disc

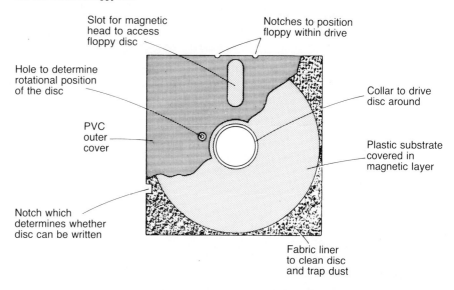

Slot for magnetic head to access floppy disc

Notches to position floppy within drive

Hole to determine rotational position of the disc

Collar to drive disc around

PVC outer cover

Plastic substrate covered in magnetic layer

Notch which determines whether disc can be written

Fabric liner to clean disc and trap dust

Whether a floppy disc can be written to, or only read from, can be determined by whether a small foil tag is stuck over a notch in its cover; the presence or absence of this tag is established by a light-detecting system in the disc drive. For 8-inch floppies the tag has to be present to write to the disc. When $5\frac{1}{4}$-inch floppies were introduced, this policy was reversed; needless to say, $3\frac{1}{2}$-inch floppies reverted to the original decision.

The first 8-inch-diameter floppy was soft-sectored and its format as defined by IBM became a standard for all companies. Information written on to a disc from one computer could (with the right software) then be read by a different system. Unfortunately $5\frac{1}{4}$-inch discs were not standardized, and different systems cannot read each other's discs. In part this is a ploy used by companies to prevent software piracy, ensuring that customers have to buy software from the computer manufacturer. The disc for the IBM personal computer (PC) provides the nearest to a standard for $5\frac{1}{4}$-inch discs; many other personal computer manufacturers supply discs compatible with the PC format.

The microfloppy

Developments in storage technology have meant that smaller and smaller discs can hold useful amounts of information. Microfloppies are being built in a

121

variety of formats from 3 to 4 inches, but the 300 r.p.m. 3½-inch format, originally introduced by Sony, seems to be becoming the accepted specification for personal computers. The Sony microfloppy has a hard plastic shell rather than a soft cover, and a metal shutter which protects the area that is read by the magnetic head. This means that discs can be safely carried in a pocket. As data densities increase, even more efficient ways to exclude dust will need to be found. Despite many discussions, the format has not been standardized, and again there will be no method of exchanging information between different computer systems.

Winchester discs The Winchester disc drive uses an inflexible aluminium substrate for the magnetic layer of its discs, and both its heads and its discs are sealed inside a container of clean air to exclude dust. The air is kept clean by being continuously passed through filters inside the sealed chamber. Under these dust-free conditions the magnetic head floats very close to the rotating surface so that the bit patterns can be written densely. Several disc platters can be stacked on the same motor shaft, and there is a detection head for each magnetic surface. The disc rotates at about 50 revolutions every second, giving a better speed and storage capacity than a floppy disc drive.

The Winchester disc cannot normally be removed from inside its protective box, and should its surface become damaged it is expensive to repair. The disc

The Winchester disc

The Winchester disc drive is made up of the magnetic disc used to store the information, the head that is able to read from and write to the disc, and the electronics that control the whole process and link the disc to the computer. The heads and discs are sealed inside a box and the air is kept dust-free by being constantly passed through filters.

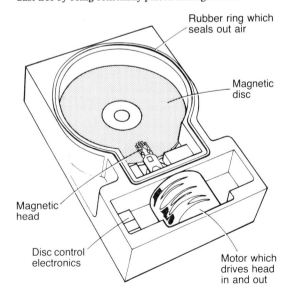

Rubber ring which seals out air

Magnetic disc

Magnetic head

Disc control electronics

Motor which drives head in and out

Clean conditions for the construction of Winchester disc drives

A Winchester disc drive is being assembled. The iron oxide material used for the surface layer is a very dirty material, yet once this is bonded to the aluminium substrate of the disc, no dust can be allowed near the disc.

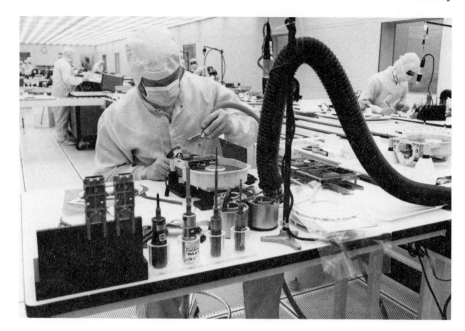

has to be assembled or repaired inside a clean room (see p. 96) to avoid being contaminated by dust. Winchester discs have become more and more reliable, however, lasting more than five years with ordinary use.

Because of its high speed, the Winchester disc drive is ideal for storing heavily used information, such as the operating system of a computer. The combination of a Winchester and a floppy disc drive in a computer system is ideal. Since the Winchester disc cannot be removed from its container, for safety the information on it must be duplicated on to another disc ('backed up'). Although they do not store as much information, floppy discs can be used to store this duplicate information.

Mass production has lowered the price of Winchester discs considerably, but both they and the electronics which link them to the computer cost considerably more than a floppy disc drive. Winchester discs are available with diameters between 3 and 14 inches, and with capacities ranging from five to several thousand megabytes. Winchester discs with a diameter of 3 inches are now being mass-produced and their price is falling dramatically.

Removable hard discs

The removable hard disc dominated the computer scene until the mid-1970s, since when its position has been eroded by the floppy and Winchester discs. Its magnetic surface is usually protected from dust by a mechanical shutter, which is opened when the disc is put into the disc drive. In some systems, any dirt and dust are swept away with a blast of clean air when the disc is loaded.

Data density

Two factors determine how much data the magnetic material on a disc can store: how closely the data can be stored around each track, and how near together the tracks can be packed. The longitudinal method of storage enables about 15,000 bits per inch to be packed around each track. Better control of the shape of magnetic particles may allow densities of up to 40,000 bits per inch to be obtained. At densities higher than this, the small magnets representing each bit will start to reduce each other's magnetization.

The limitations on packing the magnetic tracks more closely together are mechanical, rather than concerned with magnetic properties. The dimensions of a disc vary slightly with temperature and the tracks are never quite circular or centred properly. These problems limit floppy discs to about 100 tracks per inch at present. Even when the substrate material is more stable, there are problems in positioning the head over finely spaced tracks. These limit hard discs to about 1,000 tracks per inch.

In 1985, the maximum data density of a disc was about 15,000,000 bits to the square inch (1,000 tracks per inch multiplied by 15,000 bits per inch along each track). One square inch was sufficient to store about 300,000 words, or a few novels! The capacity of discs of a given physical size has doubled every two to three years for the last three decades. In 1985 the highest-capacity $5\frac{1}{4}$-inch-diameter Winchester disc could store nearly 400 megabytes of data.

Perpendicular storage

In the discs described so far, the small bar magnets lie parallel to the surface of the disc. An alternative, perpendicular method of storage promises to pack greater amounts of data on to a disc, perhaps up to 100,000 bits per inch. In perpendicular storage, the magnetization of the small bar magnets is perpendicular to the surface of the disc. Thus they do not interfere with each other's magnetization, even at high densities. Materials such as chromium cobalt (CrCo) can be magnetized perpendicularly. These very hard materials have to be sputtered on to the surface of the disc—a process where a thin coating is applied in a vacuum. Discs manufactured in this manner are always likely to be more expensive, but the extra storage capacity will in future make this expenditure worth while. Japanese manufacturers have taken a lead in perpendicular magnetic technology, which was pioneered by Professor Shin-Ichi Iwasaki of Sendai University in Japan.

The disc interface

Specialized electronic equipment is needed to link a disc drive to a computer system. This usually consists of a board—the **disc interface**—which plugs into a bus connector and can decode the signals from the CPU. To avoid having to build a different board for every combination of disc drive and computer bus, there are standard connections from disc drives. The most common are the SCSI (Small Computer Standard Interface) and Storage Module standards.

The interface board is connected to the disc drive by a cable. The board organizes the transfer of information to and from the disc, acting as an information store during the transfer, and detecting and correcting errors in the stored data. Discs (apart from floppies) are high-speed devices requiring fast electronic processing, and interface boards have to be specially built. General-purpose microprocessors are too slow to be used as controllers for these boards.

The digital optical disc

The **digital optical disc (DOD)** can store massive amounts of data, and is the only foreseeable high-density disc technology that will permit the disc to be removed from the drive. Unlike a Winchester disc drive, the storage capacity of the disc system can be increased by putting a new disc into the drive. Information is stored on the optical disc by burning small holes into a thin metal film, which is protected on both sides by a layer of plastic or glass. These holes are written by a small laser, and the same laser is used, at lower power, to read the information. A 12-inch disc will hold between 1,000 and 10,000 million bytes of information, and each removable disc costs less than £100. Text can therefore be stored on the optical disc between ten and one hundred times more cheaply than on paper. The economic consequences for any organ-

The digital optical disc

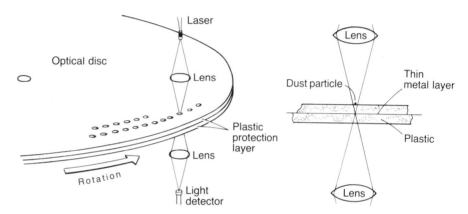

The digital optical disc stores data in the form of holes in a thin metal film protected by two layers of plastic. When the laser is used at high power it burns holes in the thin metal film. At lower power the same laser detects the presence (or absence) of holes, without damaging the metal film. Each square inch of the optical disc can store the equivalent of 10,000 typewritten pages of A4 paper.

A small dust particle on the plastic film does not block out a bit of information, because the laser beam only comes to a sharp focus at the metal film. At the plastic surface, the beam is wide enough not to be affected by a particle of dust.

Unlike high-density magnetic discs such as the Winchester disc, the optical disc is removable. Hence the capacity of the drive can be increased. Optical discs are 'write-once' because they store information by damaging the surface of the metal film. (The enlargement shows the pits in the metal film caused by the laser, each one representing a single bit.) However, there are prototype optical discs that can be rewritten.

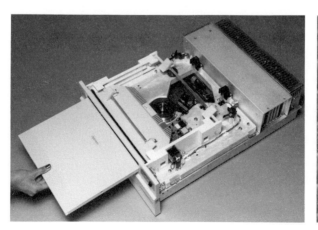

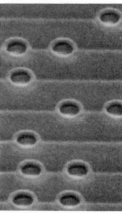

izations manipulating large quantities of text scarcely need spelling out; such equipment will eventually cause the wholesale restructuring of, for example, the administration of large corporations.

The DOD is a 'write-once' device; once full the disc cannot be reused in order to store new information, although information can be erased from the disc by covering an area in holes. For many applications, however, the archival nature of the disc may not be a disadvantage; and, in any case, rewritable optical discs using various storage technologies are being developed in the laboratories, and may be commercially available from the late 1980s. On microcomputers, the optical disc has appeared first as a read-only memory; mass-produced discs 12 centimetres in diameter (the same size as the compact disc for audio information) store 600 megabytes of unalterable data that can be read by comparatively inexpensive equipment.

The range of memory types

The fact that each type of memory has a different set of characteristics ensures that it has its own niche in the computer world. The devices tend to be faster and more expensive the further they are down the page, but memories are so varied that they can only be characterized crudely in such a diagram. The major division is between random access memories and non-random-access memories. The former are made from integrated-circuit chips, divided into cells holding small amounts of information; each cell can be accessed quickly by the computer CPU. The magnetic disc is the archetypal non-random-access device; unlike most of the chip memories it is non-volatile, retaining information even when the power is switched off. The bubble memory is a non-mechanical, non-random-access device with a limited range of applications.

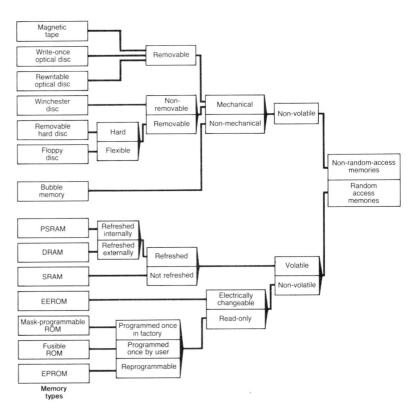

Memory types

The optical disc should not be seen as a competitor to the magnetic disc, because it is slower, and eventually will have less dense storage than magnetic technologies. But high-density magnetic discs will be non-removable. The optical disc should be seen as occupying a place between the magnetic disc and tape, similar to the disc in speed, and to the tape in price.

Nine Software

Software is the overall name for computer programs, each one of which performs a single conceptual task. Computer hardware is only important as the vehicle for software, and no matter how powerful a computer is, it is only as useful as the software that runs on it. Software is called 'soft' because of its amorphous nature; it is information, a specification for a task, and only physical in the sense that it has to be physically stored in the computer hardware. Yet there is no strict dividing line between software and hardware, since a task performed by hardware can be mimicked by software, and vice versa.

Software is an important industrial product, just as much as computer hardware. Some programs (such as Wordstar, dBase II, and Lotus 1-2-3) have sold hundreds of thousands of copies and earned their companies tens of millions of dollars. Software is expensive to develop, but very cheap to manufacture, and once perfected it never breaks down—although the hardware it runs on might develop faults.

Personal computer users are probably most familiar with programs for word processing, spreadsheet calculation, and data base management, as well as games programs. Any individual customer is also likely to need special programs, for example for accountancy, preparing statistics, image processing, typesetting, etc. Because of the general-purpose nature of the computer, the range of programs is effectively unlimited. Owners of popular computers like the IBM PC and the Apple Macintosh have a choice of thousands of software packages.

When personal computers came on to the market in the late 1970s, all the software ideas that had been developed in the previous twenty years were poured into them, perhaps creating the impression that producing novel programming ideas is a straightforward and inexpensive task. This is certainly not the case, and now that the flood of software rewritten from old programs has abated, we can expect the pace of software innovation to slow down, unless new methods of programming are developed. Most new programs will be written for microcomputers rather than for large computers, because of the huge numbers of owners of these machines.

Software can be broadly divided into two areas: applications programs and systems programs. **Application programs** perform the tasks for which a computer is bought, and **systems programs** (covered later in this chapter) are support programs that enable full use to be made of a computer.

Applications programs

Applications programs usually have to be bought as extras after a computer system is installed. Purchasers of computers often feel that they need to learn how to program, but this isn't really necessary for they can take advantage of professionally written programs, perhaps adapting them slightly to their own special requirements.

Some applications programs are so useful that versions of them are available for almost all computers. **Word-processing** programs help users to edit, format, and print text, **spread-sheet** programs are calculation aids, **data base management systems (DBMS)** are used for the storage and retrieval of all kinds of information, and **communications** programs enable computers to transmit information to, and receive it from, other computer systems. Customers of popular computers are faced with a choice of dozens of each of these types of programs.

Word processors

Word-processing programs are probably the most popular computer software of all. A **word processor** is a computer running such a program. The equivalent of about one-third of a sheet of A4 text is displayed on the screen of a VDU. As the user types text in, he or she can see on the screen an approximation of what the text will look like when it is printed out on paper. Many more facilities are available than on an electronic typewriter: for example, any amount of text can be deleted; text can be added, even in the middle of existing text; and parts of the text can be moved about easily. Existing text from another file can be brought into a document that is being written, and at any time the document can be printed out in a variety of formats. Packages linked to the word-processing software can check spellings against a dictionary of words stored on disc, point out simple grammatical mistakes, automatically produce an index and table of contents, or provide the user with a thesaurus. The main deficiency of present-day word processors is the limited display that is provided on their screens, but this should be cured by the advent of less expensive high-resolution VDUs.

A word processor is particularly useful for text that is going to go through several drafts. For short letters, however, it has fewer advantages. A common illusion is that you have to be able to type quickly to reap the benefits of word processing. In practice, for all but the very slowest typists, writing speed is determined by the brain and not by the agility of the fingers.

It is naïve to think of word processing as only a substitute for typing. The word processor can be used much earlier on in the creative process of writing. At first, users continue to develop the conceptual outline of text on paper, but as they become more familiar with the word processor it is used as a notepad for initial thoughts. One or two hours' training are sufficient to start off on a word processor, refinements being picked up slowly—the mental reorganization necessary to extract the maximum from word-processing software might take six months of steady use.

Spreadsheets

Whereas word processors and data base management systems are powerful analogues of writing and file storage respectively, spreadsheet programs provide a completely new facility. The spreadsheet allows the user to vary rapidly all the factors in a complex calculation, and see the results displayed very clearly.

Imagine a sheet divided into squares, or **cells**, as on a map, each cell having an identity number like A1, A2, etc. Into each cell the user can type either a number or a calculation (such as 54×35). In the latter case the cell displays the answer to the calculation in the cell. A calculation can also use numbers from other cells (such as the contents of cells A1 and A2), which might themselves be the results of calculations in other cells. In a spreadsheet program, this imaginary sheet is displayed on a VDU. A calculation can be broken down into a series of steps, and the intermediate results displayed in different cells.

Take a concrete example of using a spreadsheet to predict the cost of heating a house. Into each spreadsheet cell would go one of the factors involved in the calculation, such as the size of the house, thickness of the walls, insulation value of the windows, cost of gas, average temperature inside the house, and so on. From these factors the cost of the heating can be calculated with a few fairly simple formulae, and the answer displayed within a cell. The flexibility of the spreadsheet now comes to the fore: to change a factor in the calculation, all the user has to do is to alter the number in the appropriate cell (the underlying formula will remain the same, of course). To find out, for example, the effect of installing double glazing, a new value can be typed into the cell containing the insulation value of the windows. This is immediately taken into account in the calculation, and the new heating cost appears at the right point on the screen. A spreadsheet user can thus easily find the effect of varying all the factors in a calculation.

The spreadsheet has a variety of features in order to make it easier to use. Text can be put into a cell to describe the contents of nearby cells. New rows and columns can be added if some of the factors in a calculation change. The formulae behind the spreadsheet, as well as the numbers, can be saved on disc, and the results of a calculation printed out, displayed as graphs or charts, or put into a document.

The concept of the spreadsheet was invented in 1979 by two Americans, Daniel Bricklin and Robert Frankston, and the first spreadsheet software, Visicalc, was rapidly produced for the Apple microcomputer. Visicalc sold hundreds of thousands of copies, and in 1981 it was the best-selling program in the world. Success often seems to induce a fatal lethargy in companies, and within two or three years Visicalc was superseded by better spreadsheet products, such as Supercalc, and later by Lotus 1-2-3, which included graphics to display the spreadsheet results.

Data base management systems

A data base management system (DBMS) is a computer program designed to store and retrieve information of all kinds. The user can very quickly organize the DBMS to store lists of names and addresses, types of garden plants, results of experiments, etc. The data can be entered in any order, and then sorted by the computer using any of the factors stored, by name or age, for example. Unlike word-processing, spreadsheet, or communications software, the customer usually has to write programs to organize the DBMS system for a particular task, particularly in order to find or print out some particular set of information. Hence using a DBMS requires more skill than any of the other popular types of program.

The data base can be searched for specific types of data—for example, for details of all the 37-year-old people, or of all the people with five letters in their surname—and individual **records** can be sorted into alphabetical or numerical order. The DBMS does not do this by rearranging the data, but by making up an index, which the computer consults in order to find out where information is stored.

Early DBMS systems were developed for large computers and stored data in a complicated fashion, which was designed to minimize the use of computer resources but led to some loss of flexibility in searching for information. Most modern data base systems use the theory developed by Dr E. F. Codd at IBM in California in the early 1970s. His insight was to see that the data should be stored in simple two-dimensional tables, rather than in complicated structures tailored to particular types of searches. In almost all of the popular DBMS systems, especially those for microcomputers, the data is organized in the form of simple tables; one column might hold names, another addresses or ages, for example. These techniques are called **relational**, and their increased flexibility requires more processing power. The mainframe companies were slow to change from their existing software, and it was left to microcomputer software companies to popularize these relational data base techniques with programs like dBase II, which has sold hundreds of thousands of copies.

DBMS software makes large demands on computer power and disc storage, and these demands become extreme when the data being stored grows larger than a few megabytes. Furthermore, large collections of data must be treated with extreme care, because carelessness or a single disc failure (on a Winchester disc, for example) can destroy large amounts of valuable information. It is very easy to generate a small-scale DBMS system on a single-user computer, but much more difficult to produce a large-scale one for business records—which might have to be used by many people at the same time—and make it safe, reliable, and fast enough to be useful.

Communications

Another common type of software is for communication between computers, but in this case specialized hardware is also necessary. The software is able to send and receive data over telephone lines through a **modem**. To send a message, the communications software sorts out information into a stream of bits, and the modem sends the bits down a telephone line as a series of modulated tones. At the other end of the line another modem demodulates the tones back into bits; modem is an abbreviation for **mo**dulator/**dem**odulator. The software in the computer receiving the message then reassembles the bits into the message. The rate at which data can be sent depends on the quality of the telephone line; usually the limit is 1,200 baud—about 120 characters per second.

Communications facilities open up a variety of new applications for the computer. For example, **electronic mail** can be sent and received. When a computer is started up, its VDU indicates whether a message has been received. Electronic **bulletin boards** and **conferencing facilities** allow messages to be exchanged amongst groups of users with particular interests. Fairly simple communications software allows a user to search hundreds of specialized commercial data bases of information (mostly US-based), together containing tens of millions of scientific articles, magazines, legal judgements, lists of available software, etc.—a mass of information equivalent to an encyclopaedia 10 miles thick, and growing by one foot every hour!

Integrated software

Different software packages were originally developed by different manufacturers, and so programs for separate applications were completely independent. The user ran one of the programs at a time, and information could not be conveniently exchanged between them. **Integrated software**, which is now available from several companies, amalgamates several different programs; the user might be able to word process, do spreadsheet calculations, and perform data base work, all with a single package of software. The two best-known examples of integrated software are Symphony and Framework, from companies that have succeeded with other microcomputer software. However, the word 'integrated' is rather flattering, because the individual software modules do not necessarily fit together well. As yet, we have only a limited understanding of how the disparate programs should be presented to the user.

Linking to the mainframe

Within a large organization, the computer department will offer versions of these popular software packages running on a mainframe computer. But these packages will not be as **user-friendly** (clear and simple) as the microcomputer versions, because they have to work with a variety of simple computer terminals and the mainframe provides less processor power per user than an individual microprocessor.

Problems arise if a microcomputer user tries to link in with the mainframe. For example, a piece of text written on a personal computer may need to be sent to several dozen people within a company, or part of the company's data base may need to be copied to the personal computer. The hardware links are no problem; boards which allow communication with the mainframe can be plugged into the personal computer. But the software packages on the microcomputer and the mainframe are likely to be incompatible. Not unnaturally, companies are rushing to fill this gap in the software market.

Systems programs

The systems programs of a computer provide help for a variety of tasks performed on the computer system. Examples include **compilers**, which translate programs so that they will run on the particular machine; **editors**, which help programmers to write software; and **linkers**, which join existing to newly developed programs. These programming aids usually come with the computer (on discs) when it is purchased.

Operating systems

A particularly important systems program is the **operating system**, which controls the detailed operations of a computer and its peripherals, and allows the user to perform basic tasks like making copies of programs, examining the contents of discs, etc. Applications programs use the facilities provided by the operating system, which is therefore an essential program. Most users need not concern themselves with systems software in general, but are forced to have a limited understanding of the operating system.

This program is written either by the manufacturers of the computer hardware, or for them by a specialist firm. With the help of the operating system, users can examine the contents of discs, copy programs (from one disc to another), delete or update files, or run programs. However, the casual user has no interest in the operating system, except as a means to control applications programs, and therefore it should be as invisible as possible. As the capabilities of computer systems grow, operating systems are being extended to control areas such as graphics, networking, data base management, and communication with other systems. Operating systems are absorbing more and more computing power, particularly for the graphics needed for advanced man–machine interface techniques.

Even when some other program is running, the operating system is normally in control, ready to take over if the program threatens to disorganize the computer system, for example by using memory reserved for another program. Rather than running the computer directly, other programs are actually using existing functions of the operating system. The operating system contains a host of **primitives**. These are small subprograms that can each perform a simple function, like writing a set amount of information to a disc, raising the disc head from or lowering it to the disc surface, or reading information typed in at the terminal. Any operation that is repeatedly needed by applications programs should be part of the operating system. This set of routines is often called the **kernel** of the system. Because these primitives are needed by so many programs, they must be efficient or else they will slow down the whole system. If the system has more than one user, there must also be a **scheduler**, a program that shares out the computer's time between the users.

The man–machine interface

The display on a computer screen should give a clear view of the state of the piece of software that is running at that moment; it should show the options the user has, and also how to choose between them. Nowadays this must include good use of diagrams and pictures, because text alone is too complex to understand. The **man–machine interface (MMI)** is the combination of software and hardware that organizes the presentation of the computer system to the user.

At one time the MMI was the last part of a computer system to be designed but now it is so important that it is often the first. Computer programs are becoming more powerful and more difficult to understand, and we are relying upon them more. Someone designing a car component on a computer might wish to see the current design of the part, rotate this to see it from another viewpoint, or change a dimension and see the effect. The processor power for this type of display can only be provided by 32-bit microprocessors, as well as specialized graphics chips. As computers are mass-produced, the level of user interest in technicalities decreases. This calls for software which makes the equipment easier to use, or more 'user-friendly'. After all, you don't need a manual to operate the television or the telephone, so why should the computer be any more difficult?

A video game involving a car race provides an excellent example of an MMI. The user is presented with colour pictures of the race viewed from a racing car, and allowed a few simple controls (left, right, accelerate, and brake). On the personal computer these controls are operated by pressing keys. In the amusement arcade versions of the game, the MMI inputs are reduced to the familiar steering-wheel, and brake and accelerator pedals. Because these are so familiar, the player can interact with the game almost immediately and needs to learn little of the details of the computer to use the system fully. The car race is modelled by a complex program, and the display is merely an output from that model; but it is critical in allowing the user to control the computer without detailed knowledge of its workings.

The problem for designers of complicated software is how to provide such an easy MMI for a range of other tasks. Because the MMI controls should operate in a similar way for every program that runs on a computer, the MMI must be a general-purpose program supplied by the manufacturer, and not left to suppliers of individual programs.

The man–machine interface for new software will use more and more graphics, and hence greater processing power. Graphics are produced most efficiently by specialized chips built into powerful personal computers with 32-bit microprocessors.

As programs become more complex and software costs rise, it is becoming increasingly important that the same operating system can be used on many different types of computer. If an operating system is **portable**, then the software for that function can be transferred easily, and programmers and computer users can switch machines without having to learn a new system. Portability is usually achieved in one of two different ways: either by writing the operating system in a high-level language (a compiler for the language would be needed for the particular computer), or by writing the operating system in the machine language of a popular microprocessor chip, which is likely to be incorporated into many different systems.

There are three main types of computer operating system: single-user, multi-user, and distributed systems. These are different both in their software and their hardware, with each structure having advantages and disadvantages depending on the situation.

Single-user systems

Single-user operating systems organize a computer to be operated by one person at a time. Typical examples are CP/M, MS-DOS, and PC-DOS. A big advantage of single-user over multi-user systems is that none of their processing time is spent on organizing how the computer shares its resources between users. With poorly organized multi-user operating systems, more than half of the computer's power can be absorbed by this task. In single-user systems both the applications software and the operating system itself are easier to write and much less complicated. Furthermore, because the user's terminal is (usually) close to the computer system, there is no restriction on the rate of communication between the user and the computer, as is necessarily the case with a mainframe. For example, loading a digital picture on to a television display takes only a second or so, instead of the few minutes it would take through a remote link with a large computing system. Other advantages for the user include total control of the system, the ability to make and remove copies of important software, and unlimited access to the system's resources.

However, there are disadvantages to single-user systems, particularly those that cannot link to other computer systems. Problems are bound to arise when an organization has centralized information sources which many people need to maintain and examine, but the company uses many different computers. Such an organization must carefully co-ordinate the purchase and use of computer hardware and software to minimize the difficulties of linking them together, and to the centralized computer.

The single-user system

The single-user computer system is a self-contained system that looks after one user at a time. Excellent software packages are available for popular single-user systems (such as the IBM PC or the Apple Macintosh). They are usually much easier to use than the software on large computers. The operator of a single-user system is in total control of its resources, and can take copies of important software. However, he or she is cut off from the resources provided by a mainframe system, such as expensive peripherals, electronic mail, and centralized information.

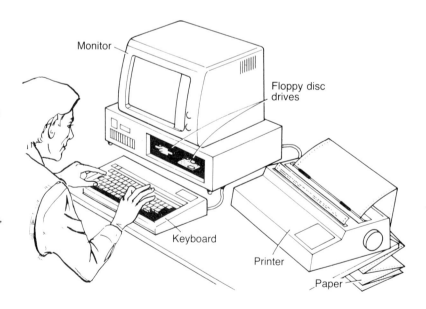

Monitor

Floppy disc drives

Keyboard

Printer

Paper

CP/M   CP/M (control program for micros), produced by Digital Research, is an example of a straightforward single-user operating system. In the 1970s, there was only one CP/M—the CP/M-80, which used the instructions of the Intel 8080 microprocessor—but Digital Research has since produced versions for other microprocessors, such as Intel's 8086 and 8088, and Motorola's 68000 micro. It has also brought out Concurrent CP/M for the IBM PC, which can organize the processing of several tasks on one computer.

The central command processor (CCP) element of the CP/M software analyses and processes commands typed in at a VDU. For example, the user can command the system to run a program, obtain a list of the software on a disc, or print a file. The basic input/output system (BIOS) provides a set of primitive operations to link the computer to peripheral equipment. These are used by the CCP when necessary. The basic disc operating system (BDOS) organizes the disc system to store and retrieve disc files. BIOS must be tailored by each microcomputer manufacturer, but the rest of CP/M-80 was written by Digital Research in a high-level language. CP/M-80 can be implemented easily on most of the microcomputers that use either the Zilog Z80 or the Intel 8080 series of chips.

CP/M-80 is the Model T Ford of computer operating systems, crude, functional, and popular. Hundreds of megabytes of useful software are available for nothing through CP/M-user clubs, and if you take just about any program you can think of, there is a version commercially available which will run under the CP/M operating system. The Z80 and 8080 microprocessors are now obsolescent, and little more software will be written for them. However, this will not mean the end of CP/M, for Digital Research has produced CP/M+, which is able to use larger amounts of memory if these can be managed by the hardware. With new, powerful processors like the Z800, which can run all the old software, CP/M+ will survive for many years.

The biggest blow to Digital Research's pride came when IBM chose Microsoft's PC-DOS operating system for its PC. PC-DOS (and MS-DOS, which is used on PC-compatible computers) has replaced CP/M-80 as the most popular operating system simply because of the massive sales of the IBM machine. PC-DOS is still a simple single-user operating system, with a few improvements on CP/M. For example, each file is marked with a date whenever it is changed, and groups of similar files can be organized together. The operating systems for 8-bit processors are necessarily simple and crude, because the processors do not have enough power for more user-friendly software and complex graphical displays. The high-powered IBM PC/AT computer uses an operating system that can support several users.

Multi-user operating systems

A multi-user operating system enables one computer to be shared between several users. If enough processing power is available then the computer can switch from one user to another quickly enough so that each appears to have unrestricted access to the machine.

Multi-user systems have many potential advantages. Communal information need only be stored on the central computer in order to be available to all. The cost of expensive and rarely used equipment and software can be shared. There are few problems with incompatibility in hardware and software between different users, because both must be centrally authorized before used as part of the system.

The multi-user system

The multi-user system shares out the resources of one large computer (usually a mainframe or supermini) between many users. Both software and hardware are shared. The popularity of such systems is declining, because they cannot give sufficient processing power to each user.

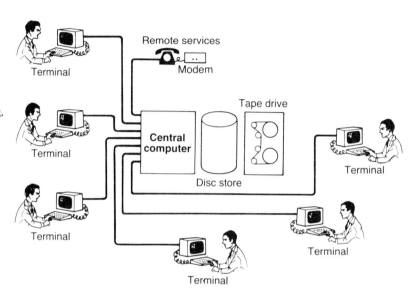

In practice, however, there are many disadvantages to multi-user systems. The operating systems are very complex, and expensive to write. A considerable part of the total processing power of the computer is taken up by the task of allocating processing time: in order, for example, to prevent a single user monopolizing the computer's time. As a result, the processing power available to each user is often much less than if each has a small microcomputer. The individual user is also not allowed more than a set allocation of memory, disc space, and computer time. Most users of multi-user systems are unhappy with

Multi-tasking and windowing

While a multi-user system caters for several users at the same time, a multi-tasking system allows a single user to control several tasks on a single computer system. Multi-tasking software often has **windowing** facilities, i.e. the outputs from several programs can be displayed at the same time on one screen. For example, while a program is being tested, the high-level language version of the program can be followed, so that the program can be immediately corrected when a fault is found. A display of the time might appear in a corner of the screen. Of course, the processor is only performing one of the tasks at a time, but swapping so quickly between them that it appears to be performing them all simultaneously.

the service they obtain; the systems simply do not provide enough computing power. The tendency is to move towards more distributed systems, in which many computers are linked together so that information can be transferred between them. But the worst fault of larger systems is their software. This is far less user-friendly than for small microcomputer systems, and also far more likely to be out of date, since it is more complex and takes longer to develop.

UNIX—a portable multi-user operating system

UNIX is a good example of a multi-user operating system. With the backing of the giant American communications firm AT&T, it seems likely to become the most common system for 16-bit microprocessors. It also represents an interesting trend: the development of the portable operating system. Most of UNIX is written in a high-level language, C, rather than in assembly language. The process of putting UNIX on to a new computer system involves providing a C compiler for the system, and linking up peripherals (like disc drives or VDUs) using the native machine language of the particular computer. UNIX is available on almost all popular computers, from micros to the Cray supercomputer. Although Burroughs has been writing operating systems for its computers in a high-level language since the early 1960s, UNIX is the first operating system which can be implemented fairly easily on to any suitable computer system.

Existing programs written in the C language can be compiled on a UNIX system on a new computer and run immediately (in theory). Therefore as soon as UNIX becomes functional on a computer system, a large number of applications programs are already available. If a company wants to avoid committing itself to the hardware and software of a single firm, UNIX is the only realistic choice.

UNIX was initially written in 1969 by Ken Thompson, a Bell Laboratories engineer, for the PDP-7, an obsolete DEC computer that he found abandoned in his laboratory. With the help of colleague Dennis Ritchie, a multi-user operating system that proved practical was produced. In 1973, with Dennis Ritchie, he rewrote UNIX for a PDP-11 minicomputer, deciding to do so in a portable language rather than the assembly language. They invented C for the purpose, and the whole of UNIX, except the software for the input and output devices, is written in C. Perhaps the prime reason for the success of UNIX is its conceptual integrity, a consequence of the fact that the original system was designed and implemented by only two people.

We can imagine UNIX as a series of concentric layers, like the coats of an onion, each performing the same computing function, but becoming less abstract and more related to the particular computer as we approach the centre of the system. At the surface of UNIX is the **shell**, which interprets the commands given by the user of the computer system. The shell reads and writes files, sends text to printers, calls up programs from discs, and shares out the computer's time between users. The shell is essentially a program which lies at a more abstract level than the basic operating system; it combines operating-system primitives into more abstract functions, making UNIX easier for the user.

At a lower level is the kernel of UNIX, the set of basic functions used by the shell. Each operation of the kernel performs a simple function, similar to the primitives of CP/M. Sets of these kernels can be built up into programs to control discs, printers, and disc directories. There is also **resource-scheduling** software to share out the processor time between the users.

UNIX stores files on disc in a tree-like structure, which enables the system to accommodate many users and yet keep overall control. Each user (a 'branch' on that tree) has his or her own file directory.

UNIX has many problems, reflecting both its age and the fact that it was originally developed for scientific rather than business work. It is a difficult system for the beginner to learn, at least in its basic form. The commands that the user has to enter into the system are terse and incomprehensible, and hence must be learnt by rote. More 'user-friendly' software will surely be necessary for UNIX to become a commercial success. Although a considerable amount of UNIX software is available, none of it is integrated. UNIX is a complex system requiring 5–10 megabytes of storage (and hence a Winchester disc) for all its files. Furthermore, there are many incompatible versions of UNIX, although Version V from Bell Laboratories may become the *de facto* standard.

Since 1980, many commercial firms have produced UNIX 'look-alikes' (such as Cromix, Coherent, and Idris), which attempt to provide the same facilities, and are marketed much more vigorously. However, the new commercialism of AT&T, Bell's parent company, must threaten these firms' success.

Distributed systems

A distributed system consists of many separate processors linked together by software and hardware, and usually based around a local area network. Such systems are the third type of computer organization, and are likely to become increasingly important. Many different computers can be connected to a distributed system, each of which can serve one or many users. The most advanced systems are those where all the computer hardware and software is purchased from one manufacturer. However, most large computer systems show only some of the features described: they can transfer data from one to another but mutual sharing of facilities is limited. Whatever the distributed system, it is usually necessary to have a central machine that can provide communal information and specialized equipment—but not processing power.

A **local area network (LAN)** is a data highway specifically designed to transport information from computer to computer; computers can be distributed along the LAN. Each user can be provided with an individual computer (often referred to as a workstation), relying on the network only for central services, such as a system of electronic mail. Distributed systems enable a computer system to combine many of the best features of personal computers and big multi-user computers. Users can retain a large amount of processing power and yet communicate with one another and share expensive facilities such as high-quality printers and large discs and programs. One big advantage of LANs is that they are specifically designed to transport information, and so they perform this task much faster than general-purpose computers, which are structured for processing rather than distributing information.

In 1985 LANs could transport data at a rate of between 1,000,000 and 10,000,000 bits of information per second. Each point on a LAN that receives or transmits information is called a **station** (or node), and the cabling between each station can be a simple twisted pair of wires, a heavy-duty coaxial cable, or even a fibre optic link, depending on the distances involved and the data rates required. A telephone link will not transfer data fast enough, and so a LAN is normally confined to one location, such as a large office block or factory.

Extra processing power can be added to a distributed system as the number of users increases, simply by adding more computers. The amount of power per user can be kept constant, or increased. Furthermore, the new processing power is concentrated where it is required, rather than at the end of a communication link with a slow transmission rate. The failure of an individual

The distributed system

The distributed computer system is more advanced than the multi-user system. Firstly, processing power is completely divorced from the transfer of information, which is carried out by a local area network (LAN). Secondly, processors can easily be added at stations around the LAN, increasing the amount of processing power available. If these can all run the same software, then many of the advantages of a centralized system can be retained. A completely distributed system is possible, in which the resources of the whole network are available to each user, but few systems have reached this stage. The role of the mainframe computer is clearly changing: it is increasingly being used as a centralized supplier of information and expensive peripherals, rather than as the source of a computer system's processing power.

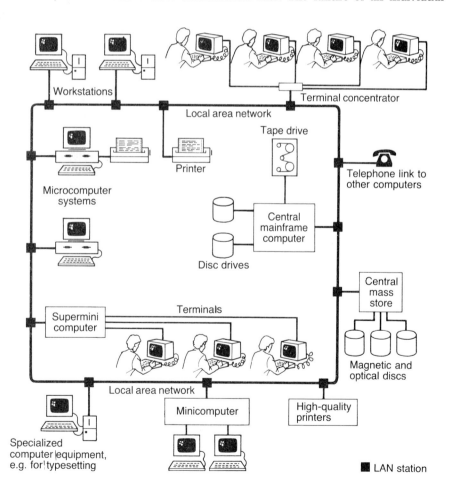

Workstations

Local area network

Terminal concentrator

Tape drive

Printer

Telephone link to other computers

Microcomputer systems

Central mainframe computer

Disc drives

Central mass store

Supermini computer

Terminals

Magnetic and optical discs

Local area network

Specialized computer equipment, e.g. for typesetting

Minicomputer

High-quality printers

■ LAN station

computer in a distributed system is not catastrophic—most users will be un-affected—and it may even be possible to substitute another computer. But the irresistible drive behind distributed systems is that the power of the single-chip microprocessor is increasing by 60 per cent each year. Processing power is much more inexpensively supplied by many small processors rather than by a few large mainframe computers.

The OSI reference model

Many organizations encounter problems when they try to link a range of computers from different manufacturers. Writing software to transfer files from one part of the network to another is easy, but users may wish to share resources such as mass storage or programs.

The International Standards Organization has defined a seven-layer reference model of abstraction for computer networks. This is called the Open Systems Interconnect (OSI), because it allows computers from different manufacturers to communicate openly with one another. The bottom layers are concerned with the physical connections, the middle layers with communication between the computers, while the upper layers deal with the more abstract concept of applications software. If a manufacturer converts to the OSI model, then its computers should (in theory) link up to all other compatible systems. In 1985 layers one to four were well defined, and ISO subcommittees were working on the other three. Adherence to the OSI standards is the only chance that smaller firms have of standing up to IBM, which is promoting its own System Network Architecture (SNA) as the *de facto* standard in this field.

At level three of the OSI standard (concerned with communication), there are three LAN standards. One (Ethernet) is a bus system, and the other two are varieties of ring systems. Ethernet is backed by the might of Xerox, Intel, and DEC, and seems likely to be the most successful. Unfortunately, because of the long gestation period for LANs, elements of all three LAN systems were technically obsolete before the systems became popular.

The ring LAN

The ring system was developed into a commercial product during the mid-1970s. Information is transferred in packets (or slots), which circulate continuously round all the stations connected to the ring. The information is inserted into the first empty packet to arrive at the transmitting station. A full packet contains the information to be transferred, the address of the destination station, and a few bits of control information. As it moves around the ring, it is examined at each station to see whether it has arrived at the correct destination. When it does arrive, the station concerned accepts it and empties it of its data. The station immediately retransmits the empty packet to the originating station with the message that the data has been correctly received.

The Ethernet LAN

The Ethernet LAN system was developed in the early 1970s at Xerox's Palo Alto Research Center (PARC). Ethernet is a bus system, in which every station is connected to a communal data highway, such as a coaxial cable, and is listening continuously to see if it is required to receive information. To send information from one station to another, an individual station has to take control of the bus; there is no master controller of the network. As soon as the bus is clear, i.e. no data is being transmitted along it, a station can transmit a message down the bus asking for control of the bus for a data transfer. If this request is successful, the station transmits a string of data to another station within the system. The other stations are switched off during this process.

There are two main problems with such a system. The first is the possibility of two or more stations asking for control of the bus at the same time. Chaos is avoided through the use of collision-detection hardware, which detects when such a situation arises, assumes control of the bus, and forces the would-be communicators to wait for a random length of time before trying again. Eventually information transfer starts. For obvious reasons, this is called the 'cocktail party' effect. A second problem is that, unlike ring systems, there is no innate protection from one device monopolizing the LAN. Division of the LAN's resources has to be enforced externally by hardware or by rigorous software standards for each attached processor. Despite these deficiencies, Ethernet seems likely to be very successful, given the marketing power of the American firms that are backing it.

Ten **Programming Languages**

Computers are far away from being able to comprehend human languages, and so as yet we cannot specify what computers should do using our everyday language. It requires more than a dictionary and a knowledge of grammar and syntax to understand a sentence: we also need a considerable amount of interpretive ability, a background knowledge of the particular language, and the possession of similar cultural experiences to the author of the sentence. At present a computer does not possess enough of these attributes to be programmed using everyday languages.

Computer programmers must instead use more straightforward languages, which have vocabularies of only a few hundred words, all with well-defined and unambigous meanings. A program written in such a **programming language** is the specification of a task that a computer is to perform. It can not only be understood by humans, but also be automatically translated by another computer program into the electronic logic of the computer. Wherever possible, programs should be written in a standardized language, making them portable and thereby spreading the high cost of programming.

The **compiler** or **interpreter** program of a computer performs the task of translating programs written in a programming language into a machine-operable form. If a programming language is well defined, i.e. it has a standardized syntax and functions, then the same program can be run on different computers. But the implementation of the compiler or interpreter is performed individually for each language and type of machine, and so will vary in quality.

Thousands of programming languages have been developed, and almost all rapidly abandoned. There is always a temptation to develop an efficient language specifically for one task, such as for the control of robots or the analysis of images. However, for a language to be widely useful, it requires far more than just a language translator for a particular computer. A successful language needs supporting manuals and textbooks, a rigorous and accepted definition of its structure, a number of programmers trained to use it, and its own 'literature' of programs which are known to perform common tasks. Even given these factors, the widespread acceptance of a language is a somewhat random process.

If the world were perfectly organized, perhaps only a dozen or so computer languages would be sufficient to cover almost every computer task. An integrated set of computer support programs ('tools') could be created to help develop programs in this limited set of languages. However, the use of languages is conditioned by inertia as much as by efficiency. The choice of language for a software project often depends on which language the programmer was trained in, or which language his or her firm prefers to use.

Three languages—FORTRAN, COBOL, and BASIC—dominate the world of programming. These were all designed as specialist languages, used primarily for scientific applications, commercial applications, and personal computing respectively.

FORTRAN is an attempt to translate scientific formulae into machine instructions, while the vocabulary of COBOL, with its imperative verbs, reflects the functions needed in the commercial world. BASIC was originally designed to help non-technical students write programs for simple numerical calculations. All three languages are technically outmoded, and could be replaced by more efficient and more easily comprehensible languages.

An alternative approach to language design is to reflect the structure of the algorithm for solving a problem, while using standard mathematical symbols. A print-out or 'listing' of a program in an algorithmic language gives a clear view of its intention. Further efficiency is gained by designing the programming language to allow tasks to be easily broken down into small independent sections (modules), each of which can be perfected, even by unreliable human beings. Modularity has been shown to be the single most important feature of a language for reducing the cost of programming. This algorithmic approach has usually come from the computer science departments of universities, and unfortunately has never been fully accepted commercially. Languages such as ALGOL and Pascal are based on this approach; Modula-2 and Ada also encourage structured programming techniques of breaking a large program into simple understandable elements.

As with human languages, an individual needs to make a considerable effort to become fluent in a programming language. A month or two may give enough familiarity to write programs, but performance continues to improve over several years. The years of education needed to understand a language, the investment in software written in it, and continued support from computer manufacturers ensure that outdated languages survive, and that new languages, whatever their theoretical advantages, will not be easily adopted. Despite the fact that superior languages to FORTRAN and COBOL have been developed, only BASIC has become as popular. Instead of being replaced, both languages have slowly evolved to incorporate new ideas.

High-level and low-level languages

Programming languages can be broadly classified into high- and low-level types, which have opposite properties. A **low-level language** is close to the primitive machine instructions of a particular computer, and details of the machine being used are built into the language. For example, the low-level language will often know about the interrupt structure of the computer, or the size of memory available. Thus we can define a program in a low-level language as a list of instructions for the computer to perform.

A **high-level language** is more remote from the machine instructions, but easier for a human to understand. Programs written in a high-level language can be translated to run on a variety of machines, because the language is not specific to a particular computer. This portability has great advantages, but it does mean that the understanding of a particular computer is not built into the language. In a high-level language a program is a mathematical statement of the task to be performed; because it is exact, it can be translated into different sets of machine instructions.

A single program line (**statement**) in a high-level language is translated into more machine instructions than a similar statement in a low-level language. For example, multiplication is not often available as a machine instruction on a computer, and so it has to be programmed by a whole series of computer instructions. A high-level language enables multiplication to be specified by a single statement, which is sufficient to initiate the many machine instructions needed for multiplication.

The length of time taken to write a statement in a computer program is roughly the same for each type of language, and therefore since each high-level statement translates into more machine instructions than a low-level one, the higher the level of the language, the greater the productivity of each programmer. Because the cost of hardware is decreasing relative to that of software, the level of languages is certain to become higher, in order to contain software costs.

The higher the level of a language, the easier it is for non-specialist users to program in it. Rather than worrying about the detailed control of the computer, the programmer using a high-level language can concentrate on the real challenge—developing the intellectual ideas behind a program. Nevertheless, professional programmers, especially those working on microcomputers, find it helpful to be able to understand and write in assembly language, the symbolic representation of the computer's actual instructions.

Machine code languages

The lowest-level language available to a programmer consists of the machine instructions themselves. When a program is running in a computer, it functions by switching electrical voltages. The electronics directly mimic Boolean operations like AND, NOT, and OR, as well as simple arithmetical operations, such as ADD and SUBTRACT. A machine code instruction is simply a binary number (such as 10111001) which fits into a memory cell of the computer; the computer interprets the contents of the cell as an instruction to perform one of its basic operations.

The first programmers had to generate these binary machine instructions themselves, translating their programming requirements into streams of arcane binary instructions. Each step in a program had to be transformed into many machine instructions. As computers became able to process thousands, then millions, of instructions every second, the task of writing programs in terms of machine instructions became impossible.

Assembly languages

The first step in making programs easier to write and understand was the development of assembly languages in the late 1940s. In an assembly language, each machine instruction is represented by a symbolic name, in order to make programs more comprehensible. If a programmer wanted to add the two values 53 and 75, then he might write the following two lines in an assembly language program (the semicolons indicate the end of a statement line).

LOAD A, 53;
ADD A, 75;

A computer has a special program (called an **assembler**) which analyses each assembly language statement and translates it into machine code. After being translated into machine code, the first statement above causes 53 to be loaded into the A register, and the second causes 75 to be added to it and the result left in the A register. A simple two-line example is used here merely for illustration; assembly language programs often run to thousands of statements. Thus some of the difficult, repetitive work can be taken away from the programmer, as can be seen by looking at what would need to be written in machine code to perform the addition above. This consists of the codes for the instructions (LOAD and ADD) and the two numbers themselves. Our simple two-line example might translate into the following four machine code instructions, which would be put directly into the memory of the computer.

11010101	(Load the A register with the next value)
00110101	(53 in binary)
10100011	(Add the A register to the next value)
01001011	(Binary representation of 75)

The assembly language version of the program is shorter and clearer! Each instruction in an assembly language program is a symbolic representation of one computer operation, and in this case we can see how the data values need to be dovetailed as well. In a machine language program each binary number is either a data value or an instruction.

Efficiency of assembly languages

Because of the direct relationship between assembly language statements and operations that the computer actually performs, an assembly language program can be as efficient as the machine code instructions. The programmer can select the machine operations which will perform the task quickest, or which will occupy the least amount of memory. In contrast, all higher-level languages must by their very nature be less efficent than a perfected assembly language program, because they must always take account of the most general case that they might be used for. For example, a programmer may be writing a program to calculate sums of money, and know in the particular case that the sums will never exceed £1,000. If the program is written in an assembly language, it does not have to use more memory than necessary to store the values concerned. If it is written in a high-level language, however, the amount of memory used will inevitably be greater, since the designers of the language could not so restrict the scope of its variables.

Yet assembly language programs can in practice be inefficient, especially if they are long. They are difficult to write and to alter, or to understand after they have been written, because the instructions represented are arbitrary, reflecting operations that are easy to fabricate from transistors, rather than the more abstract tasks that we would like to specify in a program. Long assembly language programs are simply too complex for humans to cope with. Hence there is a strong trend towards high-level languages. There is also a tendency within languages for each statement to perform more and more as the languages evolve.

However much one might wish to avoid using them, assembly language translators are always required for professional work on a computer system. Some of the details of the hardware are so specific to individual computer systems that they cannot be encapsulated in a high-level programming language. For example, the task of linking a disc drive or a printer to a computer invariably involves getting to grips with the assembly language of the machine.

The prime problem facing programmers writing assembly language programs is not how best to tackle the task for which the program is being written, but rather how to exercise detailed control over the computing machine itself. Assembly language programming might then seem rather boring, but programmers tend to enjoy the challenge, which can easily be absent when writing in more straightforward high-level languages. The intellectual pleasure of writing an assembly language program is akin to that gained from solving a crossword puzzle, or taking a car engine to pieces—a mystery to those who do not indulge.

Symbolic representation

The symbolic representation in an assembly language of individual computer instructions is easily extendable to allow additional features to be added to the assembler. For example, an appropriate name can be used to represent a number in a program, thereby making the program more comprehensible. Suppose a program constantly employs a temperature value. This value can then be called TEMP, and set early on in the program by a statement such as the following:

TEMP = 75;

The name TEMP can be used for the temperature throughout the program, and an assembly language statement for addition could appear as

ADD A, TEMP;

This would add 75 (the value for TEMP) to whatever value happened to be in the A register—the assembler program that translates statements into machine instructions substitutes 75 wherever it finds the word TEMP. The advantage of this technique is that throughout the program the programmer is dealing with an immediately understood name, rather than a number, which will always make him stop and think. If the programmer wishes to change the value of the temperature throughout the whole program, then the single statement

TEMP = 80;

at the start of the program is sufficient. This brings out another advantage of symbolic representation. Without such a system, the programmer would have to search for all the values of 75 in the program and alter them to 80, perhaps missing one of them, and causing a program error. An even worse error could be introduced if the programmer finds a number 75 and alters it to 80, when the value 75 did not refer to temperature. This type of program 'bug' can be extremely difficult to track down and eliminate.

A tenet of good programming is that programs must be comprehensible, both to program writers and outside observers. The use of names for program elements such as variables is a step to this end. Programs in a language like BASIC become unintelligible as they get longer, one of the main reasons being that variables can only be represented by one letter in this language. A statement in BASIC setting the day (A) to Tuesday (3) on line 128 of a program might be

128 LET A = 3

Even this single BASIC line is much less clear than an equivalent line in the Pascal language (Pascal programs don't have line numbers).

Day : = Tuesday

When there are 20,000 lines in a program, clarity is essential. Although some versions of BASIC allow more flexibility in naming variables, programs using this feature become non-portable because of the lack of standardization. If the programmer is the only person who can understand a program, then there is no external discipline on programming standards.

In a Pascal program, good programmers would never need to make such statements as

Day : = 3

for the entirely legitimate reason that the two sides of the statement refer to totally different types of information, one a number and the other a day of the week. A computer manipulates symbols, and not just numbers, and so should manipulate the symbols (such as Tuesday) that we actually use. A day is a special 'data type' with properties of its own, and the programmer should not mix it up with numbers, which represent completely different entities. In any case, one year after the BASIC program has been written no one will remember what the 3 represents, but most of us will still know the day of the week. As a major part of the cost of a program is taken up by its 'maintenance' many years after it has been written, it is critical that programs are designed to be easily understood and altered.

Subroutines

A simple operation such as multiplying two decimal numbers may take many hundreds of machine instructions on a small computer. This is because such a machine (usually) does not have an inbuilt machine instruction to perform the operation, and will instead need to carry out a series of additions. Even adding two floating-point numbers together can require a whole set of computer instructions. Small computers can only handle 8 bits of data at a time, and a floating-point number is typically encoded with either 32 or 64 bits. Hence they have to add two floating-point numbers in a series of steps, each of which manipulates eight bits at a time. This process is normally invisible to the programmer using a high-level language—except that it takes longer than it would if the machine had a wider data range.

For each programmer to write a program for multiplication would be a waste of his or her time, and leave plenty of room for error. Early on, general **subroutines** for this and many other functions were written for the computer, in order to save on effort in the future. Their general applicability does, however, mean that they are certain to be more inefficient for specific tasks than specially written assembly language programs. Subroutines are kept on discs to be brought into a program when needed.

There has to be a standard format for a program to tell the assembler program to take a subroutine off the disc. These formats became a primitive programming language. Both the use of English language names for the processes and the retention of normal mathematical notation ensure that the meaning of a subroutine is clear, even to the non-specialist. For example, the subroutine to print out a number might be called PRINT. The standard way of asking for such a subroutine to be inserted is often the word CALL. The combined statement CALL PRINT, followed by some value, will cause that value to be printed. The assembler program automatically inserts the relevant machine instructions into the program when it finds this line. Hence in order to print out the value of TEMP + 2, the 'subroutine call' in an assembly language format might be

CALL PRINT (TEMP + 2);

The value TEMP + 2 in the subroutine call is usually referred to as the **parameter** or **argument**. Thus a single statement in an assembly language program can invoke a complicated set of machine instructions.

High-level languages

Because machine instructions are different on different computers, programs written in assembly languages differ from one computer system to the next, whether subroutines are used or not. A standardized language is therefore needed if the same program is to be used on different systems. AUTOCODE, the first high-level language with a program that would translate it into machine language, was developed in 1952 by Alick Glennie, a UK Army scientist working on the Manchester University computer. The mid-1950s saw a revolution in computer programming with the arrival of COBOL and FORTRAN, two languages which have dominated the field ever since.

Languages, both high- and low-level, can be translated into machine instructions through one of two different processes, either **compilation** or **interpretation**. Compilers and interpreters are the programs which perform the respective translations. Compilers translate a program totally, so that it is ready for use when required; interpreters do so one statement at a time, as it is being used. Running a compiled program is analogous to reading a complete translation of a foreign novel, whereas running an interpreted program is like reading the same book, stopping at the beginning of each sentence for someone to translate it for you. A compiled program is more polished, and once the initial translation has been done we are not slowed down by the translation process. However, interpretation produces results more quickly, since we do not have to wait for the whole program to be translated, and is often more convenient for the programmer. The division between compiling and interpretive *languages* is practical rather than philosophical, and most languages could actually be implemented in either way.

Compiling languages

A program in a compiling language is written on a computer with the help of the editor, a systems program that allows programmers to write, view, print, and correct the text of the program being developed. Once the programmer deems his efforts satisfactory, the program is then passed to the compiler, which attempts to translate it into the machine code of the computer.

The process of compiling a program into machine code is naturally enough performed by a computer program. The compiler examines the syntax of the program statements and then attempts to translate them; if the programs call for subroutines, these are brought off a computer disc and inserted into the program. The compiler is itself stored on disc, and only brought into the main memory when needed. Initially, there are usually errors in the programmer's use of the programming language, and the compiler is able to detect these and warn the programmer. These are called syntax errors to distinguish them from errors in the logical flow of the program, which the compiler cannot detect. However, the computer can detect some logical errors which only produce absurd results when the program is run—these are called **run-time** errors. For

Stages to producing a working program

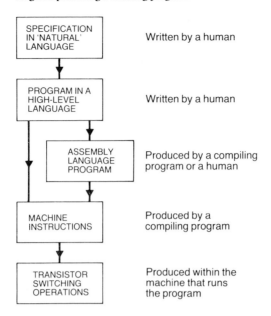

Before writing a computer program, there should be a specification of what the program aims to do. This is often written in 'natural' or everyday language, perhaps in a formal style. The specification is then converted into a high-level language program, a comprehensible but rigorous formulation of the task. This is often translated automatically (by a compiling program) into an assembly language, a symbolic representation of the operations that the machine can perform. Sometimes, however, the assembly language stage is missed out and the high-level language translated directly into machine instructions. The next stage of translation is into the binary code; the computer program is stored on disc in this form. The final transformation is into the electrical switching operations performed by transistors as the computer runs the program.

The diagram represents the same task at different levels of abstraction. Despite their different nature, each of the representations can be loosely called the program. Only the final one actually performs any physical operation, but it is so complex and specific to the particular machine that it is virtually incomprehensible to human beings. If the program needs to be changed, this must be done at a higher level of abstraction.

example, if the computer is directed to divide zero by zero, then it cannot proceed; the error leading to such a problem can easily be found.

There are many advantages to using compiling languages, primarily because the process of translation is completely divorced from that of running the program. The compiler can link in existing programs held in large libraries on disc drives. Routines that are not used in the particular program need not be loaded unnecessarily into the RAM; interpretive languages have to have all such routines ready to use when the program is run. Computer programs can be painstakingly checked by the compiler, because the program analysis is a one-off process, completely separated from the time-critical process of running the program. Thus compiled programs are shorter and faster than interpreted programs, and because these qualities were so critical for the programs run on early computers, the early computer languages, like FORTRAN and COBOL, were all compiling languages.

A problem with compiling languages, however, is that the correction of even a single error in a program is a time-consuming process. The errant program has to be stopped, the editing program called up, the error in the program found and corrected, and the whole program recompiled—and rerun. This is a slow process, but it does ensure that the programmer has to think carefully before writing the program. With some languages **incremental compilers** can be used, which need only recompile the bits that have changed since last time, and on some computer systems the editor used to create the program examines the program's syntax as it is being typed, and points out errors to programmers—this is called a **syntax-related editor**.

The linker

The compilation of a program is usually a two-stage process. In the first stage, the compiler often performs only a partial translation. The second stage involves linking into the program those subroutines which are to be part of the program. A program extracts the correct subroutines from a library of subroutines held on disc. Not surprisingly, this systems program is called the **linker**.

Interpretive languages

In an interpretive language, all the possible computer operations defined within the language, such as multiplication, division, and printing, are already compiled and are in the semiconductor memory ready to be used. When a program is run, it is analysed one statement line at a time to determine which particular routines are needed.

In a personal computer, these routines are often fixed into a permanent memory (ROM), and so are immediately available when the machine is switched on. Interpretive languages are therefore ideally suited to simple computer systems, which do not have discs. The editing program, used to write the software, is an integral part of the whole interpretive package, and is invisible to the user. The lines of a program are simply typed on to a VDU screen with line numbers to indicate this correct order. Once the program is written, each line in turn is translated into machine instructions and run. The classic example of an interpretive language is BASIC, which is often built into personal computer systems.

To run a BASIC program, the user types the word RUN, followed by a carriage return, which marks the end of a BASIC line and calls the interpreter into action. The BASIC interpreter takes RUN as an instruction to run the current program, and it starts this process by analysing all the line numbers of the statements written by the user, and putting them into numerical order. Then each line in turn is scanned and checked against the syntax of the language, and translated into machine code. The required operations are performed immediately, before the next line is examined.

A short program in BASIC

The term 'program' covers both the specifications written in a high-level language, and also the machine language version that actually runs on a computer. A small program written in BASIC is now shown; when you tell it which year you are born, this program works out how old you are. This is a simple numeric program, ideal for BASIC.

First you have to start the BASIC interpreter, which signals that it is ready to start by typing > at the beginning of a line. The first line that you type in sets the current year, which we will assume is 1987:

    10 A = 1987

The second line prints a question asking you in which year you were born:

    20 PRINT "IN WHICH YEAR WERE YOU BORN?"

And the third line makes the computer wait until you type in the answer:

    30 INPUT B

Once this is done, the computer subtracts the year of birth from the current year then prints the answer given by the value C with a little explanatory text around it.

    40 C = A − B
    50 PRINT "YOU ARE ",C," YEARS OLD"

This is not necessarily correct, however, for you may not yet have had a birthday this year. But it is easy to alter the program to cover this situation with the following additional statements, which fit in between lines 40 and 50. If you haven't yet had a birthday, one year will be subtracted from the calculated age.

    42 PRINT "IF YOU HAVEN'T HAD A BIRTHDAY
       THIS YEAR, TYPE 1"
    44 INPUT D
    45 IF D = 1 THEN C = C − 1

You can also add a comment line at the top of the program:

    5 REM THIS PROGRAM CALCULATES YOUR AGE

This line simply serves as a reminder of what the program does. The program seems complete, and we can print it out by typing LIST.

    5 REM THIS PROGRAM CALCULATES YOUR AGE
    10 A = 1987

    20 PRINT "IN WHICH YEAR WERE YOU BORN?"
    30 INPUT B
    40 C = A − B
    42 PRINT "IF YOU HAVEN'T HAD A BIRTHDAY
       THIS YEAR, TYPE 1"
    44 INPUT D
    45 IF D = 1 THEN C = C − 1
    50 PRINT "YOU ARE ",C," YEARS OLD"

Typing RUN starts the program off, and the computer calculates your age. Of course there are a few problems: if you show it to eight-year-olds, they will quickly start putting in ridiculous numbers and will be told that they have an age of hundreds of years, an age below zero, or even a fractional age. If the program was not just for amusement, all of these 'illegal' inputs would have to be checked for and eliminated, and error messages given to the user. For example, you might check whether the person is claiming to be over 110, by inserting the following program lines between lines 45 and 50.

    46 IF C > 110 GOTO 48
    47 GOTO 50
    48 PRINT "YOU'RE TOO OLD, TRY AGAIN"
    49 GOTO 20

Although each check is simple, together they add substantially to the size of the program. BASIC allows you to enter non-integral numbers (such as 1,982.5) and, if the program was serious, you might like to add a few extra checks to see that the answer typed in is integral.

    5 REM THIS PROGRAM CALCULATES YOUR AGE
    10 A = 1987
    20 PRINT "IN WHICH YEAR WERE YOU BORN?"
    30 INPUT B
    40 C = A − B
    42 PRINT "IF YOU HAVEN'T HAD A BIRTHDAY
       THIS YEAR, TYPE 1"
    44 INPUT D
    45 IF D = 1 THEN C = C − 1
    46 IF C > 110 GOTO 48
    47 GOTO 50
    48 PRINT "YOU'RE TOO OLD, TRY AGAIN"
    49 GOTO 20
    50 PRINT "YOU ARE ",C," YEARS OLD"

This thirteen-line program illustrates several facets of BASIC: how easy it is to start to write a program, how simple it is to alter the program as you go along, and how rapidly the standard conditions assumed by BASIC become a hindrance rather than a help. We should really have been dealing with specific information types, such as years, months, and days. The whole numerically oriented structure forces the use of unnatural names, and the poor data typing forces the programmer into making checks which could be performed automatically. Only when the program is heavily used, will you find that sometimes the program won't give the right answer for someone who was born on 29 February.

Interpretive languages are much easier for the beginner to learn and use than compiling languages, because there is no need to learn about compilers, editors, or linkers. The process of correcting errors in a program is also simpler and less time-consuming. Because the editing program is immediately available, there is no need to go through the rigmarole of stopping the program, calling up the editor, finding and correcting the fault, recompiling the program, and running it again. If a BASIC program is run with a syntax error, the BASIC interpreter finds it, and indicates its position. It might display:

ERROR 93 IN LINE 56

The programmer then views line 56, looks at the manual to find out what kind of mistake has been perpetrated, and corrects it immediately. You may well ask why the BASIC interpreter cannot perform the purely mechanical task of finding out what error 93 is!

Programs written in interpretive languages tend to be slower than those written in compiling languages. There are many reasons for this, the main one being that time is wasted interpreting the program each time it is run.

Because interpretive BASIC programs are easy to write, but run slowly, manufacturers have also produced a compatible BASIC interpreter for some types of computer. A program can be developed quickly in an interpretive version of BASIC, and when satisfactory it is compiled, so that it will run faster than the interpreted version.

FORTRAN

FORTRAN (FORmula TRANslator) was developed at IBM under the direction of John Backus and released for customer use in 1957. IBM's domination of the computer market ensured that FORTRAN pushed aside all other contemporary languages (except COBOL). The language still dominates scientific programming, and FORTRAN compilers and support programs are available on most computer systems, even micros. As its full name implies, FORTRAN was first developed for scientific use, particularly for numerical calculations.

FORTRAN is an extremely powerful and flexible language for numerical work. Almost any operation can be programmed in the language; indeed there is often a choice of half-a-dozen different ways to program a function. Although

153

it was designed specifically for IBM machines, the language was rapidly taken up by scientists using other equipment and it remains the *de facto* standard for scientific work. FORTRAN has been extensively revised at regular intervals (1966, 1977) by the American National Standards Institute (ANSI). ANSI is working on a new definition of the language, FORTRAN 8X, which should correct many of the faults of the present version. This combination of strong definition and slow evolution has made FORTRAN extremely successful. Computer pioneer Gordon Bell, one of the founders of DEC, has commented 'I don't know anything about the most popular programming language in the year 2000—but it will be called FORTRAN.'

However, FORTRAN is unnecessarily complicated, which makes learning the language a long and difficult process. Long FORTRAN programs are almost unreadable, even by their original programmer. This leaves plenty of scope for error: in 1962 an unnoticed substitution of a full stop for a comma in a FORTRAN program is believed to have caused a NASA rocket to crash rather than soft-land on the planet Venus. Today's FORTRAN still carries elements of its early heritage. The line structure of the language derives from the days of punched cards, each of which held eighty characters. The programmer can only use capital letters in a program, and is restricted to words of six or fewer letters. This makes the programs unpleasant to read and prevents variables from being given names which clearly identify them—we should have to use TUESDA instead of Tuesday. FORTRAN is a difficult language to learn, requiring knowledge of computer software such as the editor, compiler, and linker. Even a simple task, like printing out a line of text, may need an almost incomprehensible set of instructions. ANSI has gamely struggled to bring elements of modern thought into newer versions of FORTRAN, but the language was defined and implemented before modern programming concepts developed.

Ratfor   Ratfor (*Rationalized FORTRAN*) is an interesting attempt to graft the concepts of a structured language on to FORTRAN, while still taking advantage of all the available FORTRAN support, such as compilers, linkers, libraries, and manuals. The programmer writes a program in the structured Ratfor language, and the program is then automatically translated ('cascaded') into normal FORTRAN statements, which are thereafter compiled as a FORTRAN program, and can rely on all the support programs available to FORTRAN programmers. Ratfor is therefore one step more abstract and removed from machine instructions than FORTRAN.

COBOL

The principles behind COBOL (COmmon Business Oriented Language) were developed by Grace Hopper and her team working for the American firm Univac during 1954–7. A Pentagon committee on data systems languages formalized COBOL in 1959. Its vocabulary and structure were defined after an extensive analysis of programs already in use for commercial applications. In 1985 a new version of COBOL was struggling through the ANSI committees; legal action was already being considered by those companies whose old software would need rewriting to conform to the new standard.

COBOL programs have paragraphs, sentences, full stops, and commas, all used for familiar purposes, because a primary aim of COBOL is to make programs readable, even to non-experts. The use of long descriptive words for data names aids comprehension, but also means that programs are extremely verbose. A major deficiency of COBOL is the constant increase in the number of 'reserved words', i.e. those which the COBOL compiler recognizes as asking for particular functions to be performed. A computer may not run old programs which used those words as variables.

The Federal Compiler Testing Center in the USA checks the COBOL compilers supplied by manufacturers for the US Government; 225,000 lines of standard programs are run through each compiler, and 5,500 individual tests performed in order to check how well the compiler conforms to the ANSI standards. If a compiler has not been through this severe test it has no chance of succeeding in the commercial market-place.

COBOL is still the most common language used commercially, and has fended off superior competitors because of the huge investment in it. In 1985 about $100,000,000,000 were invested in COBOL programs, and so we may expect the language to be with us for some decades to come. Its slow evolution should also enable COBOL to keep its dominance. Despite its commanding position in the area of data processing, COBOL is rarely taught or studied at universities.

BASIC

BASIC (Beginners' All-purpose Symbolic Instruction Code) was developed in the mid-1960s by John Kemeny and Thomas Kurtz for students at Dartmouth College in the USA. Most Dartmouth students were not scientists or engineers and did not want to learn a complex computing system, but they could be tempted to use a computer if it wasn't too difficult. BASIC fulfilled the need for a simple programming language that would not put off beginners. The casual user of BASIC does not have to learn unnecessary details of the language. For example, numbers are assumed to be real numbers (like 1.76858), whereas integers (exact numbers like 23, −1, or 121) have to be specified when they are needed. The statement to print a line is simple: the user might type the one-line BASIC program:

100 PRINT 'THIS IS A BASIC STATEMENT'

(The numbers at the beginning of BASIC statements define the order in which the statements are processed.) The program can be made to run by the command

RUN

(This is a command to the program, rather than a part of it, and so doesn't need a line number.) The BASIC interpreter then follows the single instruction of the program to print

THIS IS A BASIC STATEMENT

This program has taken only a minute for a beginner to produce and run. The editor used to write the program is contained within the language, and so all the programmer needs to do is type the single line on to a VDU.

Although originally designed as a compiling language, BASIC is now almost invariably interpretive. Once the programmer types RUN, the BASIC interpreter starts to translate the program line by line, starting at the lowest line number. Each statement is performed after it has been decoded. Often the interpreter checks whether the program line is correct immediately after it has been typed in, and before the program is run, and so can give a warning to prevent programmers from repeating any mistake. BASIC is a good language for short programs, and also for programs solely concerned with numeric calculations. It is ideally suited to personal computers because the interpreter can be contained in EPROMs, whereas compiling languages need disc drives. Thus a fairly powerful language can be provided for a small computer without resorting to disc drives.

However, BASIC has many disadvantages. Variables are restricted to one letter, and the range of data types is poor, except for numbers. The limitation of only being able to write programs in capital letters is a hangover from FORTRAN and the days when computer terminals had no lower-case letters. The standard definition of the language does not allow the use of procedures (groups of program lines that perform specific tasks, and can be called on by a main program), a technique which is essential in order to dissect a program into discrete modules. Together these factors make programs difficult to read. Another problem with BASIC has been the lack of any standard definition of the language—many of the complaints discussed have been corrected in individual dialects, but these are non-standard, and programs written in them are non-portable. ANSI has defined a standard version, but few BASIC implementations adhere to this. Perhaps the worst fault of BASIC is that because it is so alluringly easy it encourages novices to think of computers as solely processors of numbers.

ALGOL

ALGOL (ALGOrithmic Language) is an interesting example of a language which was a failure in the computer industry, but which has influenced almost all language designers (except perhaps those of BASIC) since 1960. Whereas FORTRAN was originally designed only to run on IBM computers, ALGOL was the result of an international collaborative effort. The designers of ALGOL attempted to produce a language as close to mathematical logic as possible, and were not concerned to mimic the simple operations that a computer can perform. An ALGOL program is written as if it were a mathematical algorithm.

ALGOL-60, the first practical version of the language, was strictly defined in a formal manner, using a mathematical notation specially developed for the purpose. Unfortunately no standards for input and output (for example from and to discs) were set out, and so the language never became popular. At the time, the methods for input and output varied wildly according to the type of computer, and no one could imagine how to encapsulate them all within a language. FORTRAN therefore had a big advantage over other languages since it was designed for the machines of the largest single company (IBM).

Despite its lack of success, ALGOL has often been used in scientific papers to describe the outline of a program, even though that program has probably been written in another language. This is a tribute to the clarity of the language. The ideas behind ALGOL have also survived in other languages, either directly through its offspring, such as Ada and Pascal, or indirectly by influencing languages like C.

Pascal

Pascal is the language used most in the teaching of programming at universities, mainly because it embodies advanced ideas of structured programming (see Chapter 11), so beloved of computer scientists. It was first designed by Professor Niklaus Wirth of the Zurich Technical Institute. The university has a history of producing advanced programming ideas: Heinz Rutishauser, one of the designers of ALGOL, worked there. Pascal is clearly a descendant of the ALGOL series of languages.

Pascal has excellent 'typing' of variables: the programmer must state which types of variable will be used in a program, and the Pascal compiler checks that different types are not being mixed up. For example, the programmer can define the months of the year as a data type, and then be prevented from mixing this data type with others not referring to months. Pascal allows the user to define new, more complicated types of data, reflecting real-world data types, whereas other languages tend to allow only a restricted range. For example, the records of an individual customer might be defined as a combination of a name, an address, and an account number.

Translating from a high-level to an assembly language

This example illustrates the translation of part of a Pascal program into an assembly language. The assembly language is that of the DEC PDP-11 computer, and the compiler is Oregon Software's Pascal. The few Pascal statements that we will translate manipulate a pair of variables, *count* and *extra*. First the value of count is doubled, and then the value extra is added. The new value of count is tested to see if it is greater than 3. If it is, then extra is given the value 6; if it is 3 or less, then extra is made equal to count plus three. In itself the following section of the program is pretty meaningless, but it is typical of what might appear in the middle of a Pascal program.

```
count : = extra + count*2;
IF count > 3
THEN extra : = 6
ELSE extra : = count + 3;
```

The Pascal compiler takes these four lines and translates them into the assembly language for a DEC machine. The result is the cryptic set of statements below, with each group of assembly language statements corresponding to one line of the Pascal program. The three capital letters on each line (for example MOV or ASL) are a mnemonic that refers to a single assembly language instruction, and the characters to the right refer to the numbers that those instructions operate on, or the locations in the memory of those numbers. Each assembly language line represents one instruction and the data that it processes. L1, L2, and L3 mark locations that can then be referred to by other parts of the program.

```
Assembly language     Pascal
MOV 48 (5), %0     ⎫
ASL %0             ⎬  count : = extra + count * 2;
ADD 50 (5), %0     ⎭

CMP 48 (5), # 3    ⎫
BGT L1             ⎬  IF count > 3
JMP L2             ⎭

L1: MOV # 6, 50 (5) ⎫  THEN extra : = 6
    JMP L3          ⎭

L2: MOV 48 (5), %0  ⎫
    ADD # 3, %0     ⎬  ELSE extra : = count + 3;
    MOV %0, 50 (5)  ⎭
```

The assembly language program is very difficult to understand in this form, a major reason being that the compiler has produced a very terse program. If we expand some of the more cryptic terms, then it becomes clear that the program will perform the task demanded by the original Pascal lines.

The first line of the Pascal program

```
count : = extra + count*2;
```

has been translated into lines 1 to 3 of the assembly language instructions, which can be expanded as follows:

```
MOVE THE VALUE OF count INTO register 0
ARITHMETIC SHIFT LEFT THE VALUE OF
register 0
ADD extra TO THE VALUE IN register 0
```

The first instruction transfers the value of count from the memory position it is stored in into a CPU register for processing. The data is not altered, but merely moved into register 0 of the CPU. The ASL (arithmetic shift left) instruction is next; this instruction multiplies count by two by taking the binary value for count, shifting it towards the left, and adding a 0 to its right-hand side. For example, if count is 1, it changes to 10 in binary, or 2 in decimal numbers. The third assembly language line adds the value of the variable extra to the new contents of the register.

The second Pascal line

```
IF count > 3
```

is translated into lines 4, 5, and 6 of the assembly language program:

```
COMPARE THE VALUE OF count WITH 3
BRANCH IF GREATER THAN 3 TO MEMORY
    POSITION L1
ELSE JUMP TO L2
```

If count is greater than 3, then the program performs the third Pascal statement (L1); otherwise it performs the fourth (L2).

The third Pascal statement

```
THEN extra : = 6
```

is translated as

```
MEMORY POSITION L1: MOVE 6 INTO extra
                    CONTINUE WITH THE
                    REST OF THE
                    PROGRAM
```

The alternative is the last Pascal line

    ELSE extra : = count + 3;

and this becomes

    MEMORY POSITION 2: MOVE THE VALUE OF
                                count INTO register 0
                                ADD 3 TO THE VALUE
                                IN register 0
                                MOVE THE VALUE IN
                                register 0 TO extra
                                CONTINUE WITH THE
                                REST OF THE
                                PROGRAM

Whether the third or fourth Pascal statement has been used, the program then continues on to the next part of the program, which the computer has set at memory position L3.

We can see from this example a few of the properties of high- and low-level languages. The Pascal program will run on any computer that has a Pascal compiler, whereas the assembly language program will only run on a DEC PDP-11 computer. Assembly language programs are longer and much less easy to understand than their high-level equivalents. But both programs specify the same function, and both perform the same operations when translated into machine instructions.

Pascal programs are wordy, allowing long names for the variables in the program so that it is clear what they refer to, and are therefore easy to understand. Pascal is a sparse language, i.e. it does not have a wide range of functions. A typical Pascal implementation might have perhaps a dozen mathematical functions compared to FORTRAN's fifty. This is an advantage rather than a disadvantage, because it allows a programmer to become totally familiar with all the features of the language. Any extra features can always be produced by combinations of the existing functions; if they are needed regularly they can be written as subroutines and stored on the disc drive.

The reluctance to accept new languages meant that by the time it was generally accepted, Pascal no longer embodied the advances that had been made in computer software and hardware. Its original definition by Wirth did not lay down standards for input and output. Of course, this reflects the fact that the language was designed for teaching students, rather than for real programming tasks. Nor does Pascal encourage modularity within a program, for subparts of the program cannot be independently precompiled. The whole program must be totally recompiled to correct a single error, which makes compilation a lengthy process. Bit-level manipulation of data (always needed for interacting with peripherals) is mediocre, yet the language standard does not allow interaction with assembly languages.

In practice, almost every Pascal compiler has had to extend the functions allowed in the ISO definition of the language. This in turn means that few implementations actually conform to agreed standards, and Pascal programs are not portable. Professor Wirth has since produced Modula-2, a language which overcomes most of the defects of Pascal. As the name implies, the new language is highly modular; it also allows individual sections of the program to 'hide' information from other sections to prevent them interfering in parts of the program that do not concern them. Whether this new language is successful may not depend so much upon its qualities, as upon how deeply entrenched other languages are. Given the reasonable success of Pascal, perhaps it would have been better to call it Pascal-2.

C

C is a low-level language, containing primitive operations, such as AND and OR, which are similar to the machine instructions of computers. Hence C, like an assembly language, is potentially efficient in its use of the resources of the computer. The language also embodies many modern concepts of language design, including good structure and easy use of subroutines. Large programs written in C can easily be partitioned into modules. The language was developed at the Bell Telephone Laboratories in the early 1970s, specifically for writing the UNIX operating system. C has proved to be ideal for 'systems programming', for example writing operating systems. Because operating-system routines are used intensively by almost all programs, the language they are written in must be efficient or the performance of all programs will suffer. Previously such software has been written in assembly language.

The language allows programmers considerable freedom (for example to mix information of different types), and the words and symbols used within the language are very terse. Both characteristics can lead to programs becoming totally unintelligible—such programs are wryly referred to as 'write-only'. The language provides facilities for manipulation of single bits of data, which are essential for writing programs to interact with non-standardized devices such as terminals, discs, printers, etc.

C is primarily a language for the professional who is intent on writing compact programs that will use a system's resources efficiently but are still portable. It is a small and simple language, and complicated functions have to be built from a 'tool-kit' of several small programs which can be easily combined to perform useful tasks. These are often supplied with the language compiler. Kernighan and Ritchie's book *The C Programming Language* is the *de facto* standard both for the language and for many of the software 'tools', although an ANSI standard for the language has now emerged.

Ada

Ada is the American Department of Defense's single common programming language for the 1990s, and all DOD contractors will be obliged to use it. The DOD found itself with a rapidly rising software bill—the total reached $4,000,000,000 in 1984—and the introduction of Ada is an attempt to reduce costs by making programming more efficient. With 400 programming languages in use on various contracts, the DOD decided to impose a single unified language for all its work. Ada is a complex, structured language, with the power of FORTRAN and the organization of Pascal, and is designed specifically to avoid styles of programming that lead to errors. It encourages modular programming, allows linkages to other languages to use existing programs, and has features to allow more than one processor to work on a single program. Programs written in Ada should be easy to read and understand, and data typing is strong, discouraging programmers from mixing incompatible types of information. The name 'Ada' has been copyrighted, and its use is forbidden to those versions of the language which do not fully comply with the standard definition. Subsets and supersets of the language are forbidden to use the name, and Ada compilers must pass a stringent test.

Ada will come with a complete set of 'tools' to assist in the development of programs—the Ada Program Support Environment (APSE), a UNIX-like set of support programs to help increase programmer productivity. The Ada compiler is very complex and checks each program thoroughly, which means that it compiles a program fairly slowly. Ada needs a powerful computer for compilation and plenty of disc space to store the support programs, but technological improvements should make this hardware relatively cheap in the long term.

Ada incorporates most modern ideas on language theory, and was designed by a team led by Jean Ichbiah of CII Honeywell-Bull, the winner of a competition organized by the DOD. However, one should note that previous attempts to produce such a complex language for general-purpose programming have not been conspicuously successful (Algol-68, PL/I). Past experience warns us that languages should always be kept as simple as possible, and features added only when really required.

Other languages

Many languages have not been covered by this chapter. In particular, a new generation of languages for artificial intelligence is emerging, such as Prolog and LISP. Unlike the languages described here, their use can be speeded up considerably by special computing hardware (see Chapter 16). Prolog, defined by Alan Colmerauer and his fellow researchers at Marseilles University in 1971, has been adopted by the Japanese as the core language for their Fifth Generation project for producing intelligent machines. Prolog programs are at least partially non-algorithmic. Instead of detailing the method of solving a problem, the programmer lists facts, and the relationships between them, and the program can automatically draw inferences from those facts. American workers in artificial intelligence have used LISP, a language which has probably evolved more than any other since it was first described in 1958.

Review

In 1983, the computer magazine *Byte* conducted an interesting experiment by asking readers to write the same set of programs in different languages on different computers. The results were startling. The difference in speed between the fastest and the slowest programs was as large as a factor of 700,000 times. Of course, large factors could be expected when the processors were as different as a Cray supercomputer and a small microprocessor, but the survey indicated clearly that the way in which a language compiler was implemented for a particular computer was as important as the speed of the computer hardware. In general, COBOL and BASIC came out as the languages which produced the slowest programs. Assembly languages were the fastest, followed by FORTRAN, C, and Pascal.

It should now be clear that languages are produced by a somewhat hap-hazard process, and that there is enormous inertia once a language has been established. More logical methods of language design and evolution are necessary, and any new languages must be able to link into old languages to take advantage of existing software.

Many of the basic principles underlying programming languages are now well understood, and we can expect a general trend in existing and new languages towards general-purpose algorithmic languages, on the lines of Ada, Pascal, and Modula-2. This move may, however, be pre-empted by the development of languages like FORTRAN into an updated algorithmic form. Only the emergence of revolutionary hardware, like successful parallel processors, will necessitate completely new languages. However, as the number of computer users grows, they will more and more be users of applications programs rather than writers of software, and programming languages will become less important to the average user than the man–machine interface which controls these programs.

Eleven Software Engineering

Programming may have a glamorous image, but writing lines of software is perhaps the most mundane facet of **software engineering**, the collection of techniques for producing reliable software at low cost. Experience has continually shown that more effort should be spent on the preliminary design of programs, and less on the actual programming. Designing the program while it is being written is a very entertaining, but fruitless, exercise.

In the early days of computing, programming costs were not a major part of the cost of a system, because computer hardware was so expensive. Although the programs were difficult to write, they were also relatively short. As hardware costs have diminished, software has grown increasingly complex and expensive, and consequently it is now software costs that normally dominate the overall expense of a project.

Programmer productivity

The average professional programmer only produces between ten and twenty error-free program statements per day; for programs which must be as error-free as possible, such as those controlling spacecraft or nuclear power plants, output may be as low as two lines per day. Amateur programmers can scarcely believe the low productivity of professionals, themselves claiming to write hundreds of program lines per day. Although true, this is not comparing like with like. When they are writing short, well-defined programs, professionals reach productivity rates of up to four hundred statements per day.

In a professional program, each line must be thoroughly checked for errors, any one of which could cause the program (and hence perhaps a spacecraft or nuclear power plant) to fail catastrophically. Programs must be fully documented, so that they can be understood and altered by programmers other than their original authors. They must usually be portable, i.e. easily transferrable between different computer systems. The net effect is low productivity, and high-cost software. However, to write programs in an amateurish way would be ultimately far more expensive.

The software life cycle

A program goes through four distinct phases between its conception and when it is discarded. These are its **design**, **programming**, **testing**, and **maintenance**,

Life-cycle costs of software

Programming costs account for only 10 per cent of the total expenditure on a normal professional software project between the time it is conceived and abandoned. Half of the money goes on maintenance, i.e. on making additions and changes to the software after it has been delivered. In order to reduce such costs, the software must be structured so that it can be understood and altered as easily as possible. The design and testing phases together take up 40 per cent of the cost. This percentage cannot be reduced, because skimping in either area is usually disastrous. The programming stage is one of implementation, not of design—or at least should be. Studies of large projects show that most software problems are

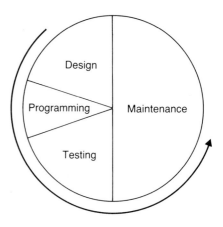

caused at the design stage, but don't show up until the programs have been written.

which together make up the **software life cycle**. If we compare the life cycle of software to that of a normal industrial product, we see that the manufacturing stage has effectively disappeared for we can replicate software simply by copying it on to an empty disc.

At the end of a program's design phase it should be clear to the customer, the designer, and the programmer what the software is to do and how it will do it. A good design results from a thorough analysis of the problem and a keen awareness of the customer's needs. The design stage is a particularly vital one because most problems with software are caused by weaknesses in design.

The programming phase is the most familiar but most misunderstood phase of the software life cycle. If software has been designed correctly, its programming should be a relatively straightforward process, taking up only about 10 per cent of the costs incurred during its life cycle. The programming should be done very late in the life cycle; a common fault is to start programming too early, before the design is finished. Again if it has been designed properly, the software can be easily written in many different languages.

On large programs, the testing phase often costs twice as much as the programming phase—the test programs may well be much longer than the program itself. A program should therefore be designed so that it can be easily tested. Errors, or 'bugs', can often be found by feeding the program with test examples, and seeing if it produces the correct answers. However, there are usually so many combinations of information that could be given to the program that they cannot all be checked. The fact that no program can ever be regarded as totally 'bug-free' has important implications. For instance, computers control nuclear missiles in both the East and the West. It is possible that the launching of these missiles could be triggered by some combination of information to which their organizing programs have never previously been exposed. In 1979 and 1980 several software and hardware failures in the computer systems of the North American Air Defense Command (NORAD) caused nuclear alerts. A single failure resulted in a full-scale alert, which meant that nuclear bombers started taxiing down their runways, and nuclear submarines were told to stand by.

The maintenance of the program after it starts working is the most expensive part of the software life cycle, and often five times as much is spent on this phase as on the original programming. Maintenance is a poor name for this stage, however, because the effort is mostly spent on modifying the software to meet new requirements, rather than on repairing faults. Because maintenance is so costly, it is important that software is designed from the start to be easily understood and changed.

Structured programming

Structured programming is a set of techniques for developing computer software, which, if properly applied, produces reliable software efficiently. The task to be performed is defined rigorously, and divided into independent modules which allow the design of the software to be clear and easily checked. The programming stage then becomes the straightforward implementation of the design. Structured programming techniques can be useful in almost any computer language, but naturally are most successful in languages designed with them in mind, such as Modula-2, C, and Ada.

The development of a program should proceed from a general statement of the program task to a detailed breakdown of the steps necessary to achieve that task. The general statement will be a few sentences giving the aim of the program—starting with a one-line title. If you don't know what program you are going to write, how can you begin to write it? The whole task can then be split into perhaps four to six subtasks, and in turn each subtask reduced to more and more detailed operations, until all of the basic steps required to perform the main task have been identified. When this point has been reached, each small subsection of the program can be safely produced because it is now understood, for example, how it links to other modules and responds to any given input, and what it does when an error occurs.

At every point the designer is confronted only with a small element of the program, less than a single page long. When the design is finished, the programmers will have a clear view of what is to be done, the customer can view the structure of the program without being confused by details, and the program is easy to document. As in other areas of computing, graphical displays are increasingly being used in software design, and simple drawings made by a computer show the links between each module.

Modularity is an important part of structured programming, and is perhaps the most significant single ingredient in the efficient production of large programs. It can be encouraged by the right choice of programming language, the newer languages Modula-2 and Ada being particularly good. They allow a program to be partitioned into separate modules, and yet when necessary can

Software prototyping

The method of producing software varies a great deal depending on whether or not the task to be performed is well defined. Structured programming techniques are fine for problems which are clearly understood, or at least can be analysed in abstract. But all too often, the customer does not provide a detailed enough specification, and, worse, no amount of questioning can build one up, because the customer does not understand either the limits or the potential of computers. In addition, unexpected changes during the development phase are the rule rather than the exception. So there may be no fixed structure for structured programming to work on.

Another stage in software engineering is needed: the customer needs to be shown **prototypes** of the software and allowed to experiment. The prototype programs do not need to be as complicated or as efficient as the final software but should demonstrate the major elements of its design. Of course they should not be used actually to perform the task since they will be inefficient compared to a polished program. Several exploratory software tools based on artificial intelligence programs are commercially available, which help in the design of programs. The Swedish Mimer data base management system contains a program written in LISP, allowing a programmer rapidly to develop small data base prototypes, The Xerox 'Loops' software supplies a complete set of programs (an 'environment') for software prototyping. Such systems encourage a flexible approach during the early design phases of a project, allowing designers to explore possible options at low expense.

control the way in which the modules interact with one another. Both languages allow the programmer to 'hide' some information within a module, allowing others to read and write only a selection of the complete information.

Concepts of structured programming now dominate professional programming. The use of structured techniques need not spoil the intellectual pleasure of producing software, but should confine that pleasure to its proper place—in the analytical rather than the programming stage.

'Pseudocode'

A program written in a high-level language is a specification of the task we want the computer to perform. However, a long program in a high-level language is too complicated to understand, because the gap between it and what we want the computer to do is too large. We therefore need an even higher-level language, one that explains the task to be tackled.

A semi-formal language that can express a problem at a high level is **pseudocode**, which lies between a natural language and a programming language. Everyday languages are a suitable form of description, but they are not logically consistent. For example, a single word can mean many different things, depending on the context in which it is used. A more formal language is necessary to specify a program. Pseudocode cannot be translated automatically into programming languages, but if its structure looks something like the final program for the task, this transformation can be performed fairly easily.

Program design languages

Program design languages (PDLs) are one form of pseudocode, helping to bridge the gulf between human ideas and programming languages. A PDL is a distillation of our everyday language into an unambiguous form. It is ideal for defining the structure of a program, and explaining clearly what is required of the programmer, while still being comprehensible to a customer.

A PDL consists of a vocabulary, together with a set of functions needed to form a logically complete and consistent language, i.e. a language able to define any task unambiguously. There is no standard PDL, although many companies have adopted internal standards. The finished structure of a program written in a PDL should be a comprehensible statement of the work to be performed; it can therefore be analysed to see if it is what is needed, before incurring the expense of writing the program. Programs written in a PDL can be easily converted into most programming languages, although this conversion cannot as yet be performed by machines. The PDL version of the program can then serve as the documentation for the programming task. A considerable effort is being made to produce PDLs which can be automatically transformed into programs.

An example of program design using a PDL

In order to illustrate how to organize a task using a PDL, let us examine the simple process of building a wall. The approach to be adopted for this task is similar to program analysis and development, and the final blueprint for action resembles a computer program written in an algorithmic language.

One of the first things to notice is that building a wall is a completely different process for an expert as compared to an amateur. A professional will immediately be able to write out most of the construction plan, whereas an amateur must first puzzle out how one actually builds a wall. This shows how different approaches must be adopted for program development, depending on whether or not the task to be performed by the program is well understood.

The highest level of abstraction of our algorithm is the title 'build a wall'. The wall-building algorithm for the professional can be expressed in outline as:

BUILD A WALL

1. DEFINE THE TYPE OF WALL AND SITE
2. OBTAIN FINANCE
3. OBTAIN NECESSARY PLANNING PERMISSION
4. ORDER MATERIALS
5. CONSTRUCT THE WALL

This is a 'program' in a PDL; the task has been split into five modules, arranged in the order in which they should be carried out. If we can perform all the procedures satisfactorily, then we end up with a wall. The tasks might be expressed in more detail in a PDL in the following terms (procedures are in capital letters, and descriptions are in lower-case letters).

1. DEFINE THE TYPE OF WALL AND SITE

EXAMINE AND MEASURE SITE OF WALL
DECIDE ON THE REQUIRED HEIGHT
DO draw wall

```
        UNTIL drawing is satisfactory
    END OF DO LOOP
    ESTIMATE TIME-SCALE FOR BUILDING
```

2. OBTAIN FINANCE

```
ESTIMATE WALL COST
FIND MONEY AVAILABLE
IF wall cost greater than available money
    THEN approach bank for loan
    IF bank refuses
        THEN ABANDON
    END OF IF LOOP
END OF IF LOOP
```

3. OBTAIN NECESSARY PLANNING PERMISSION

```
IF planning permission necessary
    THEN apply for planning permission
END OF IF LOOP
IF planning permission refused
    THEN ABANDON
END OF IF LOOP
```

4. ORDER MATERIALS

```
list materials
    DO until all materials ordered
        order one material
    END OF DO LOOP
```

5. CONSTRUCT THE WALL

```
dig foundations
build foundations
lay the bricks on top of one another
END
```

This 'pseudo-program' is clearly only an outline of the stages needed to build the wall, and more detailed work needs to be done. However, it is important to start with a rough sketch of the task. Firstly, the analyst can see early on if any stage is impractical. Secondly, if there is a flaw in the program logic, it can be spotted easily and corrected. The correction and reshuffling of the program is still simple and inexpensive.

Such simple analysis seems obvious and trivial, but it is not always performed, even for large-scale projects. In 1588, the Spanish Armada arrived in the Low Countries to collect the troops to invade England. Only then did it discover that it did not have the small boats necessary to transfer men from land to the troop-ships—an elementary blunder which would have been avoided by structured planning techniques—or is another name common sense?

Twelve Peripherals

The combination of processor and memory forms the core of a computer system, but peripheral equipment is also needed, in order both to control the system and to see the results from the processor. **Peripherals** are the tools which allow humans to communicate with computers, and understand their complexities. A computer system without peripherals is as useless as a brain without a body.

To try to describe all the peripherals that can be attached to computers would be a futile exercise. Almost all modern machines of any complexity can be linked to, or controlled by, a computer system, and can therefore be considered in some sense as 'peripherals' of a computer. However, the basic peripherals of a small computer system are two floppy disc drives (see Chapter 8), a visual display unit, and a printer. Two disc drives are necessary because then copies can be made of important information or programs. Peripheral equipment has not declined in price as quickly as microchips, since it consists more of steel than of silicon, but mass production has steadily reduced prices. In 1985, in real terms, visual display units and printers were one-quarter of the price they were five years before and had more features, primarily as a result of improvements in their internal electronics.

The visual display unit

The most basic peripheral is the **visual display unit (VDU)**, which enables programmers or users to interact with the computer. The VDU is normally a television-like display (often called the **monitor**) that can show text, and perhaps also simple images, to illustrate processed results. Its keyboard allows the user to type in commands to control the system.

The VDU is usually linked to the computer by a serial line, which is capable of transmitting about 1,000 characters every second (a rate of 9,600 baud) to and from the computer. The most common type of VDU screen displays about 25 lines of text, each with 80 characters. When the user presses a key, an 8-bit pattern corresponding to the individual letter is transmitted from the keyboard to the computer, and normally the computer then retransmits, or **echoes**, the character that has been typed in, and it is displayed on the screen.

As a minimum, the VDU is able to display all the letters, numbers, and symbols that are on a typewriter. As their software and hardware improve, screens will display more information in graphical form, for example in the

Peripherals

The visual display unit

A modern VDU, which can display 24 lines of text, each with 80 characters. The companies making these terminals have found their business under threat from single-chip VDUs, which require only trivial construction work, and personal computers, which have built-in VDU circuitry.

Their response must be to offer terminals with more facilities, such as higher-resolution and colour displays. Unfortunately there is only standardization of the most basic facilities offered on terminals, and so software has to be organized to cope with many different types.

form of simple bar and pie charts in colour. However, colour screens show less detail than monochrome (black-and-white) screens, and this lower resolution makes them less suitable for some applications. For example, users who are word processing may spend hours staring at a screen, and so need the sharper monochrome screens.

A normal VDU only displays about one-third of an A4 page of text, and the characters shown have little of the subtlety of the printed letter, because of the screen's poor resolution. However, newer, more expensive VDUs can display a whole page of text, with sufficient resolution to show different letter founts.

VDUs increasingly use the technique of **bit-mapping**, whereby the screen is a display of that part of the memory of the computer which controls the VDU. Each individual bit in the memory corresponds to a single dot on the screen of the terminal, and the 'on' or 'off' state of the bit corresponds to a white or black dot on the screen. When a letter is typed on the keyboard, electronic hardware translates that character into a pattern of 1s and 0s, which is injected into the memory and automatically appears on the screen. By using more than one bit per dot, the screen can display shades of grey, or predefined colours. Bit-mapped screens are ideal for the display of pictures or graphics and can be altered **(updated)** much faster than those connected to the computer by a serial link. The term 'graphics' refers to images artificially generated by the computer as opposed to pictures of real objects; simple examples include line-drawings, graphs, or pie charts. When a computer is used for designing indus-trial parts, the graphics becomes really complex, displaying colour, shading, and perspective, and absorbing an enormous amount of processing power.

The design of a computer keyboard is derived from that of the typewriter, even to the extent of using the 'qwerty' layout of the keys. The quality of the keyboard is very important, and keys should be easy to press, and give the user's fingers a clear and immediate indication ('tactile feedback') that they have been pressed. A professional writer may make 5,000,000 keystrokes in a year, and wear out one keyboard. Modern typists are so used to the 'qwerty' layout that it is likely to be retained, despite the fact that other arrangements of keys can be up to 50 per cent faster. The layout of the modern keyboard was originally designed to slow down typists, because nineteenth-century mechanical engineering could not cope with the speed of typists—is it a co-incidence that the longest word that can be typed from the top line of a keyboard is 'typewriter'?

Although we imagine the keyboard to be directly attached to the display screen, this is an illusion, because it is the computer that links the two. The user presses a key, the keyboard transmits the information to the computer, and the computer decides what to do with the particular keystroke. Usually it merely echoes the letter that has been typed, and so displays the character you typed on the screen. However, a single keystroke may have been prepro-grammed to cause a whole program to run, or perform some other function within a program. Most modern keyboards are **soft**: the code that is sent when a key is pressed can be changed either by a computer program, or by the

High-resolution terminals (opposite)

This high-resolution screen of a Xerox workstation (a powerful personal computer) can display much finer detail than a normal VDU. Screens of this resolution are essential for displaying photographs, different print founts, etc. Here we see a simultaneous display of English and Chinese documents. The various choices within the computer program are in the top right-hand corner of the screen; these options are displayed pictorially (as 'icons'). The arrow has been moved by the user to select the text on pandas. The same system can create and print documents in Japanese, Chinese, Arabic, Russian, and Hebrew, as well as the languages based on the Roman alphabet.

electronics inside the keyboard. If the function of a key changes, the screen should provide an up-to-date display of what the keys will do.

Speech input   We are constantly being told that soon we will control computers by speaking to them, and that the keyboard will be redundant. This is unlikely, however. Speech is actually a rather ponderous means of control, even if the problems of getting the machine to comprehend the spoken word are solved. There may though be some instances where speech recognition will be useful; for example, it could enable an operator to keep both hands free, or a computer to answer telephone queries about airplane timetables. Present speech-input machines can recognize a few hundred words when they have been trained to the voices of the people involved. Note the use of the word recognize: it is one thing to recognize words, and another to understand the meaning of words and sentences. Until machines can understand sentences, rather than merely recognize individual spoken words, speech input will be of very limited value. Hence speech input is best suited to software organized as **menu-driven** programs, which present users with only a few options at each stage.

Printers

If the VDU is essential, the printer is scarcely less necessary for any serious work on a computer. Programs, text, and results are much more easily analysed on paper than on the 25-line display of a VDU. Printers are becoming cheaper and more flexible all the time.

Modern printers can produce letters that are bold, expanded, miniaturized, subscripted, superscripted, or have a host of other features. Almost all have bidirectional printing, i.e. they print one line from left to right and the next from right to left as the print head returns. The ability to emphasize keywords, change print founts in the middle of text, draw simple graphics, and increase the size of characters means that the once-primitive printer now has features that the simple office typewriter cannot match. But computer printers are still too noisy and slow, and their quality too poor compared with, say, printed books.

A printer is normally connected to the computer either through a serial (RS-232C) interface, or the Centronics parallel connection. These two standards cover not only the hardware connections but also the software necessary to translate computer codes into characters.

The basic text characters of the typewriter are well defined by a standard code (ASCII), but the features available on modern printers vary from manufacturer to manufacturer, which means that, for example, there are no accepted standards for printing Greek letters, graphics, or even different founts. Indeed, only expensive and specialized computers can both display and print these. Even then the software will be specific to the computer and the printer. This is another example of lack of standardization in the computer industry, which is costing users a fortune through software incompatibilities.

Be warned that about half of the problems connected with personal computer systems are with printers. If the software and hardware of a computer are not designed around a particular printer, then there is little likelihood of users being able to take advantage of more than a fraction of the features that the printer offers. Unfortunately computer manufacturers do not usually make printers, and therefore feel no commitment to write their software to take advantage of the special features that printers can offer. To minimize problems, printers should always be bought at the same time as the rest of the computer system, and from the same supplier. Otherwise the printer and computer suppliers will try to blame each other for inevitable incompatibilities.

For applications where large amounts of text are produced, the printer can limit the overall speed of a computer system. Manufacturers' claims for printing rates are usually wildly optimistic, and should be halved to obtain a realistic figure. In a single-user system, the computer will often be tied up with printing for long periods, and under these circumstances a **printer buffer** can be used. This small box or plug-in card has a large amount of semiconductor memory which accepts the printing information at the highest speed that the computer can deliver it, and then passes the text on as fast as the printer can accept it. The computer is freed to do other work while the printer rumbles on.

Two types of printer are in common use in small computer systems, both relying on small 'hammers' which strike a ribbon just as in a typewriter. The first (the **needle** or **matrix** printer) has a line of small needle hammers, and letters are formed out of the dots as this line is swept horizontally across the paper. The other type (the **daisy-wheel** printer) prints a whole letter at each strike. The needle printer is faster, much more flexible, and although it doesn't produce as high-quality print as the daisy-wheel, it is steadily improving in performance. The daisy-wheel is fairly slow and inflexible, but prints 'letter quality' text, as good as that produced by an electric typewriter.

Needle or matrix printers

Needle printers are now the most popular type of printer for small computers. As the print head sweeps across the paper, each needle can be driven on to the ribbon to make a dot on the paper, complete letters being formed from a pattern of dots. A single letter of reasonable quality can be formed from an array of nine by seven dots (hence the name matrix). The printer can print over 150 letters every second, which means that each needle could be moving in and out 1,000 times a second and perhaps 1,000 million times in the lifetime of the printer. There are usually about nine needles in the print head, forming a vertical line about 3 millimetres high, but matrix printers with twenty-four or more needles are now being sold. These produce higher-quality print, almost up to daisy-wheel standard, and it is likely that such improvements will ensure that needle printers remain the most popular type of printer.

A great advantage of dot-matrix printers is their flexibility. In principle they can generate almost any shape that can be made with dots. To improve text quality, some matrix printers have a second mode, in which they move more slowly and print more dots to form individual characters. An inexpensive

173

The needle or matrix printer

Needle or matrix printers dominate the personal computer market because they are cheap and relatively fast. The print head behind the print ribbon is made up of a vertical line of nine needles. As the line is moved across the paper, the needles are driven in and out to form the characters. Most matrix printers have two modes—a fast, low-quality mode, and a slow, medium-quality mode.

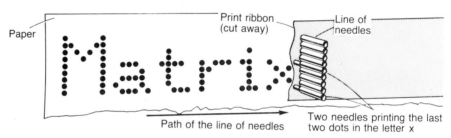

Paper — Print ribbon (cut away) — Line of needles

Path of the line of needles

Two needles printing the last two dots in the letter x

matrix printer can print 100 letters per second (i.e. a claimed 200) in the high-speed mode, and perhaps 30 in the low-speed, high-quality, mode. The low-speed results are on the borderline of acceptability for business letters. The industry cliché describes these as 'near letter quality' (NLQ), but 'not letter quality' is perhaps closer to the mark.

Daisy-wheel printers

Daisy-wheel printers are so named because of the resemblance of their print head to a daisy flower. At the end of each 'petal' is an individual letter, and the whole wheel has about 100 different characters, rather more than the typical typewriter. A small electrically driven hammer strikes one petal of the daisy on to an inked ribbon, and that character is then printed on a sheet of paper. The wheel and hammer are carried together across the paper along a horizontal slider. In order to print a different character, the daisy-wheel is rotated until the chosen petal is in front of the hammer, and stepped across the paper to the next letter space. The daisy-wheel can print up to 60 characters every second; cheaper versions for personal computers are less than half as fast.

The daisy-wheel printer is superior to the older, 'golf ball' technology, because the print head is much lighter, and can therefore be positioned more quickly. It is also cheaper and more reliable, has far fewer moving parts, and *its character set can be just as easily changed by substituting another daisy head. Special ribbons are available, which although they can only be used once, give an extremely high-quality impression. Yet, whatever its advantages, the daisy-wheel printer is probably doomed to extinction once low-cost needle printers that can print 'letter quality' text are available.*

The daisy-wheel printer

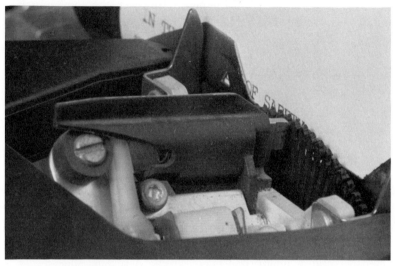

There is a single character on each 'petal' of the daisy-wheel. The daisy-wheel rotates until the correct petal is in front of the hammer, and stops before being struck. When hit, the petal drives the ribbon on to the paper.

(Below) These are the characters on the printing side of the daisy wheel, the side that presses on to the ribbon.

Printing a single letter with a daisy-wheel

The letter Q is to be printed, but it is not in front of the hammer.

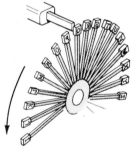

The Q is rotated to be in front of the hammer and the daisy-wheel is stopped.

The hammer strikes the back of the petal, which bends to press on to the print ribbon. The print head now moves across the paper to print the next character—the daisy-wheel is already rotating to the next letter.

175

Laser printers In the 1970s laser printers cost several hundred thousand pounds, but 1984 saw the introduction of smaller versions costing only £3,000. These quiet machines can produce text in any fount, as well as graphics, and images, all close to normal print quality. They work on xerographic principles, like photocopying machines. A metallic drum is given an electrostatic charge, which can be destroyed in selected areas by the light from a laser. Toner sticks to the charged parts of the drum, and is then transferred from the drum to a sheet of paper. Heat then fixes the image on the paper. However, the combination of hardware and software required for high-resolution screens and laser printers will not initially be cheap.

Paper The paper for printers comes in two standard widths, suitable for printing lines with 80 and 132 computer characters. The paper with 80 columns is ideal for text, easier to handle and store than the larger-width paper, and can display everything that can be seen on a normal VDU. Paper with 132 columns is better for displaying tabular information extending over many columns (as in spreadsheets), but is slowly becoming less popular. Most 80-column printers have a mode in which they can print out 132 columns with smaller, but adequately readable characters.

Paper for printers usually comes **fan-folded**, that is in continuous lengths with each sheet bent to fold over the next. **Sheet-feeders** are devices that automatically feed single sheets of paper into the printer, allowing the use of headed notepaper and standard-sized paper sheets. A reliable sheet-feeder is an extremely useful attachment—many of the first designs were mechanical disasters which worked well as paper-crumplers!

Manufacturers are forever talking of the paperless office. In practice, it will take many years for paper to be displaced by newer technologies. High-quality books are portable, pleasant to handle, contain all manner of printing subtleties which we appreciate only subconsciously, have beautiful colours in high contrast, and give an illusion of permanence. Could a message on a display screen ever replace the pleasure given by a handwritten letter from a friend? Present-day display devices do not have sufficient resolution to show the full detail of text on paper, let alone the tones and colours of a photograph, and it doesn't look as if the technology with that ability is likely to be available in the near future. Nevertheless, electronic technology is already encroaching into areas previously dominated by paper, particularly in office-work.

Menu-driven software and the mouse

In **menu-driven** programs, the user chooses one of a few options presented on the display in order to proceed to the next stage of the program. Often the choice is represented by a series of pictures ('icons')—the user might point at a filing cabinet on the screen in order to store a list, or at a rubbish bin in order to discard information from the disc. Instead of a keyboard, the user operates a 'pointing' device to make the choice.

Such user-friendly computer graphics will become increasingly common as more and more non-specialist users operate computers. Manipulating these images requires a considerable amount of processing power, and is really only feasible on 32-bit or more powerful computers. The Apple Macintosh computer system, based around the Motorola 68008 microprocessor, is the first common example of a computer that has a whole range of software based on such graphics techniques; the GEM package from Digital Research allows similar facilities on other computers, including the IBM PC.

The **mouse**, the most common pointing device, is a small mouse-shaped object, which can be held in the hand, and propelled over a horizontal surface. The motion of the mouse can be monitored by the computer in several ways, for example by a pair of small wheels which rotate as the mouse is moved. The movement is measured and transmitted to the computer (usually down a wire), which moves a marker (**cursor**) in sympathy from one option to another in the menu. When the cursor is positioned over the right option, pressing a button on the mouse signifies the selection of that option.

The mouse

The mouse is a pointing device allowing the user to choose options within menu-driven software. The user is given a series of choices on a VDU screen, and controls a cursor on the screen by moving the mouse. When the cursor has arrived at the right option on the menu, the computer is activated to follow the chosen course by pressing one of the two buttons.

The use of graphics-oriented software and pointing devices such as mice will help reduce novice computer users' fear of the keyboard. Unfortunately, for pointing devices to be of any use, the software must be designed around them. Since programs cannot always be reduced to a series of menu options, the keyboard will be with us for some time.

Thirteen The Personal Computer

The January 1975 issue of the American magazine *Popular Electronics* gave details of how to build a microcomputer system from a kit. Ed Roberts, the head of MITS, the small electronics firm selling the kit, estimated that he might sell a total of 200 kits to electronics enthusiasts. The machine was the Altair, which consisted of the Intel 8080 microprocessor linked up to a small amount of memory (usually about 4 kbytes) via the S-100 computer bus. Until then the Intel chip had only been used for professional applications, such as controlling traffic-lights, or making computer peripherals such as printers or VDUs more 'intelligent'. The Altair was the first computer cheap enough for individuals to buy, and MITS received its 200 orders in the first post. The **personal computer** was born, and within ten years millions were being sold every year.

This primitive machine was indeed only suitable for enthusiasts, because no software and little other hardware were available for the machine. Initially, there were no language compilers or program editors. The user wrote small programs in machine or assembly çode, typing them in directly from the keyboard. Programs had to be stored on paper tape because the computer did not have a disc system, although a local start-up firm, Shugart, was soon linking the Altair to its new device called a floppy disc. In practice, the microcomputer was initially totally useless, though this did not deter the computer freaks. Other firms, such as Imsai and Cromemco, then started to build microcomputers with circuit boards that could plug into the same S-100 bus connectors. The CP/M operating system had originally been designed for the Intel chip, and so was fairly easily transferred to the new microcomputer systems. Existing software for CP/M could then be used, and microcomputer sales started to take off. The computer magazine *Byte* was started up by, and for, computer enthusiasts. Now it weighs in with 600 pages every month, and in 1985 there were still 200 manufacturers making 1,000 different boards for S-100 systems.

The Apple Corporation started in a garage in California in 1975 producing a $666 single-board computer that could play simple video games, such as computerized table tennis. Three years later, Apple's second microcomputer (the Apple II) became the world's most popular computer, primarily because it was the first machine to offer a sensible colour graphics system. The market for personal computers expanded, and became large enough by 1978 to attract established electronics firms like Commodore and Radio Shack (Tandy), which brought out their own microcomputers.

Firms such as Apple, Commodore, and the British firm Sinclair initially produced single-board microcomputers, which can be used without disc drives.

Programs can be loaded from a cassette tape. These computers have a video output which allows a television set to be used as the computer display, and they also have a BASIC language interpreter in a read-only memory, enabling the user to write small programs immediately after switching the machine on. In terms of units sold, these personal computers dominate the computer market; the largest firms sell millions every year. However, without the speed, capacity, and reliability that disc storage would give them, these micros are little more than toys, suitable only for video games. They serve to introduce many people to computers, but also disillusion them because of the machines' limitations. As disc drives fall in price, they will become mandatory for more and more systems. Once someone uses disc storage, he or she will not go back to cassette tape storage willingly.

By the end of its first decade, microcomputer manufacture had changed from a cottage industry into a high-volume business in the hands of only a few manufacturers. Today the large companies make tens of thousands of micros every month, a production level which gives access to technology and economies of scale that the smaller companies simply cannot match.

In the long run, it is not the firms which assemble a microelectronics product that take over its market, but those that make its constituent chips. The rapid advances in integrated-circuit electronics usually mean that within a few years any successful electronic product can be replicated with far fewer chips, providing there is sufficient demand for it. And the firms that are in the best position to do this are those that actually manufacture the chips. In 1984, 10,000,000 personal computers were sold world-wide: and the biggest chip manufacturer of all was IBM.

The IBM PC—the empire strikes back

The IBM personal computer (the PC) was introduced in late 1981. IBM had never been particularly visionary, and had missed out on the early developments in computers, minicomputers, and integrated circuits. True to form, IBM was also late on to the microcomputer scene, but, as an IBM executive put it, 'You can't make an elephant tap-dance.' It usually produces the right product in the end, however, and when Big Blue (IBM's nickname—from the colour of its computers) introduced the PC in 1981, this was the product that the market wanted. Within a year or so, the PC had overtaken the Apple II to become the world's best-selling microcomputer. It appealed to those people who did not really understand what new personal computers were, but could sense how important they were becoming. If IBM produced the machine, customers were convinced that it must be worth while. By buying the PC in their droves, they created an enormous market for excellent software, thereby proving the truth of their convictions.

Personal computers became respectable with the emergence of the PC. They were no longer simply for home enthusiasts, and companies invested in large numbers of them. Merrill-Lynch, for example, the US stockbroking firm, bought 15,000—one for each of its brokers. The extra facilities of the PC (compared to the earlier CP/M systems) enabled more advanced microcomputer software to be written, and hundreds of companies started doing just this; the software market was flooded with programs for the new machine as well as hardware for special functions. A host of other firms produced PC-compatible computers at two-thirds of the IBM price, which could run almost all the software written for the PC. Some Taiwanese and South Korean producers went one step further, producing exact copies of the PC at 20 per cent of the price—with 'free' copies of well-known software as well. IBM was not amused.

The IBM PC

The IBM personal computer is shown in its most basic useful form—the micro itself two floppy disc drives, a display, and a printer.

The PC was not a revolutionary machine, because IBM could not afford to take any risks. In fact it was largely made up from hardware and software supplied by other companies—Intel supplied the 8088 microprocessor, Microsoft the original operating system (PC-DOS). However, the PC was an improvement on previous personal computers in that it contained no major flaws. Both the PC hardware and software are good enough for business use, especially as software was developed to link the PC to an IBM mainframe computer. It has colour graphics and an 80-column display—essential for word processing because it shows a full line of text. The keyboard has a large range of characters, including upper- and lower-case letters, mathematical symbols, and Greek letters; and it is also possible to program in new ones.

The original PC had five connectors on the bus for plugging in peripheral equipment, such as a disc drive or printer. Two rather large $5\frac{1}{4}$-inch floppies built into the processor box store only 360 kbytes each, a mediocre level of storage by industry standards. In 1983, IBM brought out the hard-disc XT version of the PC, with three more spare connectors, and abandoned the cassette interface.

The microprocessor used in the PC is an Intel 8088 chip, which has the same set of instructions as Intel's 16-bit 8086 micro. The main advantage of the 8088 over earlier microprocessors (such as the Z80) is its larger addressing range, which allows it to deal with up to 1 megabyte of semiconductor memory. However, this increase is achieved by 'paging' extra semiconductor memory in chunks of 64 kbytes, a technique which leaves many 16-bit constraints on software, which has to be organized into these blocks. IBM decided to use the slower 8088 microprocessor rather than the 8086 because, at the time the PC was designed, 8-bit memory organization was more common and cheaper than 16-bit. IBM brought out the PC/AT in 1984, an upgraded version of the PC that can run normal PC software but also support up to four users. The AT uses the Intel 80286 microprocessor, a much more powerful chip than the 8088. The PC has developed into a whole family of microcomputer systems, each suitable for specific tasks, but all capable of running the software for the first machine.

The 8087 coprocessor

For computing work that involves a great deal of number crunching the PC has a socket for the Intel 8087, a single-chip numeric coprocessor (p. 67). This chip is specifically designed to process floating-point arithmetic much more rapidly than the 8088 microprocessor. Many software packages for the PC can take advantage of the 8087 chip (and the 80287 which links with the 80286 microprocessor), but it has to be bought as an extra because it is a relatively expensive chip.

Self-checking

IBM's preoccupation with reliability is obvious throughout the PC. For example, the PC has a 9-bit, rather than 8-bit, semiconductor memory for error detection. The ninth bit indicates whether there is an error in the other eight memory bits. The PC checks all of the memory for faults when it is switched on and this process can take over a minute. Unfortunately the machine won't do more about a fault than tell you it has got one, and then refuse to operate.

PC-DOS operating system

The operating system of the PC—the program that controls the basic operations of the machine—is PC-DOS, originally from Microsoft. PC-DOS had started life as an operating system designed by the Seattle Computer Company for the 8086 microprocessor, and was sold to IBM via Microsoft. Microsoft has also produced MS-DOS, a similar operating system which is popular on PC look-alikes. PC-DOS was originally a single-user operating system, and so the computer could only be used by one person at a time. However, the PC is such a success that many other operating systems (for example CP/M-86, Concurrent CP/M, UNIX) have been fitted on to it, although none have been very successful commercially. Some of these, such as UNIX, allow many users to share the computer's resources, but the 8088 chip is not really powerful enough for heavy multi-user applications.

The most important aspect of the PC is the extra amount of memory available compared to the earlier 16-bit addressing micros. The PC can directly address up to $\frac{3}{4}$ megabyte of RAM and $\frac{1}{4}$ megabyte of ROM, instead of being limited to 64 kbytes, like 16-bit addressing systems. Larger and more complex programs can therefore be written for the PC. For example, it is much easier to write integrated programs with this amount of memory. Instead of having separate programs for word processing, storing lists, and for performing calculations, the three functions can be integrated into one program which can fit into the larger memory.

Because of the large number of machines sold, it has been worth software companies' while to write complex PC programs for computer-aided design, printing, and powerful data base management systems. However, the IBM machine is underpowered for such software, and upgraded versions of the PC system are much better for such processor-intensive tasks.

Mainframe link　　IBM did not design the PC to link into its mainframe computers, but as the machine's popularity grew, other companies rapidly developed the hardware and software needed to link the PC to large computers. Businessmen could now use much more user-friendly software, yet still take advantage of the centralized facilities provided by their company's mainframe, such as electronic mail or co-ordinated information storage. IBM was initially hesitant about encouraging this type of computer system, for fear of affecting its mainframe business. But the market potential was so large that it felt obliged to move into the field.

Acorn and Sinclair in the UK

In the UK, most of the initiative in personal computers has been displayed by small companies, such as Acorn and Sinclair. Sir Clive Sinclair is a well-known example of a successful entrepreneur producing small microcomputer systems. Largely self-taught in electronics, his small company initially produced kits for hi-fi amplifiers, transistor radios, and digital watches; these provided hours of amusement for electronics enthusiasts. Previous mass-manufacturing problems persuaded Sinclair to subcontract the assembly of his personal computers to more experienced companies.

Sinclair has made a great deal of money out of microcomputers, first with the ZX-81, a primitive, but very cheap, single-board computer, and then with the Spectrum personal computer. The latter is a more advanced computer, surprisingly good with a colour display on its monitor, but has a poor keyboard. In 1983, Sinclair sold 1,000,000 of these two types of computers, giving it 55 per cent of the personal computer market in the UK. The firm's next

The Sinclair QL

The Sinclair QL, a microcomputer which is contained in its keyboard. This machine uses Motorola's 68008 microprocessor, and has two tape cartridge systems built in. The micro can directly address 1 megabyte of memory, and this feature alone makes it technically superior to the older, 16-bit addressing micros, which are only able to address 64 kbytes of memory. The larger addressing range will mean that such home computers will be able to use more complicated and interesting software.

product was the QL (Quantum Leap) microcomputer, based on the Motorola 68008 32-bit microprocessor.

The QL is contained in a keyboard-sized box, weighs only 3 pounds, and has two 'microdrives', small cassette machines which use a continuous loop of tape. The performance of the Microdrives is inferior to that of floppy discs, but they are much cheaper. The Microdrive has 100 kbytes of memory, and an average transfer rate of 15 kbytes per second, which is reasonably fast, if not spectacularly so. The 68008 addresses 1 megabyte of memory in a more straightforward fashion than the 8088 microprocessor used in the IBM PC, and this RAM reduces the need to use discs, making the Microdrive performance adequate for many applications. Four chips specially designed for Sinclair improve performance, and these also make the micro much more difficult to copy. An extra 500 kbytes of memory can be plugged into a socket on the end of the QL. A major limitation of the machine is that it is built into a small keyboard, making it awkward to add extra cards or peripherals.

The QL package also includes the four most commonly used software packages—those for word processing, data base management, spreadsheet calculation, and colour graphics.

A major set-back for Sinclair's firm was the BBC's choice of the rival Acorn microcomputer for its series of television programmes on microcomputers. The UK is several years in advance of any other country in its use of computers in schools, because of the co-ordinated policy for school computers pursued by government education and industry departments, and the BBC. However, Acorn failed to exploit the breakthrough provided by the BBC micro and when,

183

The Personal Computer

Portable computers

The Data General One is a portable computer incorporating many advanced features. It can be run for eight hours on batteries, and the screen displays 25 lines of 80 characters, the same as a standard VDU. Two 3½-inch discs are built into the equipment. The machine is IBM-compatible, and a 5¼-inch disc can be plugged into the machine allowing programs and data to be interchanged with IBM PCs. Internally the computer uses a low-power (CMOS) version of the Intel 8088 microprocessor. The display is the weakest feature of such a portable, with much less contrast than a VDU.

at the beginning of 1985, it ran into serious financial trouble, it had to be rescued by Olivetti. At the same time, Sinclair was also experiencing severe financial problems.

Computers like the QL are products of their time rather than the work of one person or company, and equivalents have been introduced by other companies such as Commodore and Atari. The increased processing power stems more from developments in microelectronics chips than from the efforts of microcomputer-manufacturing firms like Acorn or Sinclair. In the end, microcomputer systems are simply combinations of fifty or sixty chips. The most successful manufacturer will be the one that has access to the most advanced chips, and is best at cost-cutting and marketing.

Fourteen Large Computer Systems

The mainframe

Computers started out as room-sized monsters, each of which required a host of attendants in order to keep it functional. In the 1950s such a **mainframe** machine cost what would now be many millions of pounds. Mainframe computers were designed for large-scale operations in such fields as science or business, where they calculated laboratory results or kept detailed records for banking and insurance offices. They were temperamental, and needed air-conditioning and a dust-free room to work reliably.

The size of mainframe machines remained the same until the mid-1960s, although their processing power grew steadily, and instead of a single programmer sitting at the terminal and monopolizing the machine, the computer passed into the hands of specialized computer operators. Users gave their programs to the operators as stacks of punched cards, and came back hours, or even days, later to find out the results. Large computer centres grew up around mainframe computers, which were shared between users. The computer's tasks were organized into a queue, and dealt with one at a time. This batch mode of operation is disappearing, but is still common on large multi-user systems, especially for time-consuming programs. Of course, the programs are now stored on disc.

In the 1960s, mainframe computers started to offer on-line or interactive facilities, i.e. users gained immediate access to the machine, which was organized by its operating-system software to share its resources between many users. Results were displayed immediately on a terminal, or printed out by a primitive teletype machine. The computers were often to be found organizing a reservation system for airlines, or being used by students on a university campus. Most people prefer to operate mainframes interactively, and today large mainframe computers are almost invariably multi-user systems offering interactive facilities. In 1985 the average mainframe had 120 users, and cost over $1m. Mainframes still represent a large fraction of the computer market, but their relative importance is steadily declining.

The minicomputer

The minicomputer arrived in the mid-1960s, designed for customers who didn't need as much power as contemporary mainframes could provide and

185

certainly didn't want to pay mainframe prices. The new machine had about 10 per cent of the processing power of the mainframe and was about 10 per cent of the size and cost. It was much less complicated, being simple enough for its software and hardware to be understood in detail by a computer enthusiast, who could then maintain it with little help from the manufacturer. A hundred or so companies started to manufacture minicomputers, although only a few have consistently made profits from them.

Gradually the message spread that minicomputers were not just toys for computer experts, and firms started using them in factories and offices. The more competent customers converted mainframe software packages so that they could be run on minicomputers. The minicomputer manufacturers, convinced that their products had become respectable, brought out multi-user operating systems, and hired maintenance engineers. Although 16-bit minicomputers are now obsolete, they are still sold to customers who do not want to change their software, and need compatible machines. Older minicomputers, such as the DEC PDP-11 and Data General Nova, have been turned into single-chip machines to take advantage of this market.

The supermini

The minicomputer manufacturers soon faced severe competition from microcomputers, and as a result were forced to introduce more powerful machines, **superminis**, the first of which were the VAX systems from DEC. The main advantage of the new machines was that their larger (32-bit) addressing range meant that they could run all the old mainframe programs. Superminis were a great success, and a whole generation of university students have been brought up on the VAX or similar superminis. However, computer technology

The supermini

After initially ignoring microprocessors, by the late 1970s minicomputer manufacturers like DEC and Data General found their businesses threatened by the new technology. They responded by producing superminis, very powerful 32-bit minicomputers. This is the DEC VAX-730, one of the smallest of the range of VAX computers which was started in 1977. The supermini is designed as a multi-user system; it is too expensive to be devoted to just one user.

does not stand still for long, and the superminis are now themselves under threat from newer single-chip 32-bit microprocessors, such as the National 32132 or Zilog Z80000.

The changing role of mainframes

Large computing centres are finding that the number of users of their services is continually increasing, as are the requirements in terms of processing and disc storage of each user. Mainframe computers are severely strained to provide sufficient computing power, magnetic disc storage, and semiconductor memory from a single central computer system. There are other problems with centralized processors: for example, many users have low-speed links to the central facility. Even if processing power is no limitation, the central computer might take several minutes to produce a colour image for a display.

The mainframe, supermini, and the personal computer all have advantages for particular applications, and a large computer system in the mid-1980s is therefore usually composed of all three types of machines. A fourth type of hardware used in such a system, and one that is increasingly popular, is the **workstation**. This fits between the supermini and personal computer, and in its most usual form is a single-user desk-top machine, comprising a single-chip 32-bit microprocessor, a high-resolution screen, about 1 megabyte of RAM, integral Winchester and floppy disc drives, and a LAN connection. Its virtual memory capability enables the workstation to run almost all the programs written for a mainframe computer. The processing power available to an individual user (about 0.5 to 3 MIPS) is far higher than that offered by a mainframe serving many users, and through the use of portable operating systems, excellent software has quickly become available.

The threat posed to them by such workstations is forcing the supermini manufacturers to build much more powerful machines than the single-chip computer can offer. This is becoming a harder and harder task as integrated-circuit technology is advancing so quickly. In 1985, workstations cost approximately ten times less than the larger machines per MIP (the unit of processing power), and their price was declining much more rapidly, at a rate of 60 per cent each year, compared with 25 per cent. The demand for processing power within commercial and other organizations is increasing by between 60 and 100 per cent per year. Hence organizations will increasingly adopt workstations in order to contain the rise in their computing costs. Co-ordinating the software and hardware for many processors is inevitably more difficult than organizing a single mainframe, but it will be necessary to do so simply on economic grounds.

However, the advent of distributed systems does not signify the demise of mainframes or of centralized computing facilities, rather it points to a different role for them. Instead of being a source of processing power, the mainframe will in future primarily provide essential centralized services, such as reference information and specialized equipment that is too expensive to be part of an individual workstation. When an electronic copy of the *Oxford English Dictionary*, for example, is requested, it will be accessed from the central system. As software becomes more 'intelligent', the mainframe will be able to give expert advice, based on its data base of information. Some degree of central control will also be needed in order to ensure that the software and hardware for the microcomputer workstations are compatible, thereby allowing them to communicate with each other, and use joint facilities. Of course, there will always be some large problems that require a very powerful computer, and for these the central mainframe will still be essential.

The old boundaries between mainframes, minicomputers, and micros are rapidly disappearing. Certainly they are no longer defined by size or processing power, but rather by price and the amount of software and hardware support provided for each system. The raw computing power of a 32-bit single-chip microprocessor such as the Motorola 68020 chip is about the same as that of one of the VAX minicomputers sold by DEC. In 1985, the former cost less than £100, and the latter several hundred times as much. But of course there are great differences between a processing chip and a complete computer system. The cost of a processor is only one factor in the choice of a computer: the reliability of the hardware and software, and the size and ease of storage must also be considered.

Commercial systems

For commercial computer systems in particular, the reliability of hardware and software is of overriding importance. Some companies simply cannot afford any breakdowns in their computer facilities. For example, a company's whole mailing list may be stored on a computer system, a set of records which is worth many millions of pounds. It is obviously worth paying for the most reliable computer system available. For very important applications, **fault-tolerant** computers, such as those made by Tandem, may be necessary, which are able to detect faults, and switch in spare computer hardware. This extra hardware takes over processing tasks without the user even being aware of any fault.

Computer systems should offer more reliable storage than paper-based systems, because it is simple to duplicate records on to digital tapes, and then remove these copies to a safe place. However, records stored on a computer are vulnerable to malice, an accident, or carelessness, if proper precautions are not taken. Most large commercial computer systems keep a continuous log on a second disc of all the operations that they have performed. After a computer breakdown, for example if a disc drive is damaged, the details in this log enable the firm's records to be completely reconstructed. At regular intervals, complete copies of the computerized records are removed to another building.

Computer fallibility

From a distance we often imagine computer systems to be perfect, and we also think that when they fail, they fail completely. In fact, computer systems are so complex that they can never be made perfect, and most operate with many small faults, or 'bugs', in both their hardware and software. Even a small minicomputer system may well have half a dozen of such problems at any one time. A particular printer doesn't work with a particular software package, a computer disc doesn't work until it has warmed up for half an hour, or a software subroutine occasionally gives the wrong answer. Any one fault could be cured with effort; but so could the rattle in your car, and if you only drove the car when it had no faults at all, you would not use it very often.

Computer users work around faults, ignoring them where possible, and avoiding the parts of the hardware and software that cause the problems. The number of these bugs is not static, but gradually increases, perhaps at a rate of one a week, or one a month, until it becomes intolerable. The computer engineer is then called in, and as many bugs as possible are cured.

In the process of repair, new faults are added. For example, an unusual software alteration (a 'patch') may cure a fault with a particular printer, but when in the course of time a new printer is installed, the patch stops it working properly. No one can understand why the printer will not function, and the programmer who altered the software has long since left for another job. As the computer hardware and software are repeatedly repaired, the conceptual integrity of the original system is destroyed, and the repairs eventually become more damaging than the faults.

To increase the reliability of their hardware, larger computers are usually monitored by a microprocessor, which looks for and warns of small faults. The microprocessor logs any faults, and prints a message telling the engineer which board to change on the next maintenance visit. Major faults on a mainframe can be diagnosed by linking it via a telephone link to a computer at the computer manufacturer's headquarters. The manufacturer's computer suggests which circuit boards need replacing. Mainframe machines also have semiconductor memories with error correction capabilities, and so can perform without error even with small hardware problems. Whereas at one time maintenance engineers were continuously employed at mainframe sites, today many large computer systems can run for years without hardware faults causing any disruption.

Manufacturing techniques

The processing power of mainframes increases fairly steadily and by 1985 a mainframe had a processing power of somewhere between 5 and 40 MIPS. The fastest mainframe computers are usually referred to as **supercomputers**; these mostly have speeds greater than 40 MIPS. Typically a mainframe computer operates on 64-bit-wide data. The processors of mainframes and superminis are not made from a single chip, or many chips on a single circuit board, but from many chips on many circuit boards. The chips are made from emitter-coupled logic (ECL) technology, based on a different manufacturing process than that for silicon chips. This produces chips which operate much

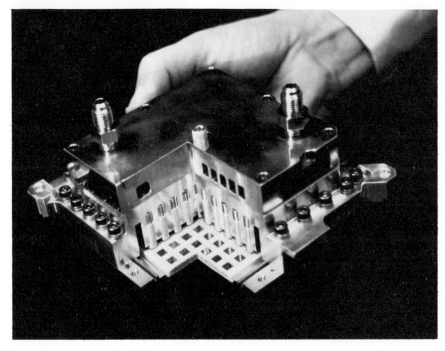

Part of a mainframe

This is a section of one of the twenty-six modules that make up the electronic circuitry of the IBM 3081 mainframe. The chips are packed closely together, and generate so much heat that the modules must be water-cooled. The small black squares are the integrated circuits, laid face down; they are cooled by the tubes that press on to their back surface. The chips are electrically linked to one another through the white ceramic circuit board, which can contain more than thirty layers of electrical connections.

Supercomputers (opposite)

Supercomputers, the fastest of all computers, are hand-built and have a very limited market. Seymour Cray (left) designed the first supercomputers for CDC, before leaving to start his own company. He later gave up the day-to-day running of his new company to concentrate on design and research work. Here Cray is with the Chief Executive of Cray Research, John Rollwagen. They stand in front of the prototype for the Cray-2 supercomputer, which generates so much heat that it runs in a bath of cooling liquid. The machine has a clock speed of 250 megahertz, pipelining facilities, and is only one-tenth of the size of the Cray-1. The smaller size helps to shorten the connection paths between the electronics of the machine—light travels only 4 feet during a clock cycle of the Cray-2!

faster than those containing MOS transistors, but which use more power and cannot hold as many transistors.

A big problem with mainframe computers is how to keep the temperature of the processor down to a reasonable level, for an enormous amount of heat is generated by its closely packed chips. In the IBM 4300 series of computers, the components are cooled with water, while in the next generation of Cray supercomputers the whole CPU will be immersed in a cooled liquid. The same liquid is used to produce artificial blood!

The Rutherford Appleton Laboratories

A large computer system at a university, or a research laboratory, may be serving thousands of users, many of whom have little need to understand computers in any detail, but simply wish to use them as a tool. The users may be social scientists manipulating statistics, astronomers accessing a data base of star images, or undergraduates learning the basics of computing science. In the UK there is a nation-wide academic computing system, providing facilities for universities throughout Britain, run through the Joint Academic Network (Janet). The heart of this network is at Chilton in Oxfordshire, at the Rutherford Appleton Laboratories (RAL) of the Science and Engineering Research Council (SERC).

The Janet network links more than 5,000 users at sites all over the UK. Each site has its own autonomous computing power, but users can still access the central Rutherford facilities through telephone lines. Various linked parts of the Janet system include an ICL parallel processor (the DAP at Queen Mary College, London), and several Cray supercomputers.

The most powerful machine at Chilton is the ICL Atlas (Fujitsu M380), an IBM-compatible computer designed and built by the Japanese company Fujitsu. This machine processes 64-bit-wide data, has a power of more than 15 MIPS, and in 1984 had 16 megabytes of semiconductor memory. Running alongside the Atlas is a second powerful mainframe, an IBM 3081 with a speed of 10 MIPS and 32 megabytes of memory. The machines are connected together and have a combined disc storage capacity exceeding 28 gigabytes (1 gigabyte = 1,000,000,000 bytes).

There are also many minicomputers at the Chilton facilities, including seven Prime 750s and five GEC 1490 minicomputers. All the computers there are linked through a ring network, which can, at least in theory, transfer data at a rate of up to 10,000,000 bits per second. Some of the minicomputers are dedicated to particular university research projects, and one is used by a local school.

Mass storage

The RAL system stores information for reference purposes on digital tape. Each roll of tape is 10 inches in diameter and $\frac{1}{2}$ inch wide, and holds between 10 and 80 megabytes of data. This is a very cheap form of storage compared to disc storage, but has its drawbacks. Considerable manpower is required—the tapes need to be selected and loaded on to the tape drive, and this usually has to be done manually—and even after the tape has been mounted on the tape drive, accessing the data takes many seconds. RAL has an interesting tape machine which reduces the extent of these problems—the Mass Store. The tape rolls in this machine have a diameter of 2 inches and are $3\frac{1}{2}$ inches long, each storing 150 megabytes. A robot arm can access any one of the hundreds of rolls arrayed in the store's honeycomb frame. Once selected by the arm, a

A robotic tape store

This robotic tape store becomes economically sensible for really large amounts of information. A robot arm can select any tape cartridge from its cell in the honeycomb, unwrap it, and load it on to a digital tape system which reads it. Tens of thousands of megabytes of information can be stored at (relatively) low cost, and accessed quickly. No human operators are required, access times are more reliable because the machine never takes a break, and the system occupies less floor space than normal digital tape stores.

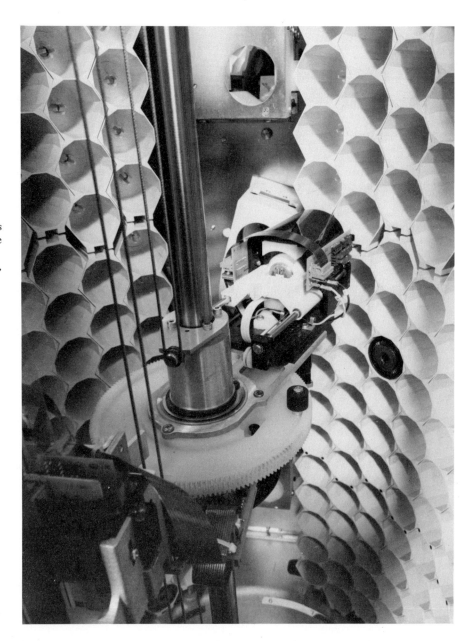

tape is passed to a mechanism which unwraps it and reads its contents on to a disc, which can then be quickly read by the computer. This wonderful piece of mechanical engineering stores 100,000 megabytes of information, needs no human operator, and costs only half a million pounds!

Communication within the Janet network

The different sites within the Janet network communicate with each other through the transmission services of the UK telephone service, British Telecom. In 1985, transmission speeds were limited to 9,600 baud, but the arrival of fibre optic links will make long-distance communication cheaper and faster. The British manufacturer GEC makes computers tailored for controlling the transmission of digital information, and a dozen of these are in use at Rutherford and around the network. However, communication systems are decreasing in price much more slowly than processing power, and so we can expect future computer systems to perform more processing on a local basis.

Software

In comparison with the centralized hardware facilities, the software facilities provided by Janet are not very extensive. All that is supplied is a basic infrastructure of operating systems, some standard software packages, and reference libraries of data. Applications software must generally be developed by users. Astronomers, however, have Starlink, a co-ordinated set of minicomputers at universities all over the UK, each running software for the processing of astronomical pictures.

The future of Janet

Given the rapid pace of technological change, the future of a large-scale system like Janet is very difficult to predict. It must continually evolve or else become technologically obsolete in only a few years. Yet to many customers, a reliable service may be more important than the system being at the forefront of technology.

As computing becomes cheaper, most of the processing will be performed locally rather than at Rutherford. The centre's function will be one of providing equipment and information which cannot be replicated locally, and perhaps co-ordinating software.

Fifteen **Artificial Intelligence**

Artificial intelligence (AI) is a branch of computer science that aims to make computer systems behave intelligently, or at least demonstrate behaviour that we might intuitively think of as intelligent. Programs already exist which show elements of intelligence—computer systems have outperformed human experts at such tasks as diagnosing diseases, matching up fingerprints, controlling the manufacture and distribution of computers, and finding mineral deposits—and it seems likely that there will be further progress in AI. If substantial break-throughs were to occur, computers would start to displace humans from work requiring mental skill, as well as from jobs requiring physical muscle. We should not exaggerate the significance of the results of present research into artificial intelligence, but they already illustrate that there is no firm division between human and machine intelligence.

Expert systems

The first commercial products in artificial intelligence were **expert systems**, in which the knowledge of an expert has been encapsulated in computer software. This software can then help decision-making by less skilled people. A better name for this type of software is **rule-based systems**, because the expertise is normally captured as a set of 'rules', which then provides the advice. The systems have been applied successfully to the diagnosis of medical ailments, mineral prospecting, the design of aircraft, buildings, and cars, and many aspects of financial monitoring and planning.

An expert system package is usually sold commercially as a general-purpose 'shell', software which can be tailored to cover many different areas of exper-tise. The software has two parts, one for capturing the knowledge of an expert, and the other for then helping the non-expert to use it. Initially, a **knowledge engineer** talks to an expert in the field of interest in order to try and structure the decision-making process into a set of rules (a **model**). The non-specialist can then use the software by supplying the program with information about particular cases; the system consults its rules and supplies the advice. Most systems seem to become useful when they have acquired a few hundred rules; below this kind of figure they are too simple to be anything but demonstration systems.

Expert systems should not be regarded as complicated, and most of the software principles involved have been used for a long time outside the AI world. Dozens of firms have already implemented their own programs, and good expert system software is available even for small machines like the IBM PC. Simple demonstration systems have been written for tasks like the medical diagnosis of blood diseases. MYCIN, a program designed at Stanford University, can perform as well (about 60 per cent of its diagnoses are correct for some diseases) as the most skilful doctors. An expert system produced by Kodak in the UK advises on the maintenance programme for complex film-processing machines, telling an engineer when the equipment needs servicing and indicating the least disruptive time to do so. If the equipment does break down, the expert system gives advice on how to repair it.

Despite their usefulness and power, expert systems still have many disadvantages. It can be difficult to break an expert's knowledge down into a series of rules. The systems have no concept of their domain of expertise; they cannot check on whether their decision is sensible or not; and they cannot yet learn from experience. At present we can therefore only regard them as knowledgeable idiots, rather than as real substitutes for human experts. We can expect expert systems to become very popular, but they are only primitive fumblings towards true artificial intelligence.

Natural language understanding

Artificial intelligence researchers have also made some progress in the understanding of natural or everyday language. Programs are available that can comprehend a limited vocabulary of a few hundred words. Such software might give advice on investments, help newcomers to operate a computer, or give an airline's customers details of a flight timetable. The natural language question asked of the computer is translated by the AI program into the programming language that would normally be used to access the data base concerned, and the DBMS provides the answer to the question. Again versions of this kind of software are available for personal computer systems.

The key to the success of the software is that it is dealing with a limited and well-defined area, that of searching a specific data base. The number of questions that the software can be asked is relatively small (if a single word is not understood, the AI software will normally fail completely). As with expert systems, a small breakthrough in AI has been achieved through having limited ambitions. The software for the DBMS is probably more complicated than that designed to understand the natural language.

Extending such software so that it can fully understand a human language is impossible using present techniques. Even if an isolated sentence is understood, this is only a start towards the comprehension of its meaning in different contexts. Context is critical for almost all interesting human communication, and computers are presently very poor at understanding context. A simple message, apparently unambiguous, may convey many associations. Consider, for example, the simple sentence 'I played tennis last night.' These five words convey a host of images: rackets, balls, sounds, fresh air, nets, and tennis kit.

Given the possession of a similar cultural background, we all know the approximate duration of play, the weather, the likely number of players, and perhaps the social implications of playing tennis. But then the same message may have a special meaning to, for instance, a regular tennis partner who hasn't been invited. None of these associations can be grasped by computer software, even if it could understand the message. Only when artificial intelligence programs gain some understanding of context will they compete with human intelligence.

The intelligent machine

Many people are still reluctant to accept the notion of an intelligent machine. A common response is that computers are essentially calculators writ large, devoid of human traits such as creativity, unexpected behaviour, and feelings—puppets slavishly performing actions according to their programmers' wishes.

This response is not based on facts, but merely reflects an understandable desire that machines should not emulate our intelligence. Computer systems have already exhibited some creativity of their own. For instance, chess-playing programs can easily outplay their programmers and have also uncovered new solutions to end-game problems. Computers played an integral part in proving that any map can be shaded in with only four different colours, after mathematicians had struggled for hundreds of years to establish this. More dangerously, programs already exist which are not understood by any one human being, either because the software is a composite program or has helped to adapt itself to perform a particular task.

One of the problems of analysing whether machines have intelligence is that human intelligence is only weakly understood. Often the human approach to solving a problem is different to that of the machine, based more on experience rather than short-term analysis. For example, before making a move in chess, humans look at only a dozen or so options in detail, quickly rejecting most possible moves. Computer programs are presently much less selective and analyse many more combinations, but in far less detail. The human being is actually employing knowledge as much as intelligence, because no matter how clever, humans do not reach championship standard without many years of practice, which engrave the patterns of the game on to the mind. Until recently, computers have not been fast enough to access the large amounts of memory required to imitate this approach, and so have been forced to employ an analytical rather than a knowledge-based approach. But this hasn't stopped the best chess programs being adequate to beat 99 per cent of human players. The increasing amounts of fast memory available to machines are now allowing the slow development of better knowledge-based chess software. The computer appears increasingly intelligent, but the algorithms employed are still fairly simple; we should not be contemptuous of the machine, but perhaps reflect that some of our own 'intelligent' actions might not be as complicated as we imagine.

Parallel processors

The serial processor is still the backbone of modern computing, performing computer instructions one at a time on a single piece of data. It can be developed a long way, to improve computer speeds by a factor of perhaps one hundred in the next decade. However, there are many problems, particularly in AI, which will need even more power than the serial machine can provide. Herein lies the importance of the parallel processor, which processes many instructions at the same time. A simple microprocessor is available for a pound or two and a few thousand of these joined together have more processing power in total than the most powerful of computers. Therefore it seems obvious that many processors should be connected in parallel and applied collectively to solve problems.

Some problems are inherently serial, i.e. each step must be performed before the next can be done. Repairing a watch is a task that will not be speeded up by setting many people to do it. Other jobs, like digging a garden can be usefully subdivided into work for more than one person. Computing problems are similar: all can be performed on a serial basis (except where time is critical), and only some are suitable for parallel processing.

Perhaps the best-known parallel processor is the Illiac IV, at the University of Illinois. This machine cost $40m. to develop and it took ten years of design, redesign, and testing before it became operational in 1975. The target speed of 1,000 million operations had been cut by a factor of four. Programming for the parallel processor was painfully slow and difficult, and the 'one-off' machine needed constant attention.

Parallel-processing machines have proved themselves in particular cases, but neither the hardware nor the software has yet been developed so that one machine can tackle a large variety of tasks. The key to building a generally applicable parallel processor must lie in an understanding of how best to organize the software to dissect a task and delegate it to many processors. The hardware of parallel processors must be structured by the software, and not vice versa, for the simple reason that the hardware is a means to an end—running the software.

The UK company Inmos has become the first microelectronics firm to announce a 32-bit microprocessor that is designed for parallel processing—the **transputer**. The 250,000-transistor microprocessor can be used as a normal serial machine, but can also be linked with other transputers to form a parallel-processing array. When a number of processors are connected up to each other, there are often problems of intercommunication, and so each transputer is designed to be as self-contained as possible. The design of the Inmos transputer was coordinated with the development of a new programming language, Occam, developed in conjunction with Professor C. A. R. Hoare of Oxford University. Occam is a general-purpose language, benefiting from Hoare's years of experience of language development, with facilities for dividing up program software for use on many processors.

The speed and power of a computer alter its response time, and this may sometimes be an important factor in apparent intelligence. The most advanced projects in artificial intelligence will require a much larger amount of power than can be provided by even highly developed serial machines. Herein lies the importance of **parallel processors**, computers which can perform many operations simultaneously. The development of inexpensive parallel-processing hardware is a necessity for the mass application of artificial intelligence software.

Self-programming software

We talk of 'intelligent machines', but although developments in the field of artificial intelligence demand powerful computing hardware, the problems to be solved mainly concern software. At present, programs are developed by

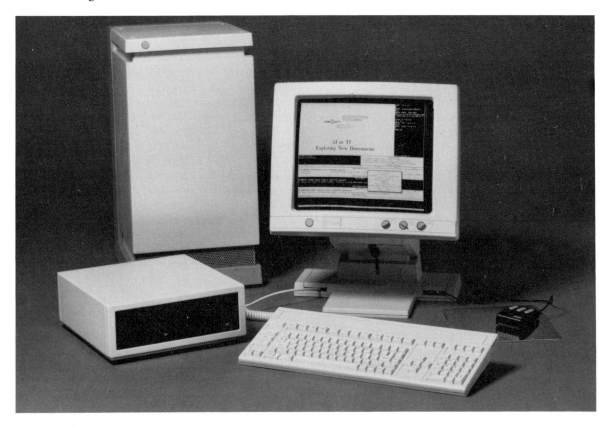

formal analysis, and then written out so that they mimic the necessary logic. This limits their use to applications that are clearly analysable. In future, programs are likely to be generated by a process of self-adaptation. By 'praising' or 'criticizing' the actions of the computer, the required behaviour will be

The Fifth Generation project

The Fifth Generation project in Japan is an attempt by that country's Ministry of Trade and Industry (MITI) to produce computers that are easy for non-experts to use. Artificial intelligence software and hardware will be needed in order that non-specialists can interact with computers in everyday language. Only in this way will computers ever reach their full market potential. In order to give enough computing power for artificial intelligence work, the core of the project is the construction of high-speed parallel-computing hardware implemented in VLSI. Prototype hardware and software are being developed by Japanese computer firms and used at the co-ordinating centre, the Institute for New Genera-

tion Computer Technology (ICOT) in Tokyo. The ten-year project, started in 1983, has a budget of $800m. The core language chosen for the Fifth Generation project is Prolog, which is designed to enable logical inference to be deduced from information.

The importance of the Fifth Generation project has been exaggerated in the USA and Western Europe. The project's aims are very ambitious for the time-scale envisaged, and it should really only be viewed as a pump-priming exercise by the Japanese Ministry. After all, only forty people work on the project at ICOT, and the US defence agencies spend far more on artificial intelligence.

This workstation from Texas Instruments is designed to provide computing power for AI work. It processes LISP, the dominant AI language in America. This single-user system contains the usual workstation facilities of Winchester and floppy disc drives, mouse, and high-resolution graphics screen, but its software is oriented to the production and use of programs for AI. The software includes an expert system, natural language software, a Prolog language compiler, and a complete software support environment, a set or programs to assist in the development of LISP software. Fifty of these workstations were delivered to the MCC project, a research venture organized by a combination of US companies to compete with the Japanese Fifth Generation project.

The 32-bit processor has many features to speed up LISP processing, and can directly access 128 Mbytes of memory, thereby accommodating very large programs. In 1985 Texas was working on a US Department of Defense project to produce a 40-MHz VLSI chip specifically designed to run LISP instructions, with processing speeds improved by a factor of ten. This single chip could perform functions which would require several hundred integrated circuits in an average computer system.

rapidly generated in much the same way as a child is taught. Computer programs will also modify themselves in the light of 'experience', to the extent that their decision-making processes will not be totally comprehensible. Humans will structure the rules that the software initially follows, but those rules will include the ability to 'learn' by experience, and even to modify the way that they learn by experience.

This may sound far-fetched, but primitive examples of such self-generating programs are already common, even outside the AI field. For example, it is no longer economically sensible for individual companies to write programs to store and sort lists of information, such as the addresses and telephone numbers of their customers. A general-purpose program for data base management can be bought for a few hundred pounds, and quickly modified to store lists of almost any kind. A simple question-and-answer sequence takes place at the keyboard, and the software itself then produces a specific package to fit the firm's requirements. The result is a composite program that has effectively been generated by the DBMS software for the particular task, and is understood by no single person.

In the future, more complex versions of such self-programming software will mean that large numbers of computer programmers will not be necessary—although taking programs past the threshold at which they can themselves write complex programs will clearly require an enormous effort. There are few long-term prospects in computer programming for our children: they should be learning how to use the computer rather than how to write programs for it.

Living with artificial intelligence

The progress made in artificial intelligence is disturbing, and we can expect attempts to ignore or stop it. Some modern philosophers have attempted definitions of intelligence that exclude machines, only to have to revise them time and again. We will be much better off if we accept the likelihood of intelligent machines, rather than indulge in the idea that they can never be developed. Even a cursory reading of this book should have dispelled any notion that the computer is a mere dumb 'number-cruncher'. Intelligent machines are almost certain to be produced—to a limited extent they exist already—and we must now start to discuss sensibly the implications of their large-scale introduction into our society.

Sixteen The Future

The microelectronics industry has always had to face cyclical changes in demand. An increase in turnover of 25 per cent in 1983 was followed the year after by the deepest ever slump—a veteran semiconductor worker commented 'You are always working overtime up to the moment that you're sacked.' In the long term, however, continued expansion seems inevitable. The penetration of microelectronics into domestic and industrial products will no doubt continue. By 1988, the value of the chips alone is predicted to be $40bn., and by the year 2000, it seems likely that the microelectronics business as a whole will be second in value only to the petroleum industry.

Improvements in computer hardware have removed many of the technical obstacles to problem-solving with computers. Computer processing power will continuously decrease in price, and more, and increasingly complex, software will have to be generated. Unfortunately, as programs become more complex they also become more expensive to write, and consequently software costs are becoming a larger part of the total cost of any computer system. However, once a software package has been produced, the cost of replicating it is then negligible. This means that general-purpose packages will increasingly take over from 'in-house' software written specifically for one company. Considerable effort is being devoted towards developing techniques for producing reliable software which can be used for many different applications, and so can be mass-produced. Much of this work is performed on a national scale or by the academic community, simply because the research is either too costly or too speculative for commercial organizations. In this area, a national commitment to producing innovatory software, such as the Japanese Fifth Generation project, may well pay dividends.

Information technology

Half of all work in the developed countries involves the selection, organization, and transfer of information in one form or another. Hence there is a huge market for **information technology** products. Powerful new microtechnology tools for storing, organizing, and transferring information are therefore certain to alter the structure of most companies. Intelligent copiers, word processors, automatic stock control and ordering, electronic mail, and computer filing systems are just some examples of the steady transformation from a paper-based to an electronic society. If microelectronics can improve a copier's performance by 10 per cent, or provide a more efficient method of sending mail, then it makes economic sense to switch to the new technology.

Computer literacy

By 1990, one American in two will use a keyboard during the course of his or her work. The work-forces of all advanced nations will need to acquire keyboard skills and a familiarity with computers. But this will not require people to learn to program, for they will simply be using computers as tools. Computers will be an aid to greater efficiency, running programs written by professional firms. Better programs and more powerful machines will mean that computers are increasingly useful tools for word processing, equipment design, document display, communication, and leisure activities. Keyboard skills will lose their present low-status image, and become a competitive advantage for each individual, just as literacy has been for several hundred years.

A steady decline in the real worth of the salaries of computer engineers in both the USA and the UK suggests the falsity of the view that there is a shortage of these skilled workers. In any case, the real need is for people with traditional skills to acquire microtechnology skills. Microelectronics is a general-purpose technology with applications in many areas of work. Engineers, agriculturalists, archaeologists, architects, accountants, metalworkers, social scientists, printers, and industrialists who understand microtechnology at the necessary level of detail will all be at an enormous advantage over competitors within their own field. Primary skills are not being devalued by the new technology, provided that computing skills are learnt as well.

Education

Computers will become a major element in education. The computer will be a supplement to the passive book, an interactive, tireless machine that can respond to the needs of individual children. Imagine a child being guided through a computerized encyclopaedia by an expert system, sensitive to the ability and even the mood of the child. Optical discs will allow the storage of many thousands of images in that 'book', each of which can be easily retrieved in a second or so. Machines need not replace the human touch, but by performing the repetitive elements of education, they will increase the efficiency of the teacher. The early use of computers will give children a familiarity with the machines that they will be working with later in life.

An amoral industry

The growth of microtechnology is a powerful amoral force that damages, and sometimes totally destroys, existing industries. If a new device is invented, and can be used to make a profit for someone, then it will be implemented, regardless of the social consequences. Of course, there is usually an overall benefit to society in the process, but not to the person fired, or the old-fashioned company that is wound up. There is nothing new about the social effects of introducing advanced technology—the Industrial Revolution had equally disturbing effects—but the pace of today's microelectronics revolution is unprecedented.

We can only see our moral and cultural values become part of the framework of the new technology if people with those values are involved in shaping it. Microelectronics is often criticized for the triviality of its applications—video and arcade games, talking alarm clocks, and wrist-watch computers—but in this respect it is merely a mirror of society, no different from many other industries. Our newspapers and television are scarcely organized for the cultural improvement of the general population. We cannot wish away the fact that microelectronics was created for military and capitalist purposes. If we want creative and cultural applications for microprocessors, creative and cultured people must take advantage of the new machines. Take the simple example of 'interactive books', stories controlled by a computer program. The computer allows the reader to enter into the story, making choices which alter the narrative. Inevitably the first such stories have not been of the greatest literary merit, but what a wonderful opportunity this new medium represents for a gifted writer! Microelectronics can be restrictively applied to trivia or missile control, but it need not be if we choose otherwise.

We regard computers as tools, which should be simple to use. But this is too functional an analysis, for they are machines that we should *enjoy* using, especially if we are to drive them to their limits. If they increase our own abilities, is it too much to ask that we should actually like computers? The computer is the ultimate machine, one that can pretend to be every machine that has ever existed, and is capable of modelling worlds that can never exist in reality. The people designing new computers, languages, programs, and chips are today's pyramid builders, at the limits of human creativity. Microelectronics will alter the world in ways we cannot yet dream of. Let us enthusiastically take up the challenge of the chip, and mould the new technology in accordance with humane and civilized values.

Glossary

addressing range: the amount of memory directly accessible by a computer's CPU. A 16-bit addressing processor can access 2^{16} (65,536) units of storage

AI: artificial intelligence (q.v.).

algorithm: a recipe for solving a problem.

analog: continuously variable (cf. digital).

analog computer: form of computer that calculates using smoothly variable data, rather than information in digital form (cf. digital computer).

ANSI: American National Standards Institution. The US national standards body, which is involved in laying down standards for computer hardware, software, and languages.

applications program: a program that performs a directly useful task (cf. systems program).

artificial intelligence (AI): computer emulation of the intelligent behaviour of human beings.

ASCII: American Standard for Computer Information Interchange. A standard representation of characters inside the computer, during transmission, on disc, and on tape.

assembly language: a symbolic representation of the machine instructions that a computer can perform, usually in mnemonic form indicating the type of operation.

AT&T: American Telephone & Telegraph Co.

baud rate: the speed of transfer of information across a computer link. Across a binary link, it is the number of bits that can be transferred every second.

BCD: binary coded decimal (q.v.).

binary coded decimal (BCD): a way of representing decimal numbers in binary, particularly used in a computer for performing numeric calculations.

binary system: the number system based on only two numerals, 0 and 1.

bit (binary digit): the smallest information unit of the computer. Each bit can be thought of as a transistor, which is switched either 'on' or 'off'; as a logic state, either true or false; or as an electrical voltage, either 5 or 0 volts. The terms 8-bit, 16-bit, and 32-bit are used to define the addressing range and the data width of a computer.

Boolean logic: the simple set of logical operations performed by computers.

bus: a standardized set of electrical lines within a computer system.

byte: a collection of 8 bits, usually grouped and operated on together. Each byte is sufficient to store a single character, such as a letter.

capacitor: a small electrical component that can temporarily store a small amount of electrical current.

CDC: Control Data Corporation.

central processing unit (CPU): the part of the computer that performs operations on data.

character: a (lower- or upper-case) letter, number (such as 0 to 9), text symbol (such as % or ?), or control symbol (such as a carriage return) stored within a single byte.

chip: an electronic circuit formed on a small thin piece of silicon.

clock: an electronic system within a computer which controls the timing of many of the computer's operations.

compiler: a computer program which translates a complete program in a high-level language into the machine code that can operate on a specific computer (cf. interpreter).

coprocessor: a processor (often a single chip) which is able to perform a process separately from, but controlled by, the main processor within a computer system.

CPU: central processing unit (q.v.).

cursor: a movable marker (often flashing on and off) which indicates a position on a VDU screen.

data base: information stored on a computer system in a structured form.

data base management system (DBMS): software that organizes the storage and retrieval of information on a computer system.

data range/width: the number of bits that a computer manipulates in parallel. For example, an 8-bit computer manipulates eight bits simultaneously.

DBMS: data base management system (q.v.).

DEC: Digital Equipment Corporation.

digital: varying in discrete steps.

digital computer: a computer that stores and processes information digitally (cf. analog computer).

directly addressable memory: that part of the memory system of the computer in which every memory element can be directly reached by the CPU.

disc: a magnetic plate on which computer data is stored.

disc drive: a mechanical system that enables a computer to store and retrieve information on disc.

distributed computer system: one with many processors, which are to a greater or lesser extent co-ordinated.

dopant: a small amount of an impurity that is introduced into the silicon crystal during the process of making integrated circuits.

EAROM: electrically alterable read-only memory. Alternative name for an EEROM (q.v.).

editor: software which assists in the creation of the text of a computer program.

EEROM: electrically erasable read-only memory. A type of semiconductor memory that retains its information after power has been disconnected. The contents of the memory can be erased and reprogrammed by the computer.

electron: a carrier of current, the movement of which makes up an electrical current.

electronic mail: a facility provided by, and between, some computer systems for transferring messages from one user to another.

EPROM: electrically programmable read-only memory. A type of semiconductor memory that can be read but not written by a computer; it retains its information when the computer is switched off.

expert system: a software system which encapsulates human expertise in the form of rules.

file: a set of information that is named separately and treated as a unit by the computer system.

floating-point representation: a system for representing numbers covering a wide range.

floppy disc: a removable, flexible magnetic disc for storing data.

gate: set of transistors that performs a simple logic function; and also the connection on a transistor that controls the current flow.

gbyte: gigabyte (q.v.).

gHz: gigahertz (q.v.).

gigabyte (gbyte): 1,000,000,000 bytes.

gigahertz (gHz): 1,000,000,000 hertz.

graphics: drawings, graphs, or pictures generated by a computer.

hardware: the physical parts of the computer, such as the disc drive and VDU (cf. software).

head: the part of a disc drive which reads and writes information to the magnetic disc.

hertz: a unit of frequency. The clock of a computer with a clock speed of 1,000,000 hertz (1 MHz) 'ticks' 1,000,000 times each second.

hexadecimal representation: a number system based on sixteen codes (0–9, A–F). Each code can replace 4 bits of a binary number, and so the whole number is shortened.

high-level language: a programming language designed to express problems in a more comprehensible form than the primitive instructions of the computer.

IBM: International Business Machines.

icon: pictorial representation of a function on a display screen.

input/output (I/O): those parts of a computer system that deal with the transfer of information to and from the computer, for example the keyboard and printer.

integer: a whole number, such as 56, −12, or 0.

integrated circuit: a small piece of semiconductor that performs the complete functions of an electronic circuit. Usually refers to the combination of the chip and its package.

interpreter: a computer program which translates programs written in a high-level language into the machine code of the computer, and then runs them immediately. In BASIC the translation is usually performed on a line-by-line basis (cf. compiler).

interrupt: a request to the computer to change its current task for a new one.

I/O: input/output (q.v.).

ISO: International Standards Organization. The world standards body whose work includes standards for computer software, hardware, and languages.

k: generally a shorthand notation for 1,024. Outside the field of computing—and sometimes within—a shorthand for 1,000.

kbyte: kilobyte (q.v.).

kHz: kilohertz (q.v.).

kilobyte (kbyte): either 1,024 (2^{10}) bytes or 1,000 bytes; the two values are not usually distinguished.

kilohertz (kHz): 1,000 hertz.

LAN: local area network (q.v.).

linker: software which joins a newly compiled program to existing compiled programs which are needed by the new software.

local area network (LAN): an information transfer system between computers and computer peripherals.

machine instruction: a binary number that represents the instruction actually performed by the computer.

mainframe: a large and powerful computer system shared between many users.

Mbyte: megabyte (q.v.).

megabyte: 1,000,000 bytes.

megahertz (MHz): 1,000,000 hertz.

memory: information storage system accessible to the computer.

menu-driven software: software in which the user is presented with a series of options in the form of a menu.

MHz: megahertz (q.v.).

micro: abbreviation for a microprocessor or a microcomputer system.

microcomputer: a small computer system based on a microprocessor.

micron: a micrometre, one-millionth of a metre, or one-thousandth of a millimetre.

microprocessor: a single chip of silicon containing the whole of the CPU of a computer.

microsecond: one-millionth of a second.

millisecond: one-thousandth of a second.

minicomputer: a computer system of intermediate size; now generally refers to 16-bit addressing equipment (cf. supermini).

MIPS: millions of instructions per second. The number of millions of (usually 64-bit) floating-point operations that can be performed by a computer system each second.

modem (**mod**ulator/**dem**odulator): the equipment which enables digital computers to transfer information over telephone lines.

MOS: metal oxide semiconductor. The MOS transistor is the commonest type of transistor used in integrated circuits.

mouse: a mouse-shaped object which can be used for selecting an option displayed on a computer screen.

multiplexing: a technique for using one set of electrical connections to transmit more than one set of data.

multi-tasking system: a computer system designed to swap between several tasks so that the results of all the processes can appear on a single screen simultaneously.

multi-user system: a computer system designed to be shared between many users.

nanosecond: one-thousand-millionth of a second.

operating system: a systems program used by almost all other programs, which performs all the elementary operations controlling a computer system.

parallel port: an input/output port of a computer, through which many bits of information (usually 8 to 16 bits) are transferred at once.

parallel processor: a computer system that can perform several functions simultaneously.

peripheral: any device attached to, but not an integral part of, a computer.

personal computer: a small computer system for use by one person.

pipelining: a technique whereby a problem is split into elements, each of which is dealt with by a separate processor before being passed on to the next one.

port: a part of a computer system which deals with the transfer of information to and from the computer.

primary memory: the part of the computer memory in which each memory cell can be directly addressed by the CPU.

program: a series of instructions forming a complete task which controls the operation of a computer.

program counter: a register in the CPU which monitors the current position of the program in the computer memory.

programming language: a notation used for writing a program.

RAM: random access memory. Either the directly accessible memory of a computer system, or those parts of the memory which can be read and written as opposed to those which can only be read.

read: examine information in a computer memory (without altering it).

register: a small amount of memory available within the CPU to avoid delays whilst transferring data to and from external memory.

resistor: an electrical component that restricts and controls the flow of electrical current.

ROM: read-only memory. Directly accessible memory which the computer can examine but not alter.

run: to operate a program on a computer.

secondary memory: memory accessed indirectly by a computer; usually discs or tapes.

semiconductors: materials (for example silicon) used for manufacturing chips. They have properties between those of insulators and conductors.

semi-custom chip: an integrated circuit designed or modified for a specific customer.

single-user system: a computer system only capable of dealing with one user at a time.

software: the programs that control a computer (cf. hardware).

spreadsheet: a program that allows the easy alteration and display of numeric calculations.

statement: a single line of a computer program.

supercomputer: a very high-powered computer.

supermini: a computer of intermediate size and power; normally a 32-bit machine with virtual memory and with a multi-user operating system.

systems program: a program used for supporting some operation of the computer rather than for performing some directly useful task (cf. applications program).

terminal: a peripheral with a screen and keyboard for displaying processed results and inputting data.

transistor: an electronic switch with three connections, one of which can be used to switch the current flowing between the other two on and off.

VDU: visual display unit (q.v.).

virtual memory: a technique making secondary memory give the illusion of being primary memory.

visual display unit (VDU): a screen for displaying the results of computer processing.

VLSI: very large scale integration. The technology for producing hundreds of thousands of transistors on a single chip of silicon.

volatile memory: a form of memory that loses its information when the power is disconnected.

volt: the unit of force that causes an electrical current to flow.

wafer: a thin circular slice of silicon crystal on which many integrated circuits are manufactured.

Winchester disc: a high-speed and high-density magnetic disc that cannot be removed from its disc drive.

word: the number of bits that a computer operates on at the same time, i.e. the data width. It is sometimes used (but not in this book) to mean 16 bits.

word processor: a software program designed to help produce, manipulate and print out text.

workstation: a small, self-contained computer system for professional use; often a more powerful system than a personal computer.

write: alter the information stored in a computer's memory.

Further Reading

The books listed here, all of which have been used as sources, are grouped into two classes: those which a non-specialist reader could enjoy, and those which go into a subject in more depth, and might only be of interest to a specialist. In this rapidly changing field, magazines such as *Scientific American*, *Byte*, and *Electronics* are also important sources of information.

Books for the non-specialist reader

Ashurst, Gareth, *Pioneers of Computing* (Frederick Muller, 1983).

Braun, E., and Mcdonald, S., *Revolution in Miniature* (Cambridge University Press, 1978).

Brooks, F., *The Mythical Man-month* (Addison-Wesley, 1975).

Clocksin, W. F., and Mellish, C. S., *Programming in Prolog* (Springer-Verlag, 1981).

Date, C. J., *Database—a Primer* (Addison-Wesley, 1983).

Dijkstra, E. W., *Selected Writings on Computing—A Personal Perspective* (Springer-Verlag, 1982).

Dretske, F. I., *Knowledge and the Flow of Information* (Blackwell, 1981).

Dummer, G. W. A., *Electronic Discoveries and Inventions* (Pergamon, 1983).

Evans, Christopher, *The Making of the Micro* (Gollancz, 1981).

Flegg, G., *Numbers, their History and Meaning* (Deutsch, 1983).

Grogono, P., *Programming in Pascal* (Addison-Wesley, 1980).

Hanson, D., *The New Alchemists* (Little Brown, 1982).

Hodges, Andrew, *Alan Turing—the Enigma* (Burnett Books, 1983).

Hord, R. M., *The Illiac IV—The First Supercomputer* (Springer-Verlag, 1982).

Kernighan, B. W., and Ritchie, D. M., *The C Programming Language* (Prentice-Hall, 1978).

Kernighan, B. W., and Plauger, P. J., *Software Tools in Pascal* (Addison-Wesley, 1981).

Kidder, Tracy, *The Soul of a New Machine* (Allen Lane, 1982).

Metropolis, N., *et al.* (eds.), *A History of Computing in the Twentieth Century* (Academic Press, 1980).

Microelectronics (a reprint of the September 1977 *Scientific American* issue devoted to microelectronics, W. H. Freeman, 1977).

Randell, Brian, *The Origins of the Digital Computer* (3rd edn., Springer-Verlag, 1982).

Rodwell, Peter, *The Personal Computer Handbook* (Dorling-Kindersley, 1983).

Smith, Anthony, *Goodbye Gutenberg* (Oxford University Press, 1982).

Sobell, Robert, *IBM—Colossus in Transition* (Times Books, 1982).

Wexelblatt, R. (ed.), *History of Programming Languages* (Academic Press, 1981).

Technical books

Date, C. J., *An Introduction to Database Systems* (2 vols., Addison-Wesley, 1983).

Hayes-Roth, F. (ed.), *Building Expert Systems* (Addison-Wesley, 1983).

Horowitz, E., *Fundamentals of Programming Languages* (Springer-Verlag, 1982).

King, T., and Knight, B., *Programming the M68000* (Addison-Wesley, 1983).

Mavor, J., Jack, M. A., and Donye, P. B., *Introduction to MOS LSI Design* (Addison-Wesley, 1983).

Meek, Brian, *Fortran, PL/I and the Algols* (Macmillan, 1978).

Motorola, *16-bit Microprocessor Manual MC 68000* (Prentice-Hall, 1983).

Muroga, Saburo, *VLSI System Design* (John Wiley, 1982).

Nicholls, J. E., *The Structure and Design of Programming Languages* (Addison-Wesley, 1975).

Wirth, Niklaus, *Programming in Modula-2* (Springer-Verlag, 1983).

Zilog Corporation, technical manuals for the Z80, S10, and P10.

Articles

Flowers, T. H., 'The design of Colossus', *Annals of the History of Computing* (July, 1983).

Gilbreath, J., and G., 'Erastosthenes revisited', *Byte* (Jan. 1983), 283.

Gupta, A., and Toong, H., 'Microprocessors—the first twelve years', *Proc. IEEE* (Nov. 1983), 1236.

Kilby, J., 'The genesis of the integrated circuit', *IEEE Spectrum* (Aug. 1976).

Noyce, R., and Hoff, M., 'A history of microprocessor development at Intel', *IEEE Micro* (1981).

Rosen, S. 'Electronic computers—a historic survey', *Computing Surveys* (Mar. 1969).

Scientific American issue on computer software (Sep. 1984).

Acknowledgements for Illustrations

The publishers would like to thank the following for permission to reproduce photographs and diagrams.

Bell Laboratories   85, 92 (top)
Cambridge Instruments   111
Cray Research   190 (top)
Data General   184
Dataquest   10
DEC   186
Deutsches Museum, Munich   28
Epson   174
Fairchild Camera and Instrument Corp.   87
Ferranti   97
Ford, Andrew   21, 175 (top and bottom)
Freytag-Löringhoff, Dr B. Baron v.   18
Hewlett-Packard   97 (bottom)
HMSO   29
IBM Corp.   22, 25, 190 (bottom)
Intel Corp.   70, 107, 120
Masstor Systems Int.   192
Microsoft   177
Motorola   78
Musée d'Art et d'Histoire, Neuchâtel   20
Plessey, Allen Clark Laboratories   103
Priam   122, 123
Royal Society   26
Shugart Associates   125
Silicon Compilers Inc.   92 (bottom)
Sinclair   183
Stevens, Richard 30, 113, 114 (magnetic head supplied by VAS), 180
Televideo Systems International Ltd.   170 (top)
Texas Instruments Inc.   198
Wacker-Siltronics   94, 95
Wentworth Laboratories   102
Xerox Corp.   170 (bottom)
Zilog Corp.   72

Index

Index

Index